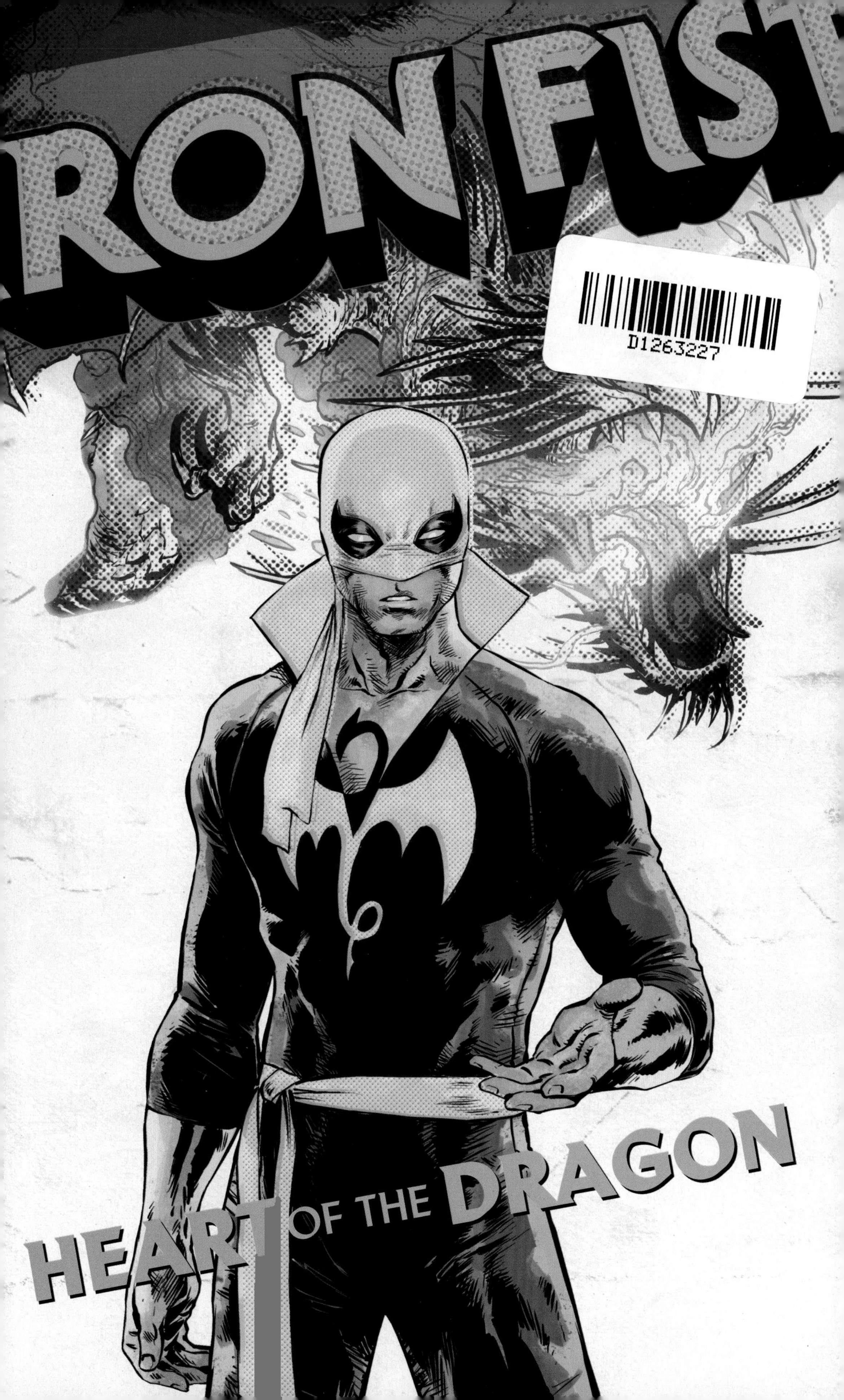
RON FIST
HEART OF THE DRAGON

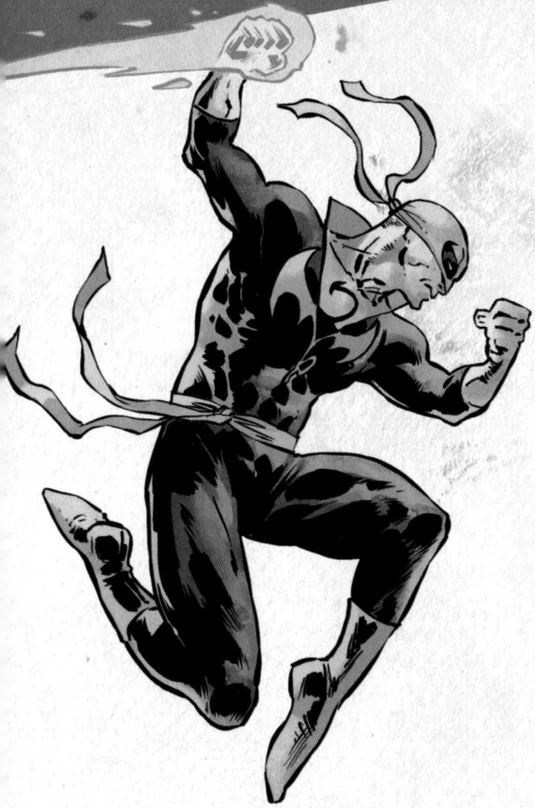

As a child, **Danny Rand** was orphaned during a tragic family expedition in the Himalayas and taken in by the people of the mystical city of K'un-Lun. He grew up to conquer a series of trials, ultimately becoming K'un-Lun's chi-powered defender: **the Iron Fist**.

Danny now lives in Rand Tower in New York with his ward Pei and his... Well, no one's really sure what Fooh is up to, but Pei and Fooh keep Danny connected to K'un-Lun.

In some ways, quite literally...

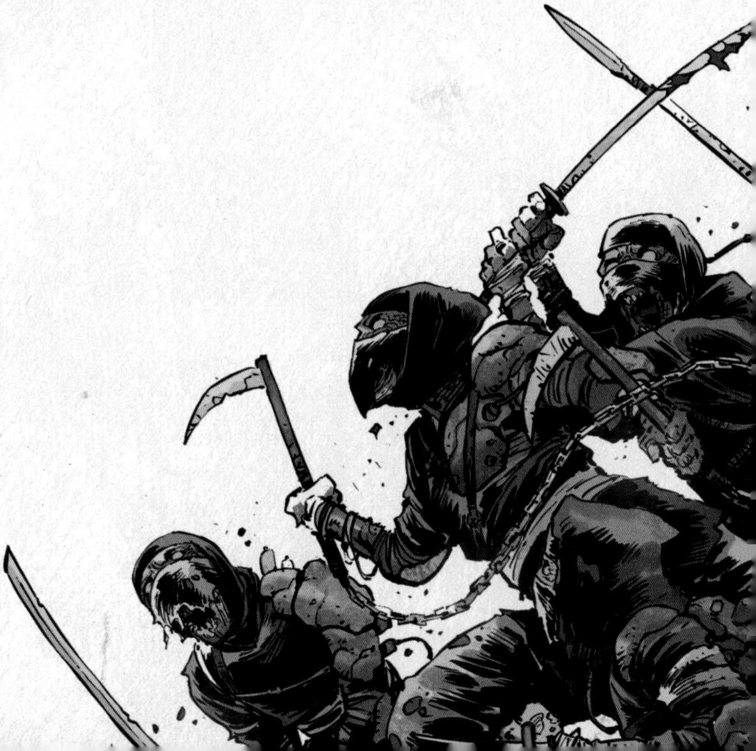

# IRON FIST
## HEART OF THE DRAGON

**LARRY HAMA**
*Writer*

**DAVE WACHTER**
*Artist*

**NEERAJ MENON**
*Color Artist*

**VC's TRAVIS LANHAM**
*Letterer*

**BILLY TAN** WITH **MONICA MU** (#1) & **LINA JIN** (#2-6)
*Cover Art*

**SHANNON ANDREWS BALLESTEROS** & **LINDSEY COHICK**
*Assistant Editors*

**JAKE THOMAS**
*Editor*

**DANIEL KIRCHHOFFER** *Collection Editor*
**MAIA LOY** *Assistant Managing Editor*
**LISA MONTALBANO** *Assistant Managing Editor*
**JENNIFER GRÜNWALD** *Senior Editor, Special Projects*
**JEFF YOUNGQUIST** *VP, Production & Special Projects*
**ADAM DEL RE** WITH **ANTHONY GAMBINO** *Book Designers*
**DAVID GABRIEL** *SVP Print, Sales & Marketing*
**C.B. CEBULSKI** *Editor in Chief*

**IRON FIST: HEART OF THE DRAGON.** Contains material originally published in magazine form as IRON FIST: HEART OF THE DRAGON (2021) #1-6. First printing 2021. ISBN 978-1-302-92469-0. Published by MARVEL WORLDWIDE, INC., a subsidiary of MARVEL ENTERTAINMENT, LLC. OFFICE OF PUBLICATION: 1290 Avenue of the Americas, New York, NY 10104. © 2021 MARVEL No similarity between any of the names, characters, persons, and/or institutions in this magazine with those of any living or dead person or institution is intended, and any such similarity which may exist is purely coincidental. **Printed in Canada.** KEVIN FEIGE, Chief Creative Officer; DAN BUCKLEY, President, Marvel Entertainment; JOE QUESADA, EVP & Creative Director; DAVID BOGART, Associate Publisher & SVP of Talent Affairs; TOM BREVOORT, VP, Executive Editor; NICK LOWE, Executive Editor, VP of Content, Digital Publishing; DAVID GABRIEL, VP of Print & Digital Publishing; JEFF YOUNGQUIST, VP of Production & Special Projects; ALEX MORALES, Director of Publishing Operations; DAN EDINGTON, Managing Editor; RICKEY PURDIN, Director of Talent Relations; JENNIFER GRÜNWALD, Senior Editor, Special Projects; SUSAN CRESPI, Production Manager; STAN LEE, Chairman Emeritus. For information regarding advertising in Marvel Comics or on Marvel.com, please contact Vit DeBellis, Custom Solutions & Integrated Advertising Manager, at vdebellis@marvel.com. For Marvel subscription inquiries, please call 888-511-5480. **Manufactured between 6/18/2021 and 7/20/2021 by SOLISCO PRINTERS, SCOTT, QC, CANADA.**

10 9 8 7 6 5 4 3 2 1

# ONE

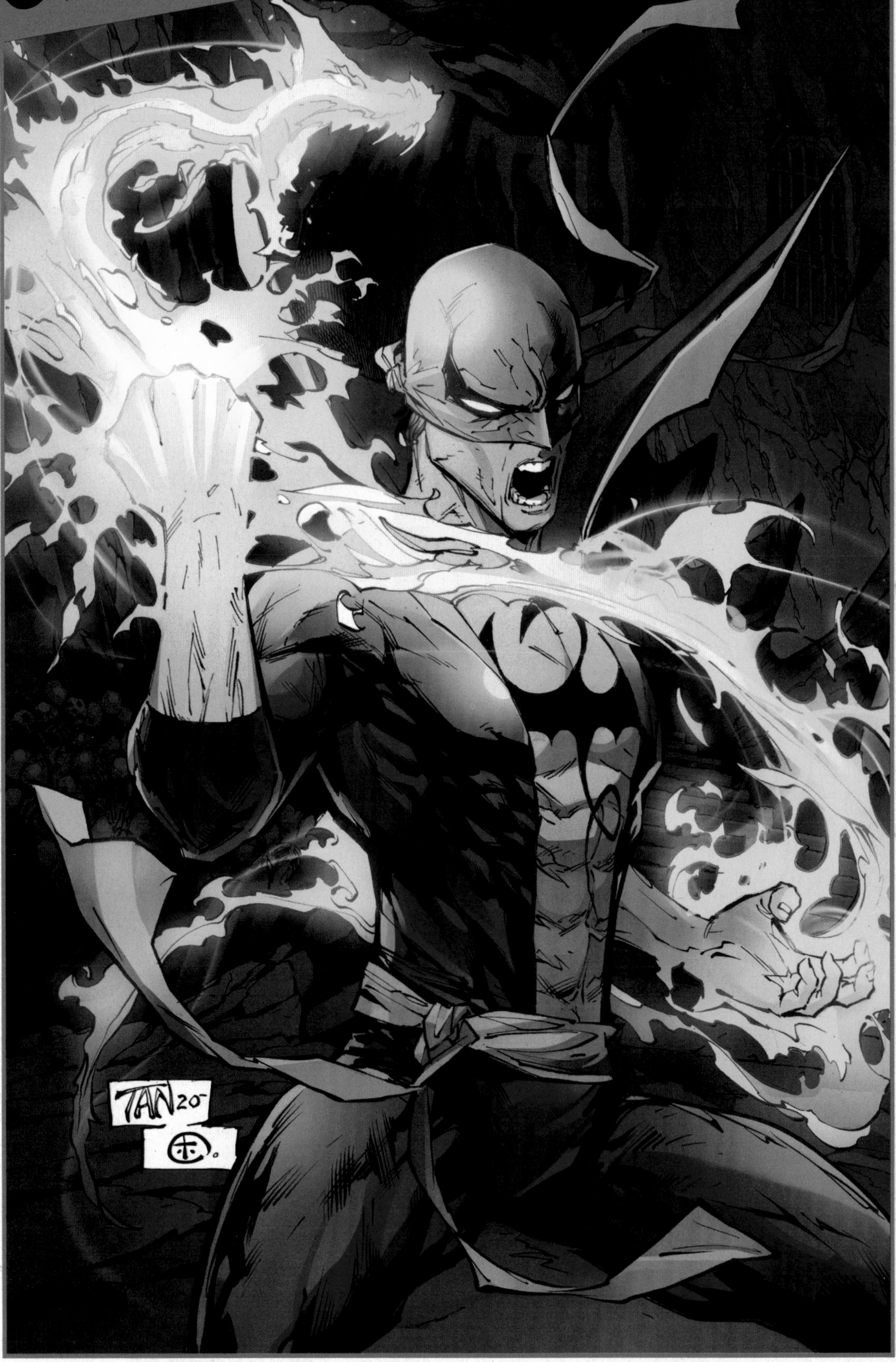
TAN 20

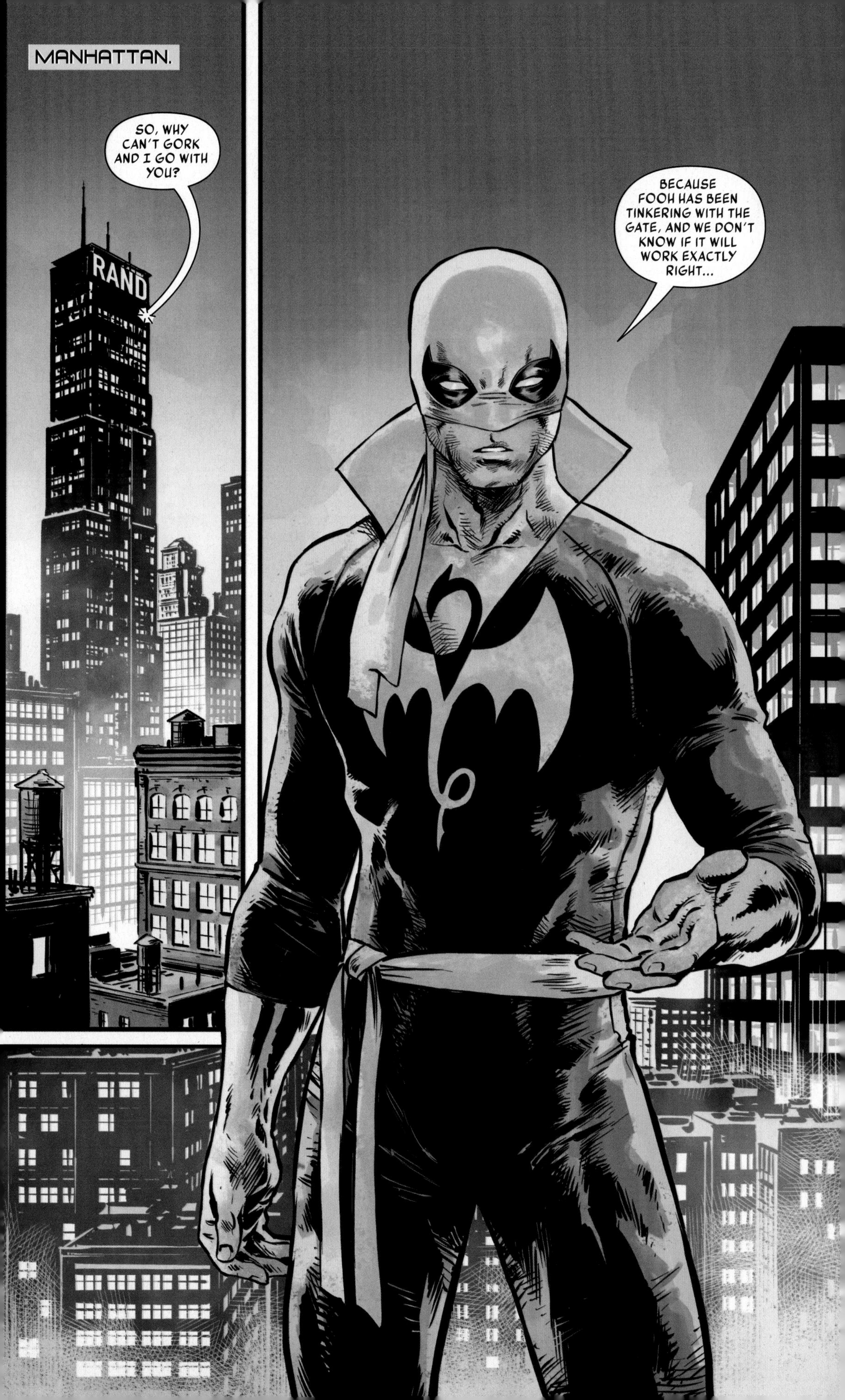
MANHATTAN.
SO, WHY CAN'T GORK AND I GO WITH YOU?
RAND
BECAUSE FOOH HAS BEEN TINKERING WITH THE GATE, AND WE DON'T KNOW IF IT WILL WORK EXACTLY RIGHT...

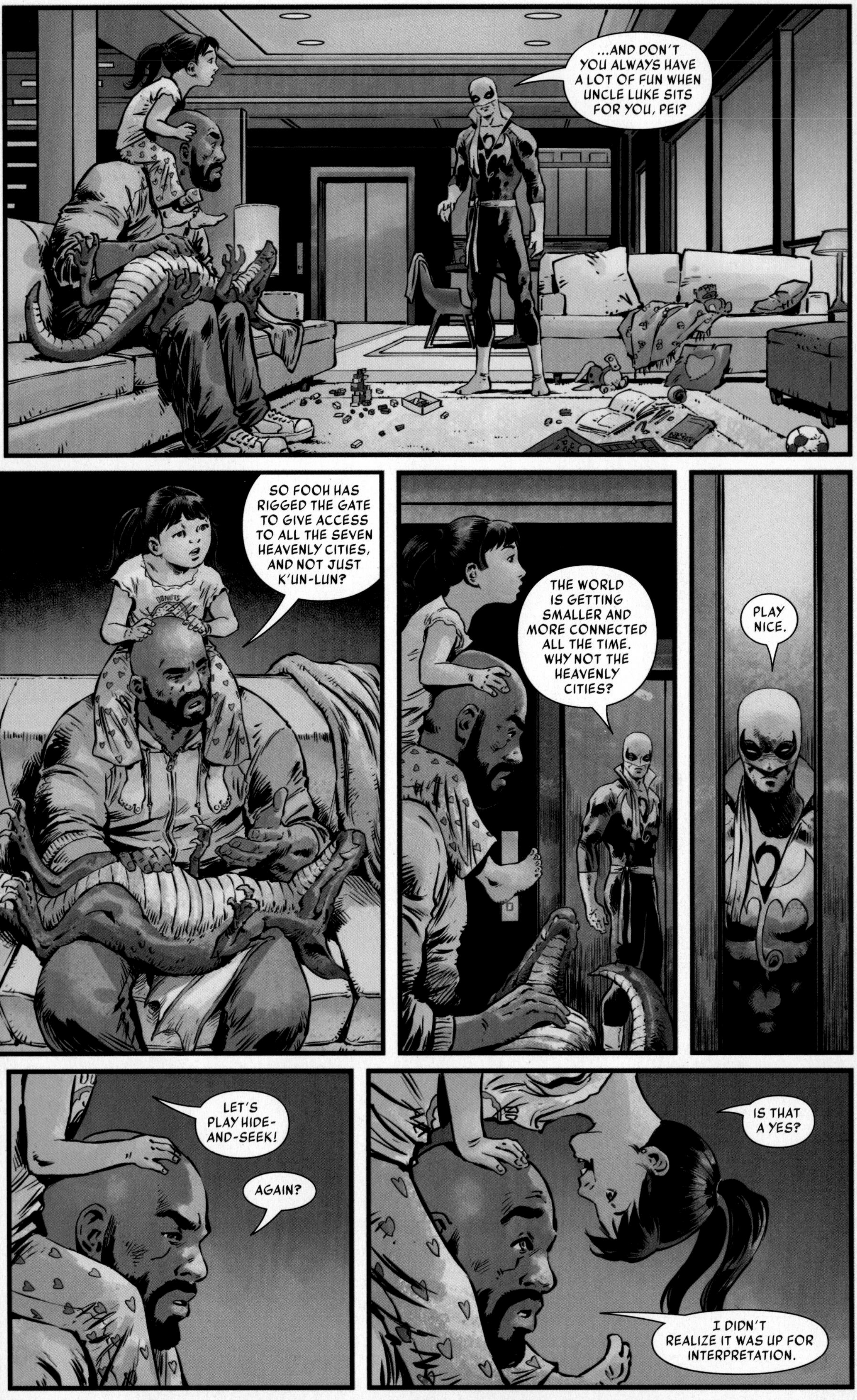
...AND DON'T YOU ALWAYS HAVE A LOT OF FUN WHEN UNCLE LUKE SITS FOR YOU, PEI?
SO FOOH HAS RIGGED THE GATE TO GIVE ACCESS TO ALL THE SEVEN HEAVENLY CITIES, AND NOT JUST K'UN-LUN?
THE WORLD IS GETTING SMALLER AND MORE CONNECTED ALL THE TIME. WHY NOT THE HEAVENLY CITIES?
PLAY NICE.
LET'S PLAY HIDE-AND-SEEK!
AGAIN?
IS THAT A YES?
I DIDN'T REALIZE IT WAS UP FOR INTERPRETATION.

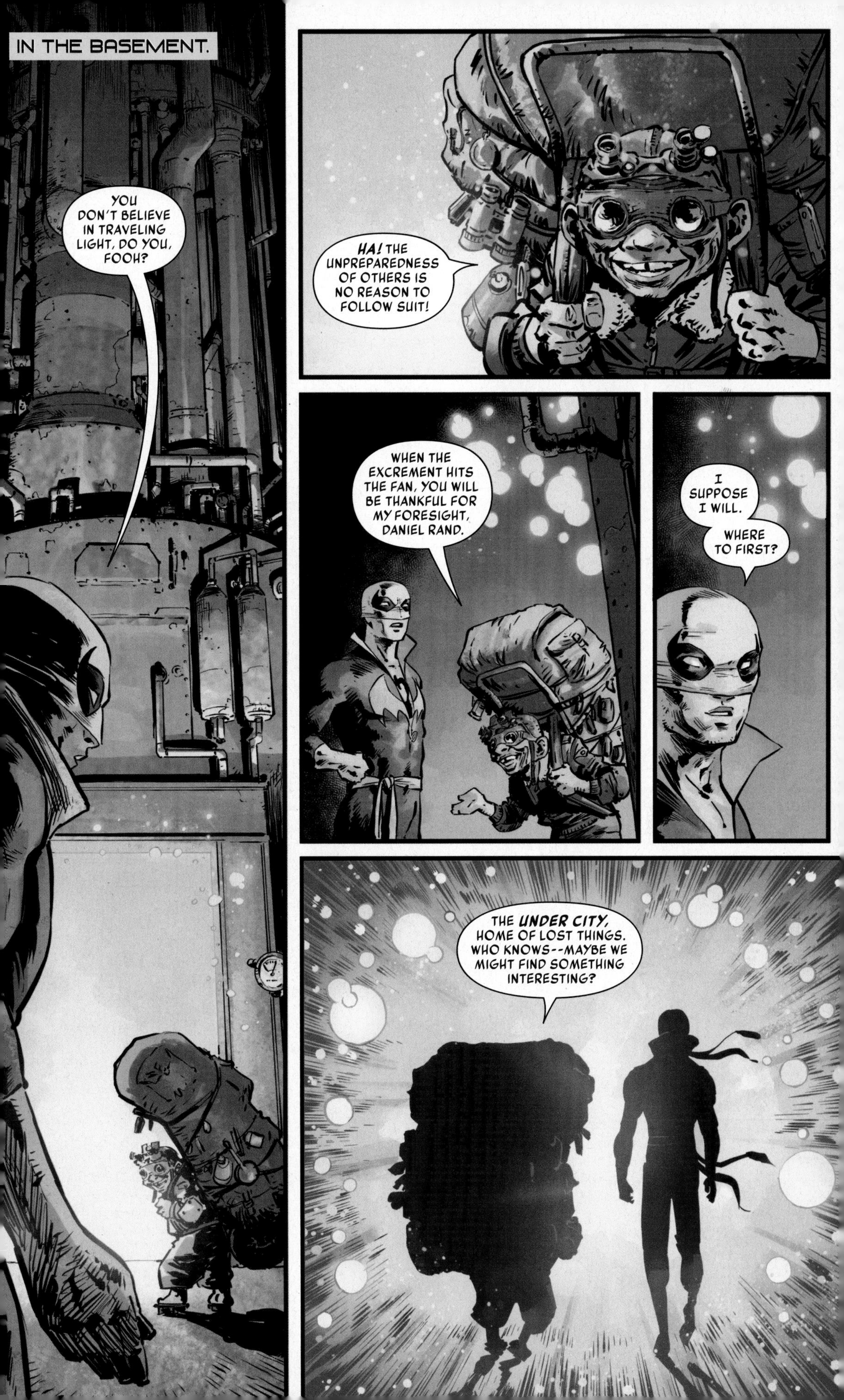
IN THE BASEMENT.
YOU DON'T BELIEVE IN TRAVELING LIGHT, DO YOU, FOOH?
HA! THE UNPREPAREDNESS OF OTHERS IS NO REASON TO FOLLOW SUIT!
WHEN THE EXCREMENT HITS THE FAN, YOU WILL BE THANKFUL FOR MY FORESIGHT, DANIEL RAND.
I SUPPOSE I WILL.
WHERE TO FIRST?
THE UNDER CITY, HOME OF LOST THINGS. WHO KNOWS--MAYBE WE MIGHT FIND SOMETHING INTERESTING?

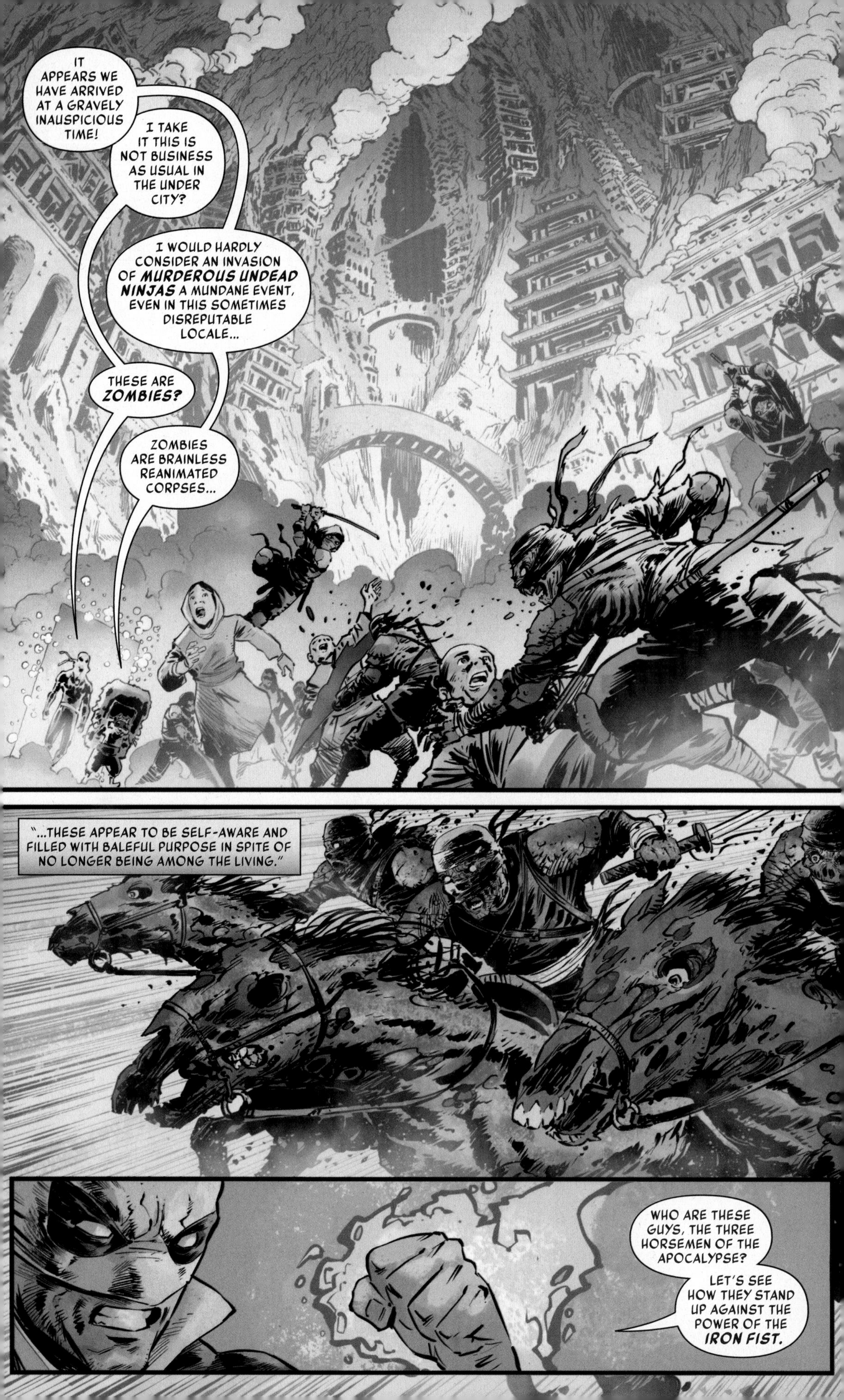
IT APPEARS WE HAVE ARRIVED AT A GRAVELY INAUSPICIOUS TIME!
I TAKE IT THIS IS NOT BUSINESS AS USUAL IN THE UNDER CITY?
I WOULD HARDLY CONSIDER AN INVASION OF MURDEROUS UNDEAD NINJAS A MUNDANE EVENT, EVEN IN THIS SOMETIMES DISREPUTABLE LOCALE...
THESE ARE ZOMBIES?
ZOMBIES ARE BRAINLESS REANIMATED CORPSES...
"...THESE APPEAR TO BE SELF-AWARE AND FILLED WITH BALEFUL PURPOSE IN SPITE OF NO LONGER BEING AMONG THE LIVING."
WHO ARE THESE GUYS, THE THREE HORSEMEN OF THE APOCALYPSE?
LET'S SEE HOW THEY STAND UP AGAINST THE POWER OF THE IRON FIST.

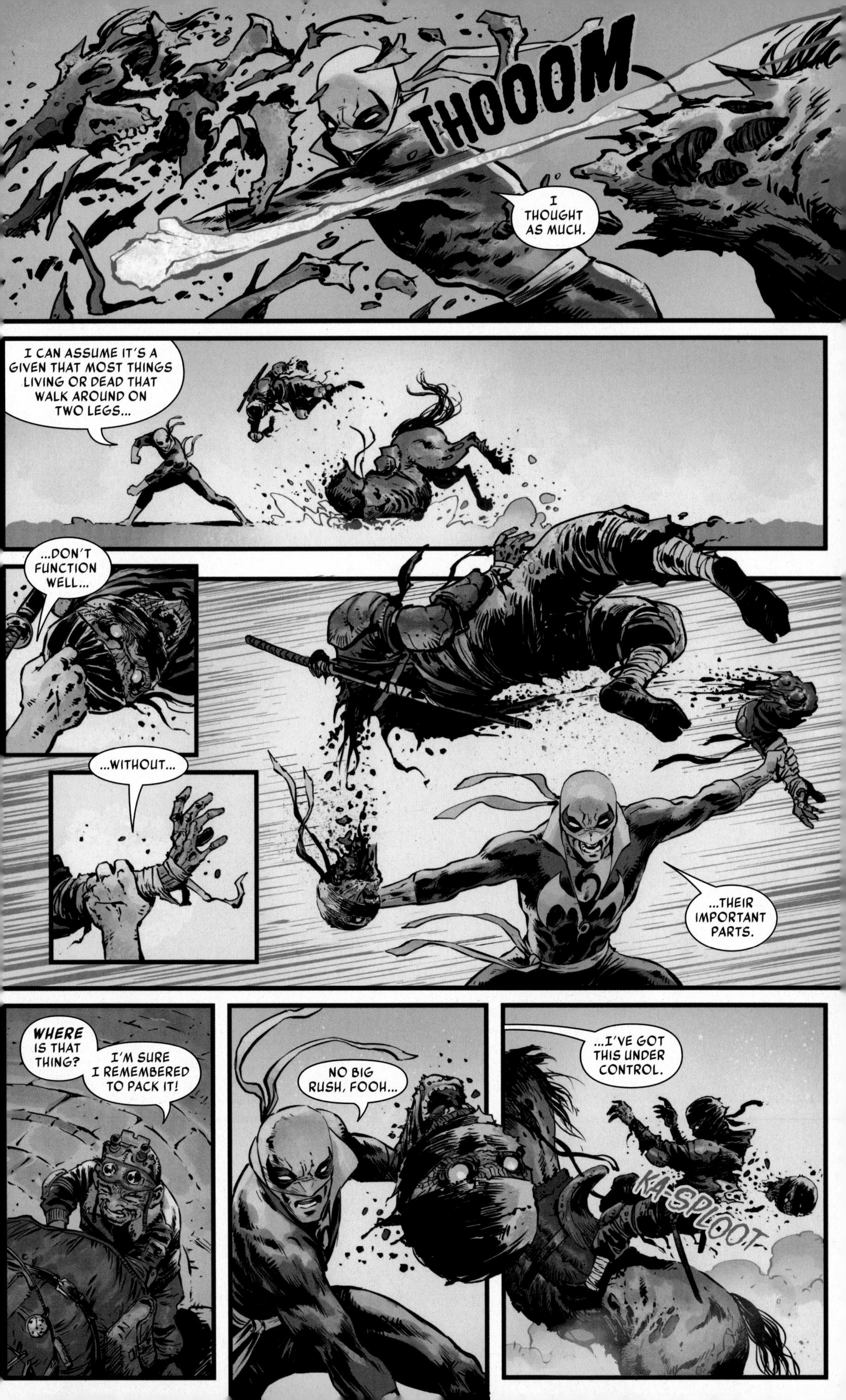
THOOOM
I THOUGHT AS MUCH.
I CAN ASSUME IT'S A GIVEN THAT MOST THINGS LIVING OR DEAD THAT WALK AROUND ON TWO LEGS...
...DON'T FUNCTION WELL...
...WITHOUT...
...THEIR IMPORTANT PARTS.
WHERE IS THAT THING?
I'M SURE I REMEMBERED TO PACK IT!
NO BIG RUSH, FOOH...
...I'VE GOT THIS UNDER CONTROL.
KA-SPLOOT

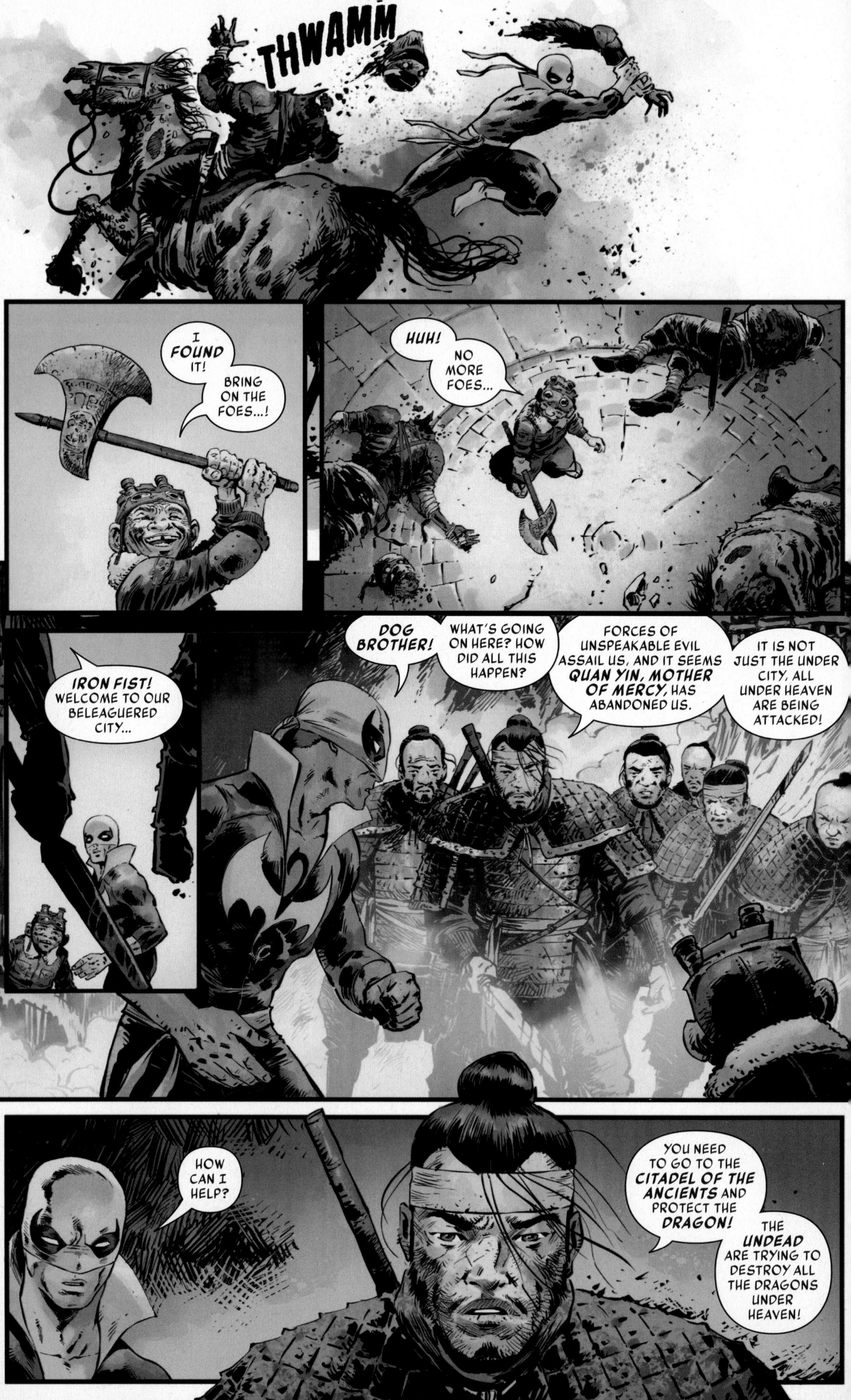
THWAMM
I FOUND IT!
BRING ON THE FOES...!
HUH!
NO MORE FOES...
IRON FIST! WELCOME TO OUR BELEAGUERED CITY...
DOG BROTHER!
WHAT'S GOING ON HERE? HOW DID ALL THIS HAPPEN?
FORCES OF UNSPEAKABLE EVIL ASSAIL US, AND IT SEEMS QUAN YIN, MOTHER OF MERCY, HAS ABANDONED US.
IT IS NOT JUST THE UNDER CITY, ALL UNDER HEAVEN ARE BEING ATTACKED!
HOW CAN I HELP?
YOU NEED TO GO TO THE CITADEL OF THE ANCIENTS AND PROTECT THE DRAGON!
THE UNDEAD ARE TRYING TO DESTROY ALL THE DRAGONS UNDER HEAVEN!

...THAT DEPENDS WHOLLY ON YOUR PARTICULAR SKILL SETS.

I'M GAME.

WHEN YOU CALL SOMETHING A "CITADEL," IT MEANS IT'S PROBABLY DIFFICULT TO GET TO.

"DIFFICULT" IS A HIGHLY SUBJECTIVE DESCRIPTION...

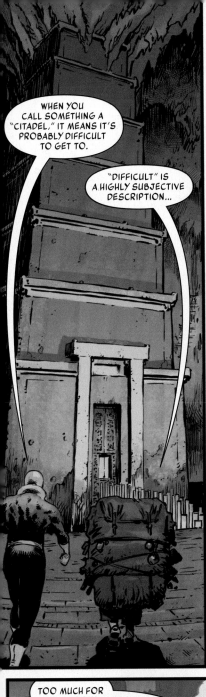

YOU, COMING, OLD MAN?

TOO MUCH FOR YOU, FOOH?

DON'T BE IMPERTINENT.

I AM ONLY PAUSING TO MEDITATE ON THE MEANING OF IMPERMANENCE...

...AND CATCH MY BREATH.

GO AHEAD, I WILL CATCH UP SHORTLY.

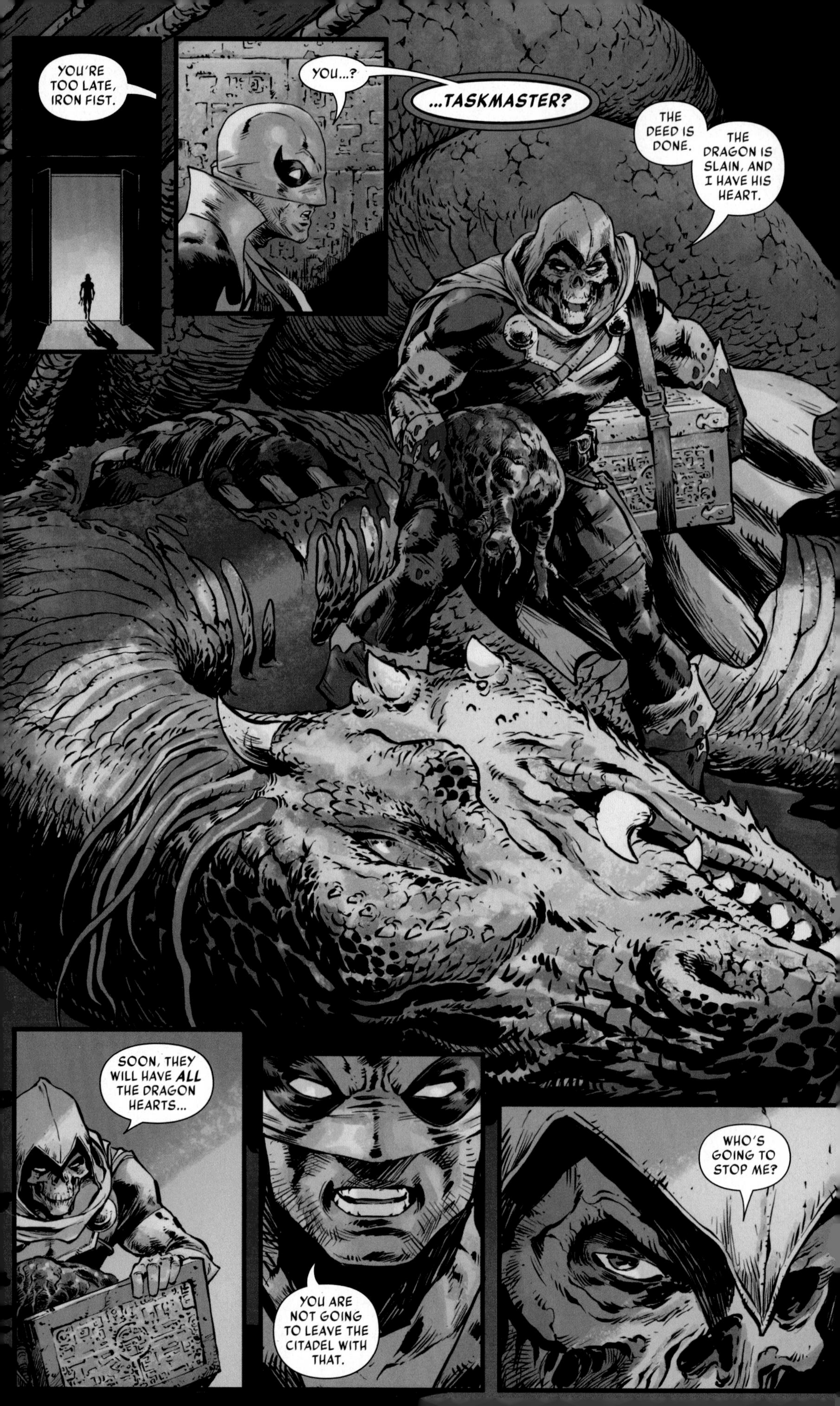

YOU'RE TOO LATE, IRON FIST.
YOU...?
...TASKMASTER?
THE DEED IS DONE.
THE DRAGON IS SLAIN, AND I HAVE HIS HEART.
SOON, THEY WILL HAVE ALL THE DRAGON HEARTS...
YOU ARE NOT GOING TO LEAVE THE CITADEL WITH THAT.
WHO'S GOING TO STOP ME?

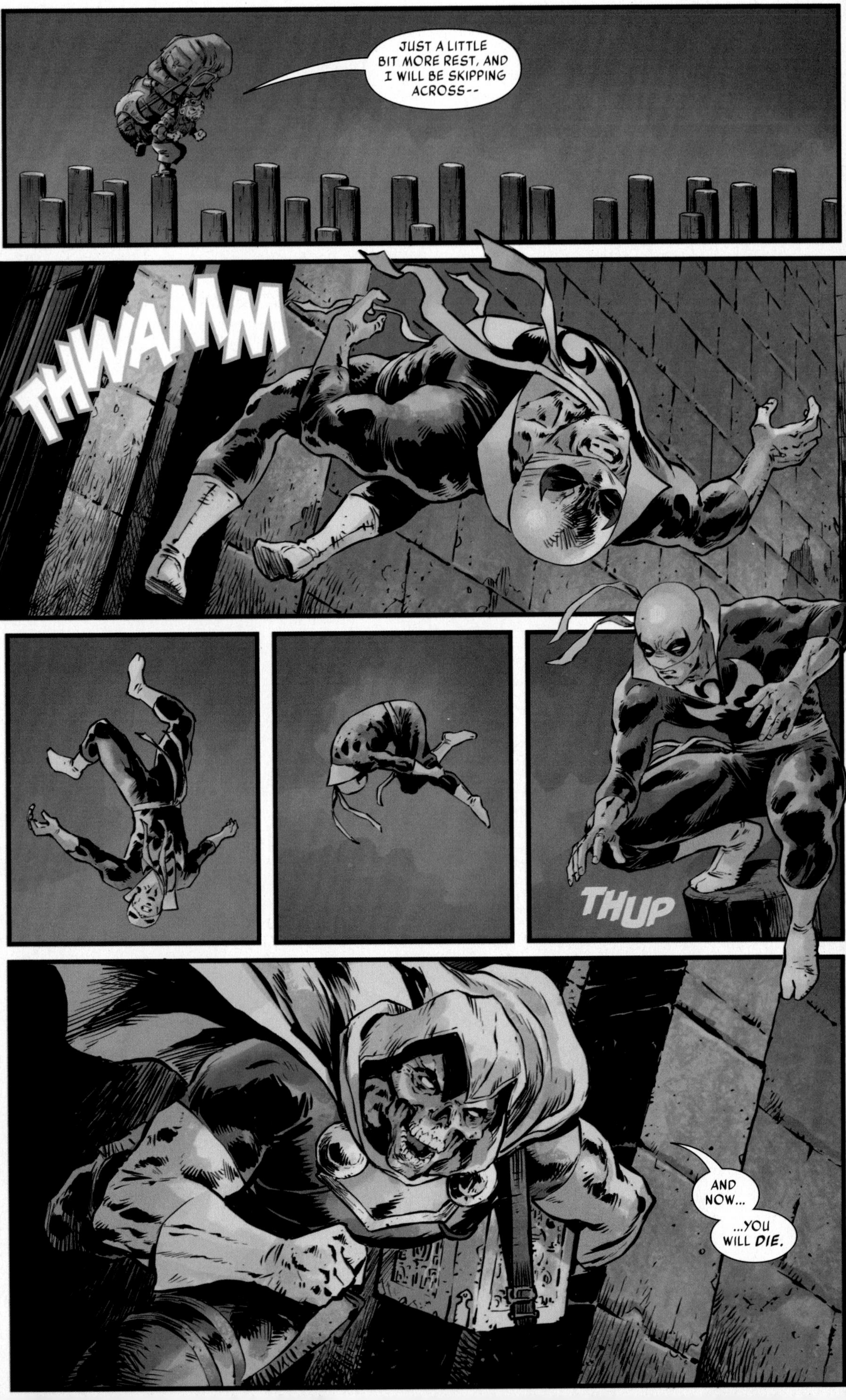
JUST A LITTLE BIT MORE REST, AND I WILL BE SKIPPING ACROSS--
THWAMM
THUP
AND NOW...
...YOU WILL DIE.

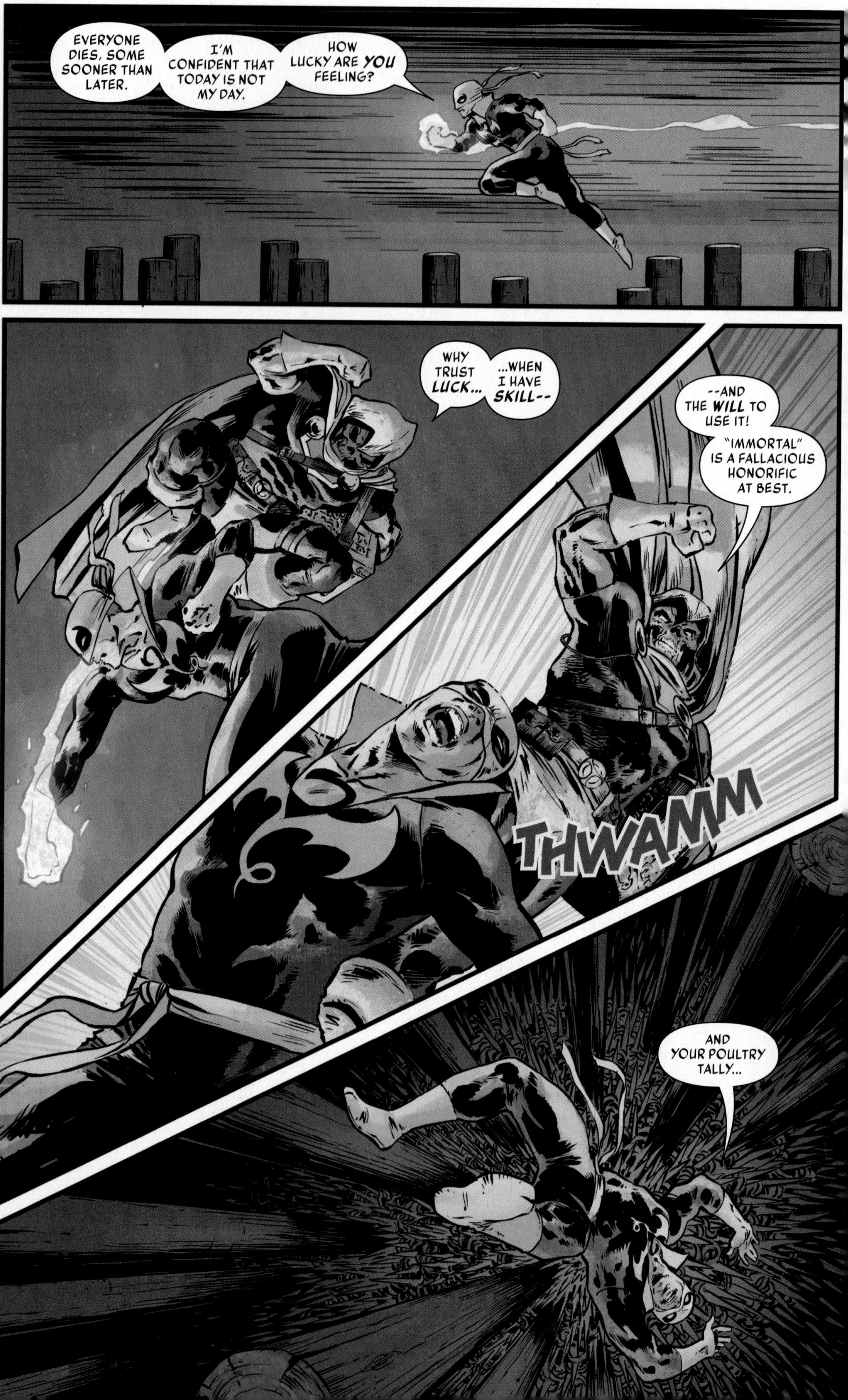

EVERYONE DIES, SOME SOONER THAN LATER.
I'M CONFIDENT THAT TODAY IS NOT MY DAY.
HOW LUCKY ARE YOU FEELING?
WHY TRUST LUCK...
...WHEN I HAVE SKILL--
--AND THE WILL TO USE IT!
"IMMORTAL" IS A FALLACIOUS HONORIFIC AT BEST.
THWAMM
AND YOUR POULTRY TALLY...

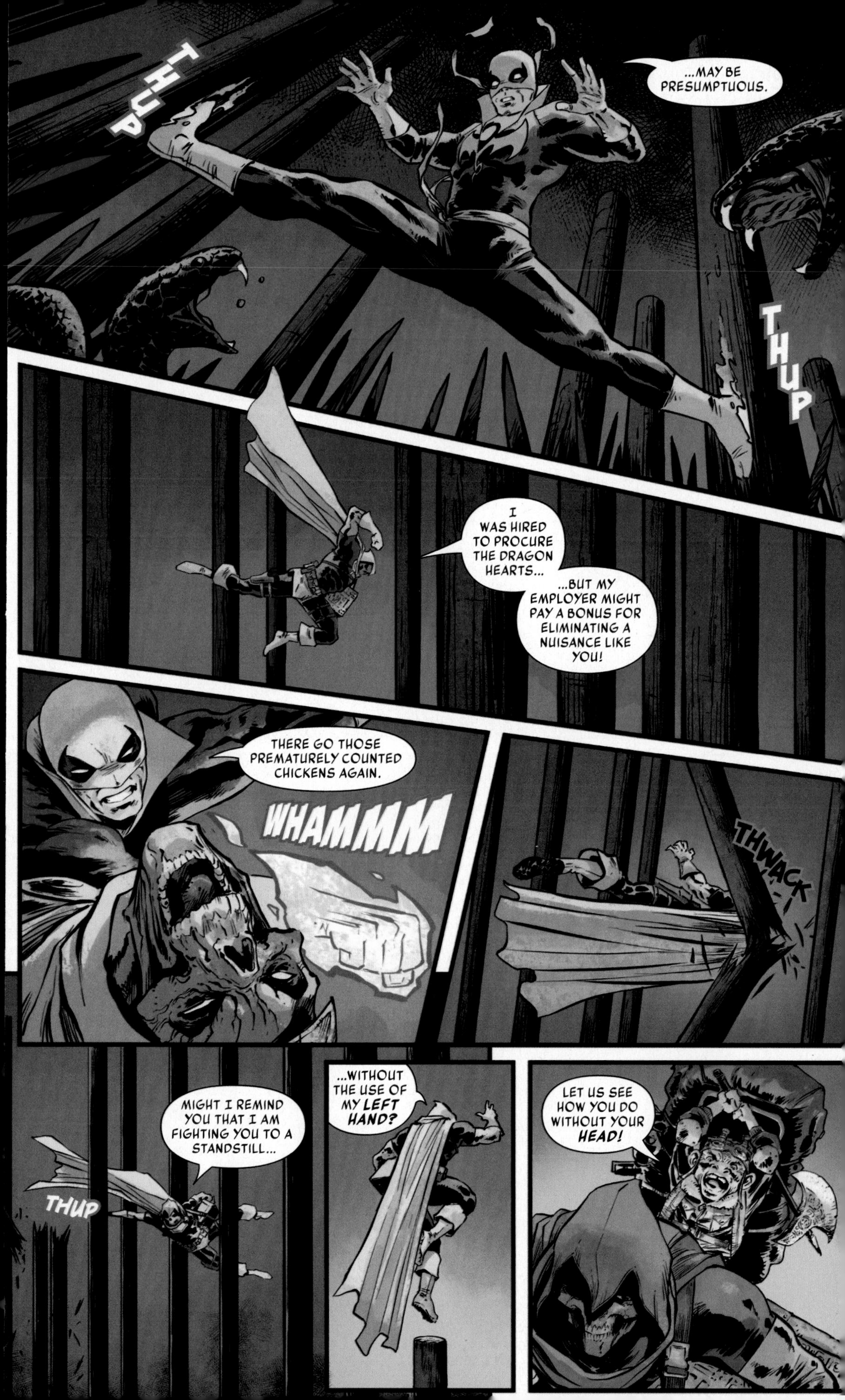
THUP
...MAY BE PRESUMPTUOUS.
THUP
I WAS HIRED TO PROCURE THE DRAGON HEARTS...
...BUT MY EMPLOYER MIGHT PAY A BONUS FOR ELIMINATING A NUISANCE LIKE YOU!
THERE GO THOSE PREMATURELY COUNTED CHICKENS AGAIN.
WHAMMM
THWACK
MIGHT I REMIND YOU THAT I AM FIGHTING YOU TO A STANDSTILL...
THUP
...WITHOUT THE USE OF MY *LEFT HAND?*
LET US SEE HOW YOU DO WITHOUT YOUR *HEAD!*

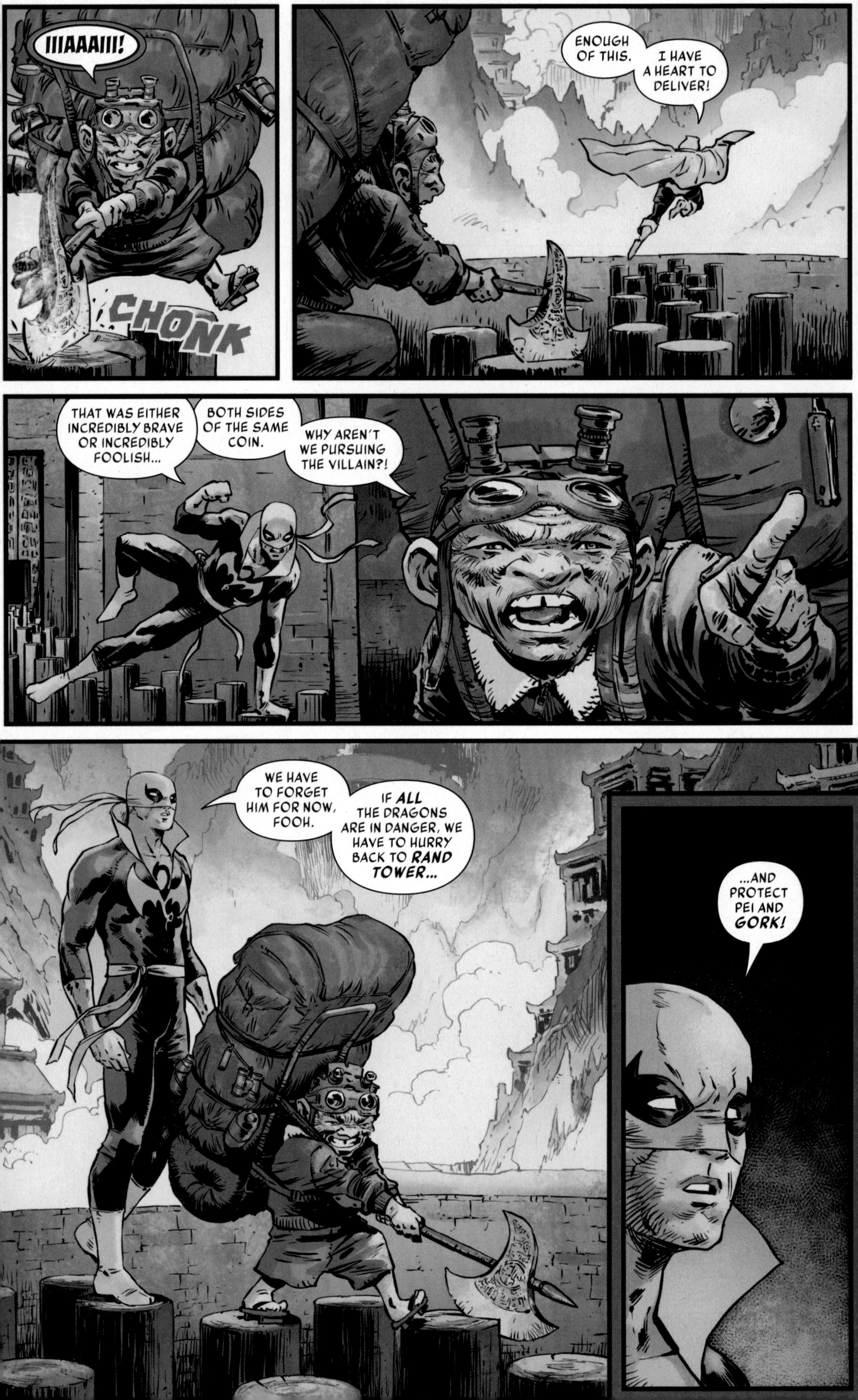
IIIAAAIII!
CHONK
ENOUGH OF THIS.
I HAVE A HEART TO DELIVER!
THAT WAS EITHER INCREDIBLY BRAVE OR INCREDIBLY FOOLISH...
BOTH SIDES OF THE SAME COIN.
WHY AREN'T WE PURSUING THE VILLAIN?!
WE HAVE TO FORGET HIM FOR NOW, FOOH.
IF ALL THE DRAGONS ARE IN DANGER, WE HAVE TO HURRY BACK TO RAND TOWER...
...AND PROTECT PEI AND GORK!

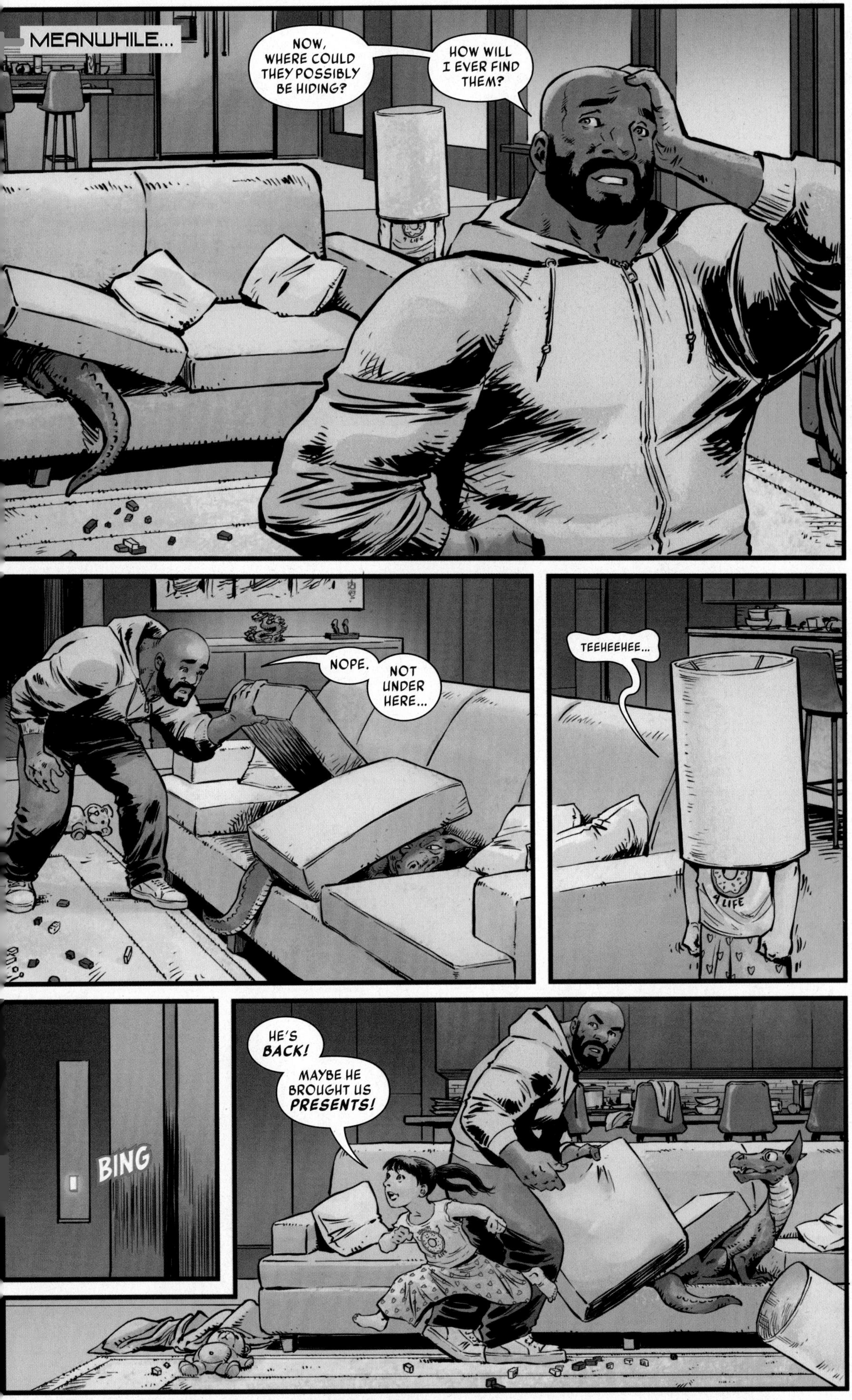
MEANWHILE...
NOW, WHERE COULD THEY POSSIBLY BE HIDING?
HOW WILL I EVER FIND THEM?
NOPE.
NOT UNDER HERE...
TEEHEEHEE...
BING
HE'S BACK!
MAYBE HE BROUGHT US PRESENTS!

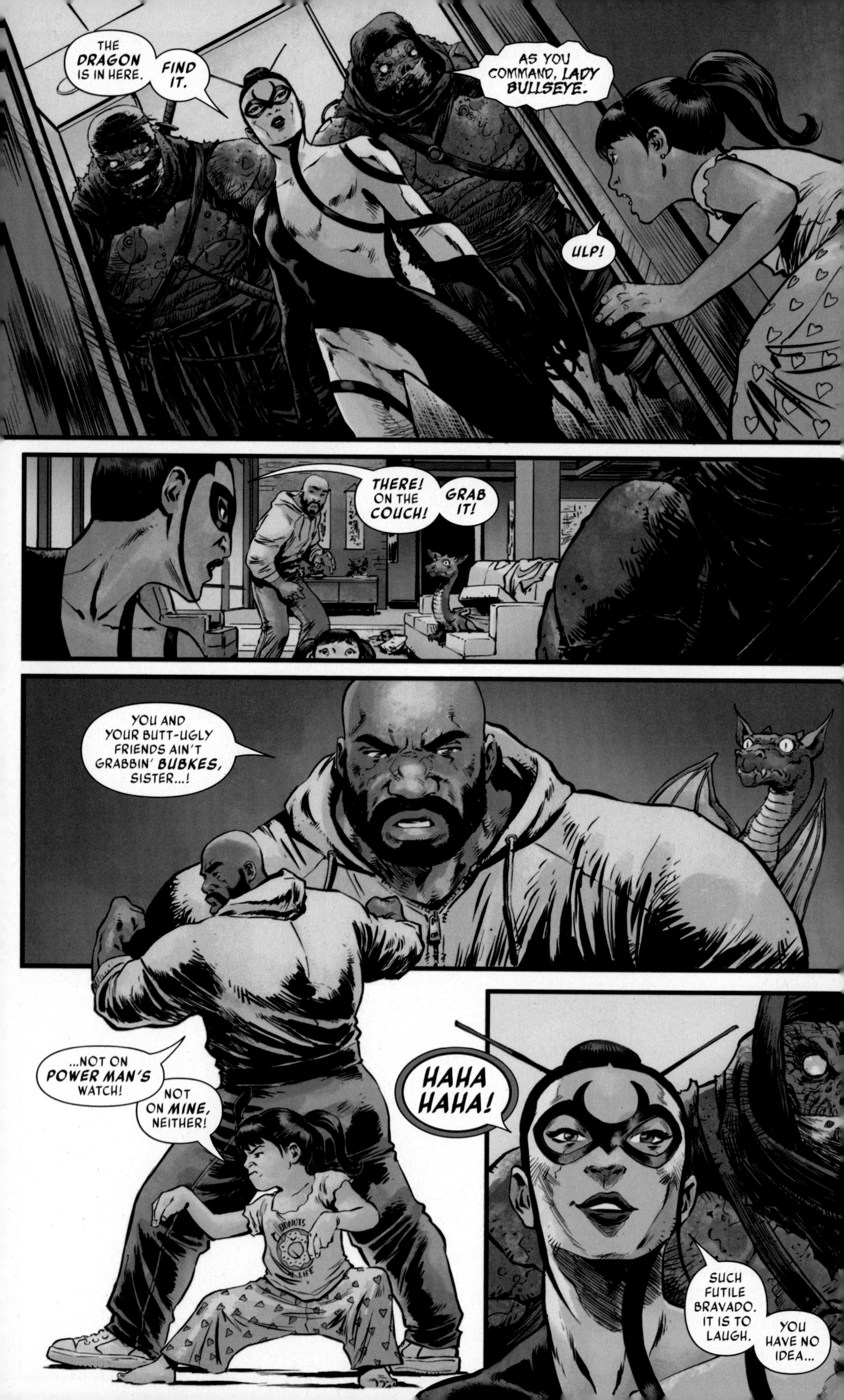
THE DRAGON IS IN HERE.
FIND IT.
AS YOU COMMAND, LADY BULLSEYE.
ULP!
THERE! ON THE COUCH!
GRAB IT!
YOU AND YOUR BUTT-UGLY FRIENDS AIN'T GRABBIN' BUBKES, SISTER...!
...NOT ON POWER MAN'S WATCH!
NOT ON MINE, NEITHER!
HAHA HAHA!
SUCH FUTILE BRAVADO. IT IS TO LAUGH.
YOU HAVE NO IDEA...

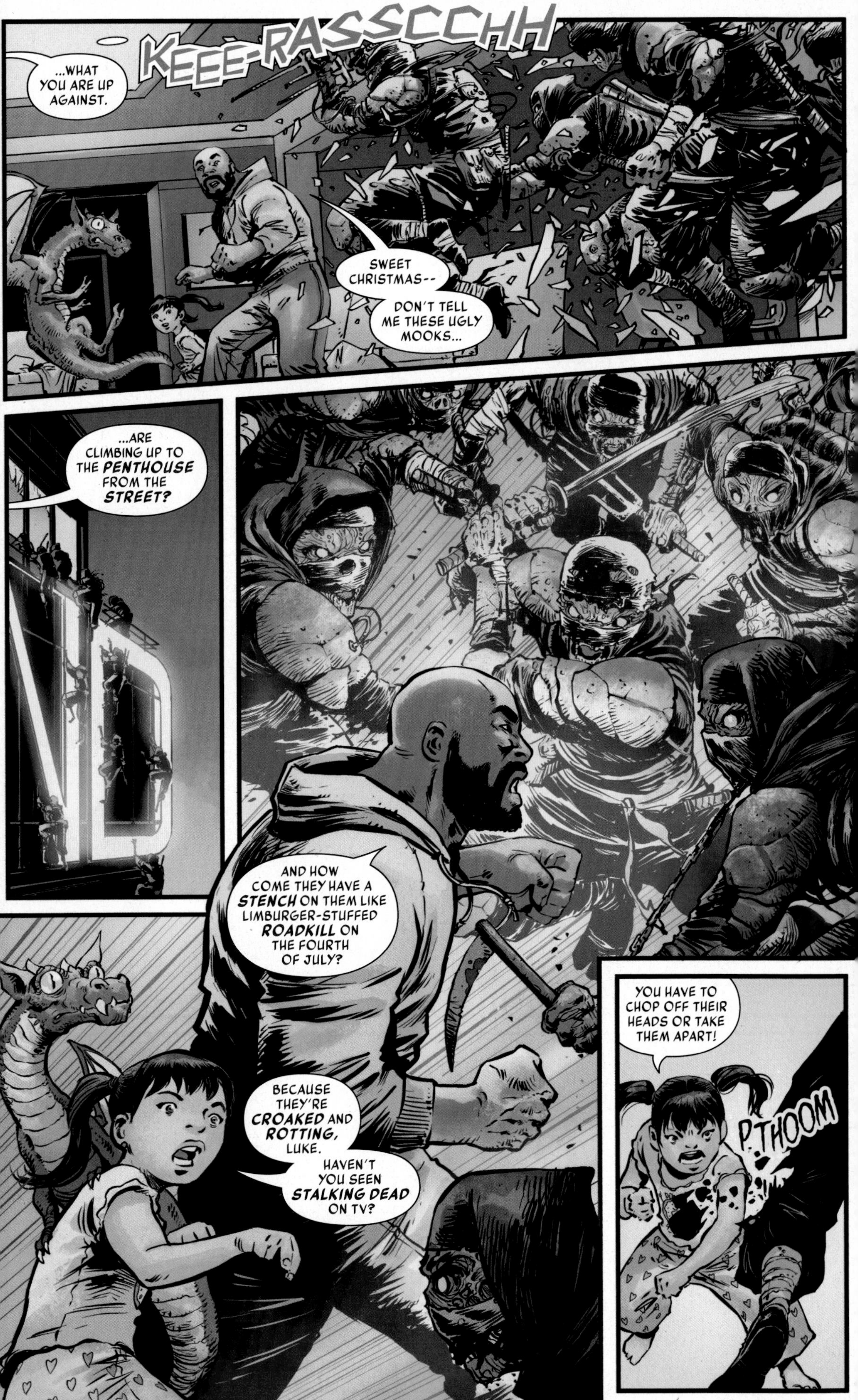

...WHAT YOU ARE UP AGAINST.
KEEE-RASSCCHH
SWEET CHRISTMAS--
DON'T TELL ME THESE UGLY MOOKS...
...ARE CLIMBING UP TO THE PENTHOUSE FROM THE STREET?
AND HOW COME THEY HAVE A STENCH ON THEM LIKE LIMBURGER-STUFFED ROADKILL ON THE FOURTH OF JULY?
BECAUSE THEY'RE CROAKED AND ROTTING, LUKE.
HAVEN'T YOU SEEN STALKING DEAD ON TV?
YOU HAVE TO CHOP OFF THEIR HEADS OR TAKE THEM APART!
P.THOOM

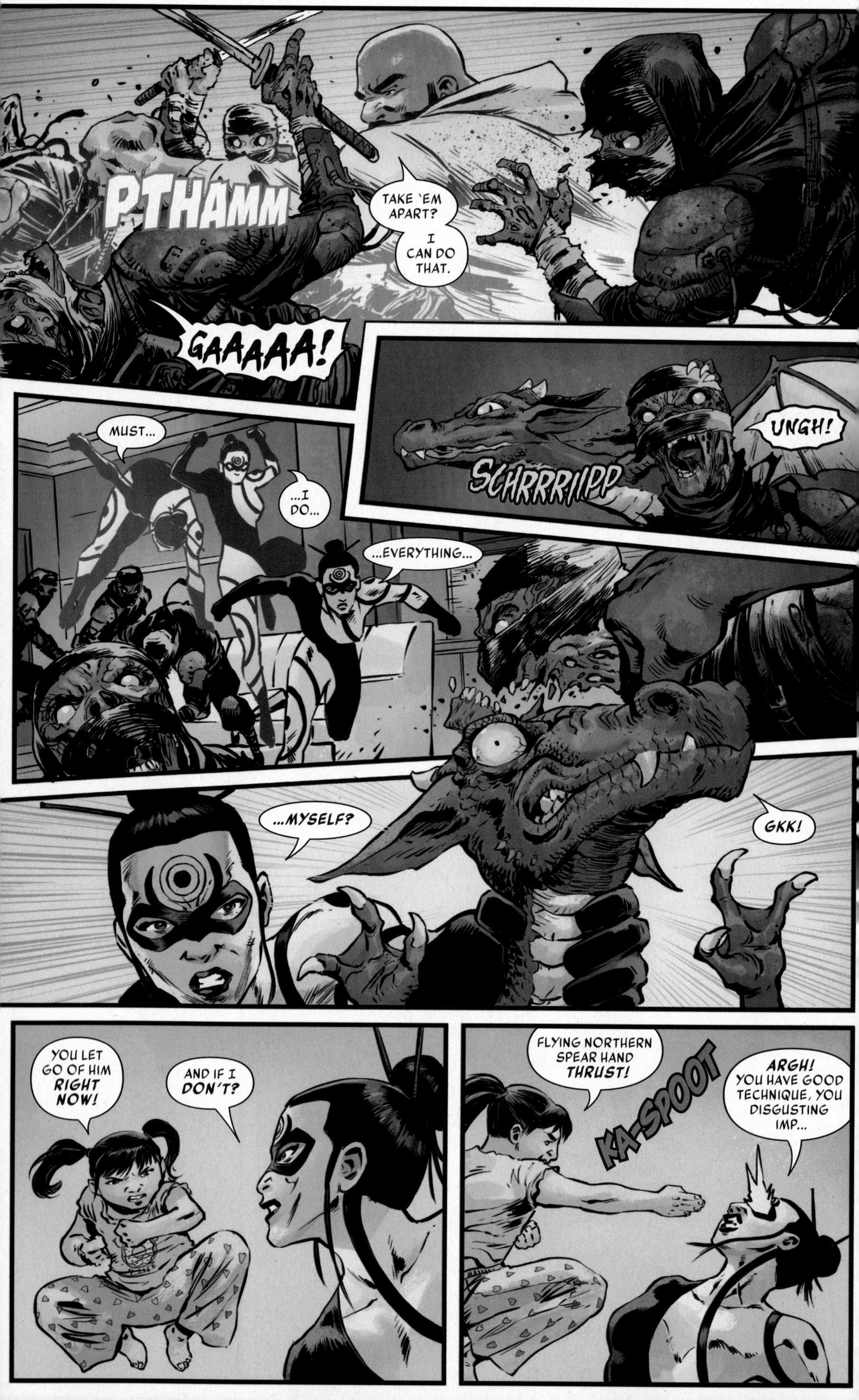
PTHAMM
TAKE 'EM APART?
I CAN DO THAT.
GAAAAA!
SCHRRRIIPP
UNGH!
MUST...
...I DO...
...EVERYTHING...
...MYSELF?
GKK!
YOU LET GO OF HIM RIGHT NOW!
AND IF I DON'T?
FLYING NORTHERN SPEAR HAND THRUST!
KA-SPOOT
ARGH! YOU HAVE GOOD TECHNIQUE, YOU DISGUSTING IMP...

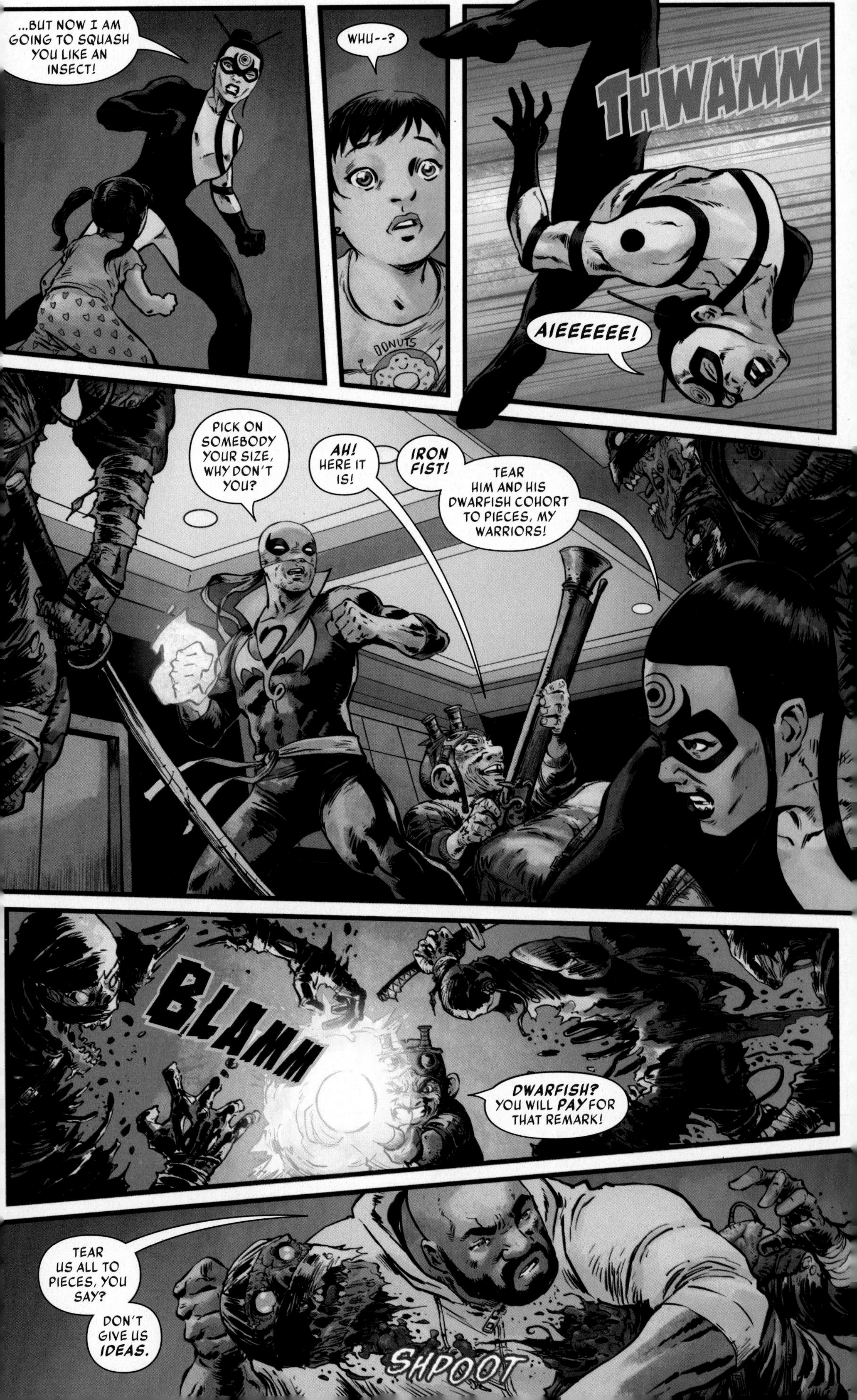
...BUT NOW I AM GOING TO SQUASH YOU LIKE AN INSECT!
WHU--?
THWAMM
AIEEEEEE!
DONUTS
PICK ON SOMEBODY YOUR SIZE, WHY DON'T YOU?
AH! HERE IT IS!
IRON FIST!
TEAR HIM AND HIS DWARFISH COHORT TO PIECES, MY WARRIORS!
BLAMM
DWARFISH? YOU WILL PAY FOR THAT REMARK!
TEAR US ALL TO PIECES, YOU SAY?
DON'T GIVE US IDEAS.
SHPOOT

RETREAT! WE NO LONGER HAVE THE TACTICAL ADVANTAGE!

TASKMASTER WAS SUPPOSED TO KILL IRON FIST AND FOOH IN THE UNDER CITY...!

...HE WILL ANSWER FOR HIS FAILURE!

MY HERO!♥

OKAY, THAT'S ENOUGH...

HEH HEH HEH.

LOOK AT THEM RUN!

DID YOU SEE HOW THEY EXPLODED WHEN I SHOT THEM WITH THAT LOAD OF SCRAP IRON?

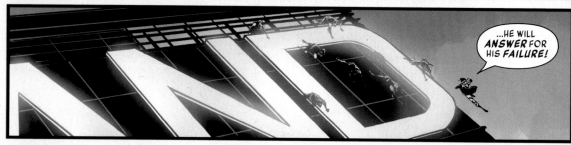

EVEN IF YOU TAKE THEM APART, THEY'RE STILL OBSTREPEROUS AS ALL GET-OUT.

GNARR!

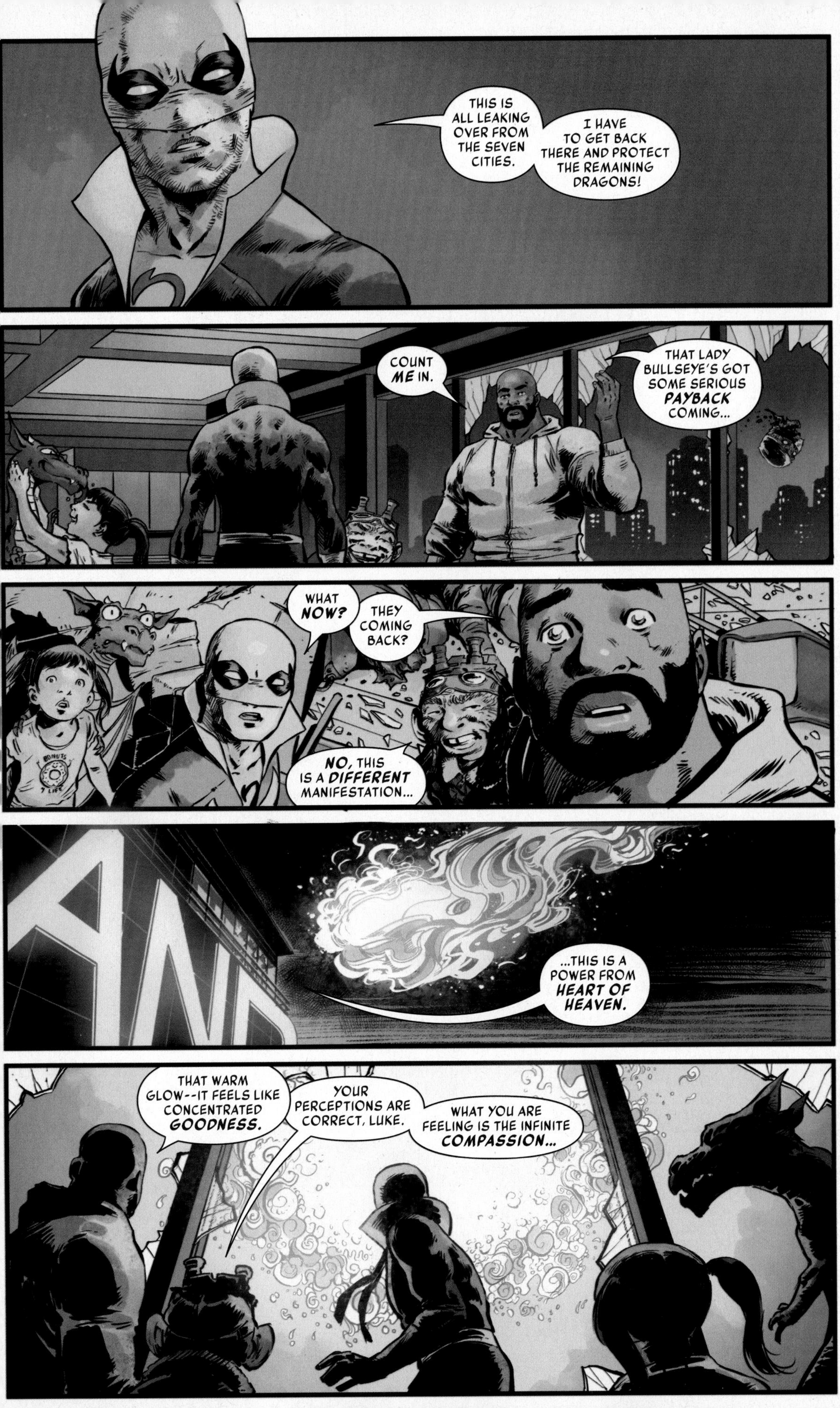
THIS IS ALL LEAKING OVER FROM THE SEVEN CITIES.
I HAVE TO GET BACK THERE AND PROTECT THE REMAINING DRAGONS!
COUNT ME IN.
THAT LADY BULLSEYE'S GOT SOME SERIOUS PAYBACK COMING...
WHAT NOW?
THEY COMING BACK?
NO, THIS IS A DIFFERENT MANIFESTATION...
DONUTS 4 LIFE
...THIS IS A POWER FROM HEART OF HEAVEN.
THAT WARM GLOW--IT FEELS LIKE CONCENTRATED GOODNESS.
YOUR PERCEPTIONS ARE CORRECT, LUKE.
WHAT YOU ARE FEELING IS THE INFINITE COMPASSION...

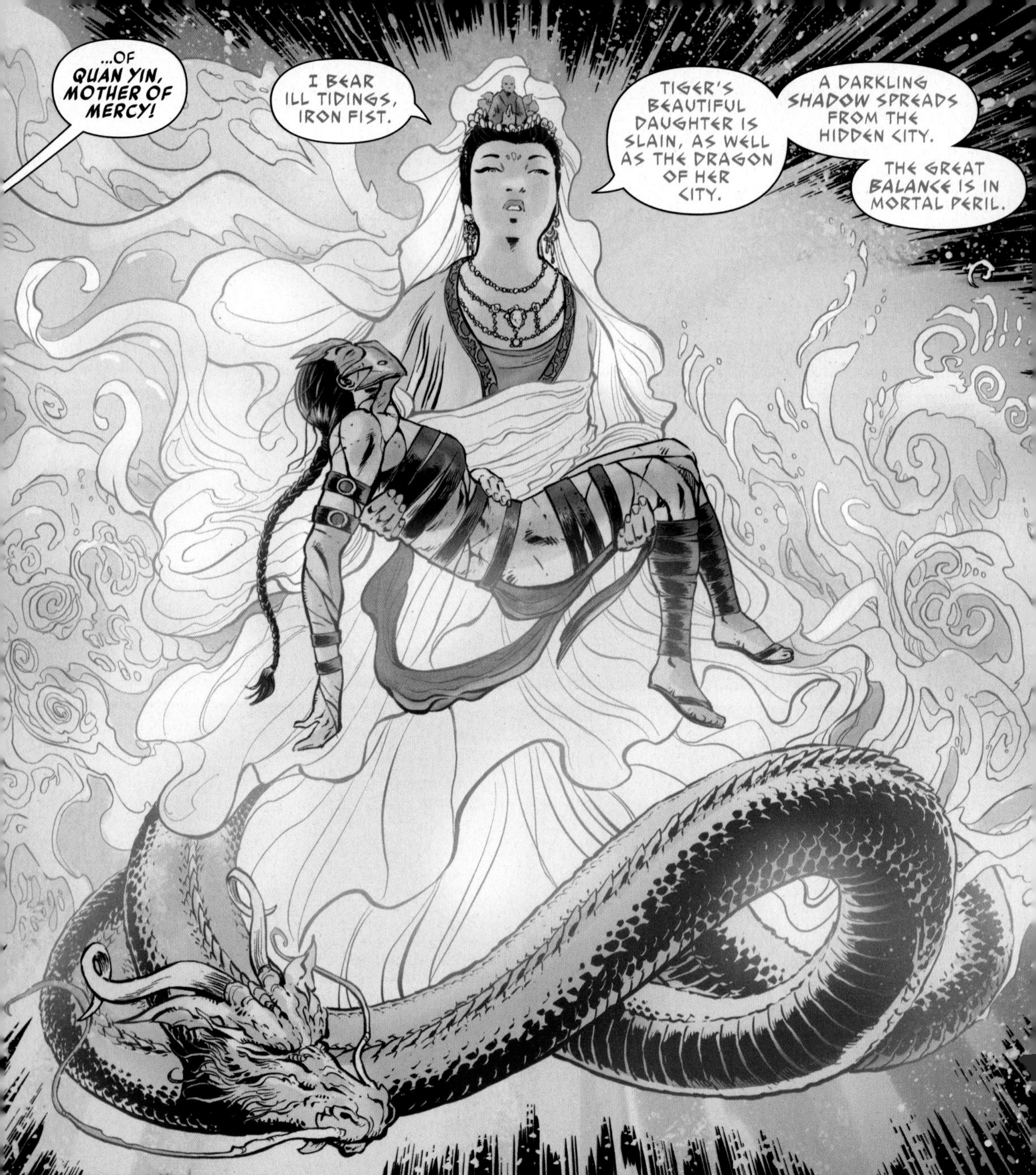
...OF QUAN YIN, MOTHER OF MERCY!
I BEAR ILL TIDINGS, IRON FIST.
TIGER'S BEAUTIFUL DAUGHTER IS SLAIN, AS WELL AS THE DRAGON OF HER CITY.
A DARKLING SHADOW SPREADS FROM THE HIDDEN CITY.
THE GREAT BALANCE IS IN MORTAL PERIL.
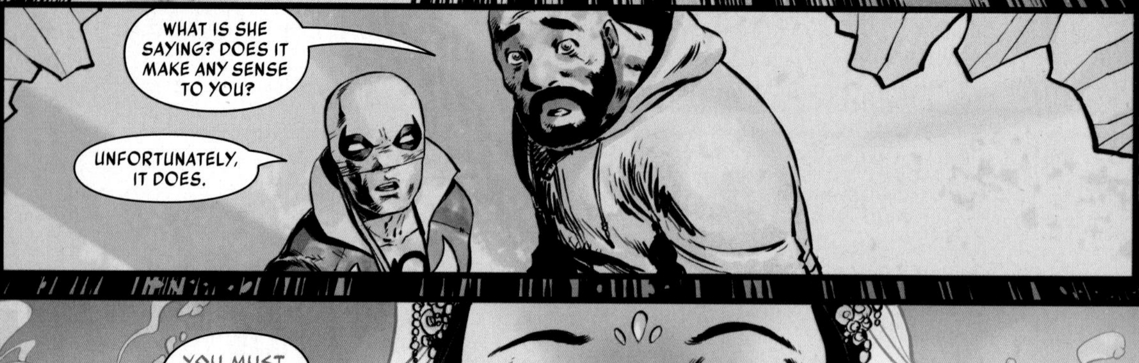
WHAT IS SHE SAYING? DOES IT MAKE ANY SENSE TO YOU?
UNFORTUNATELY, IT DOES.
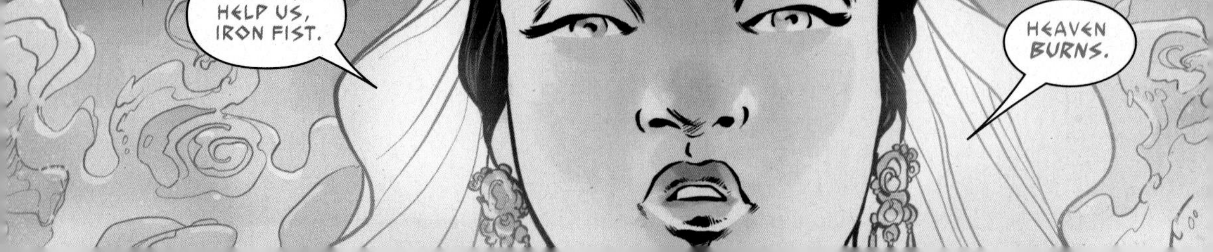
YOU MUST HELP US, IRON FIST.
HEAVEN BURNS.

# TWO

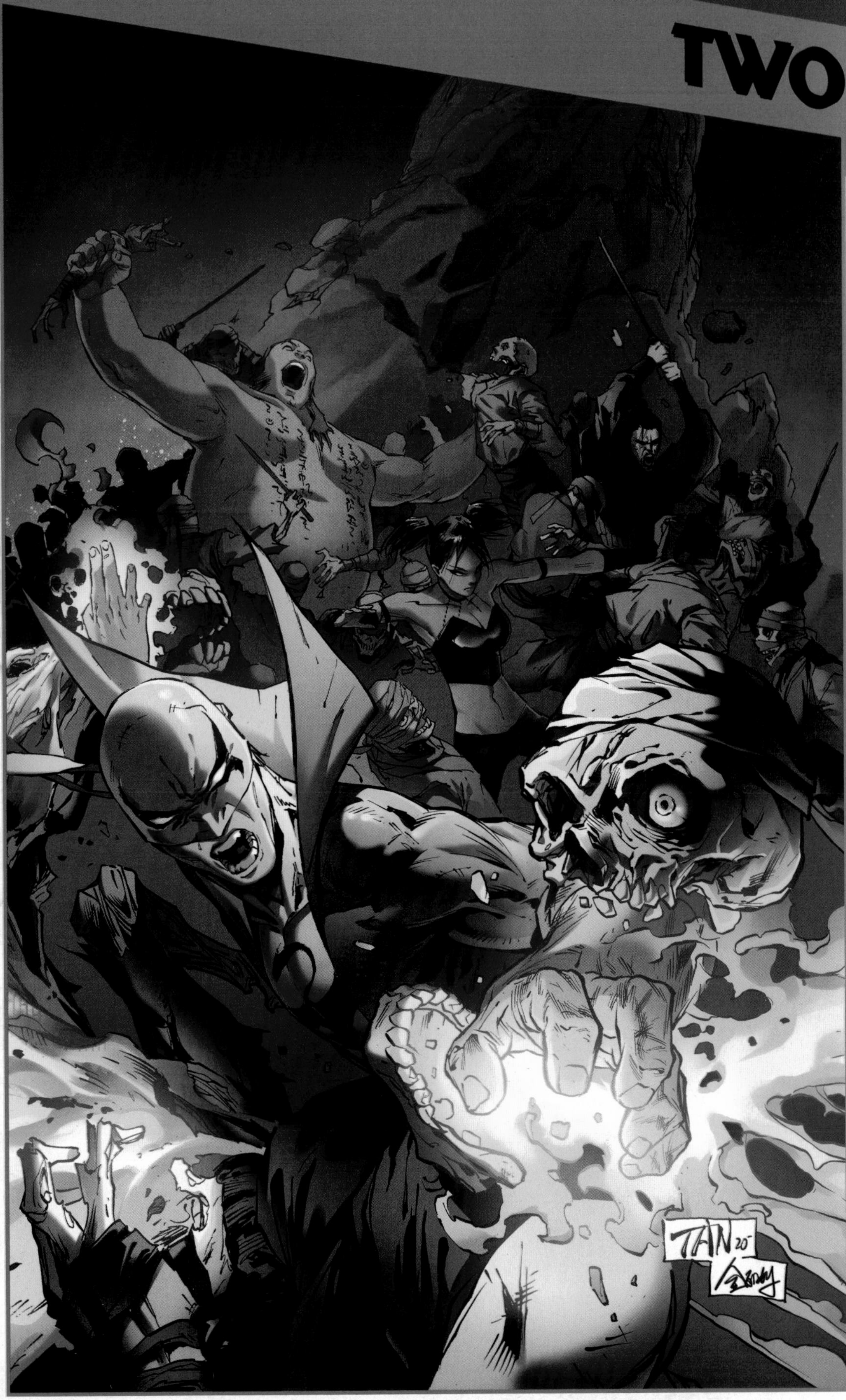
TAN 20

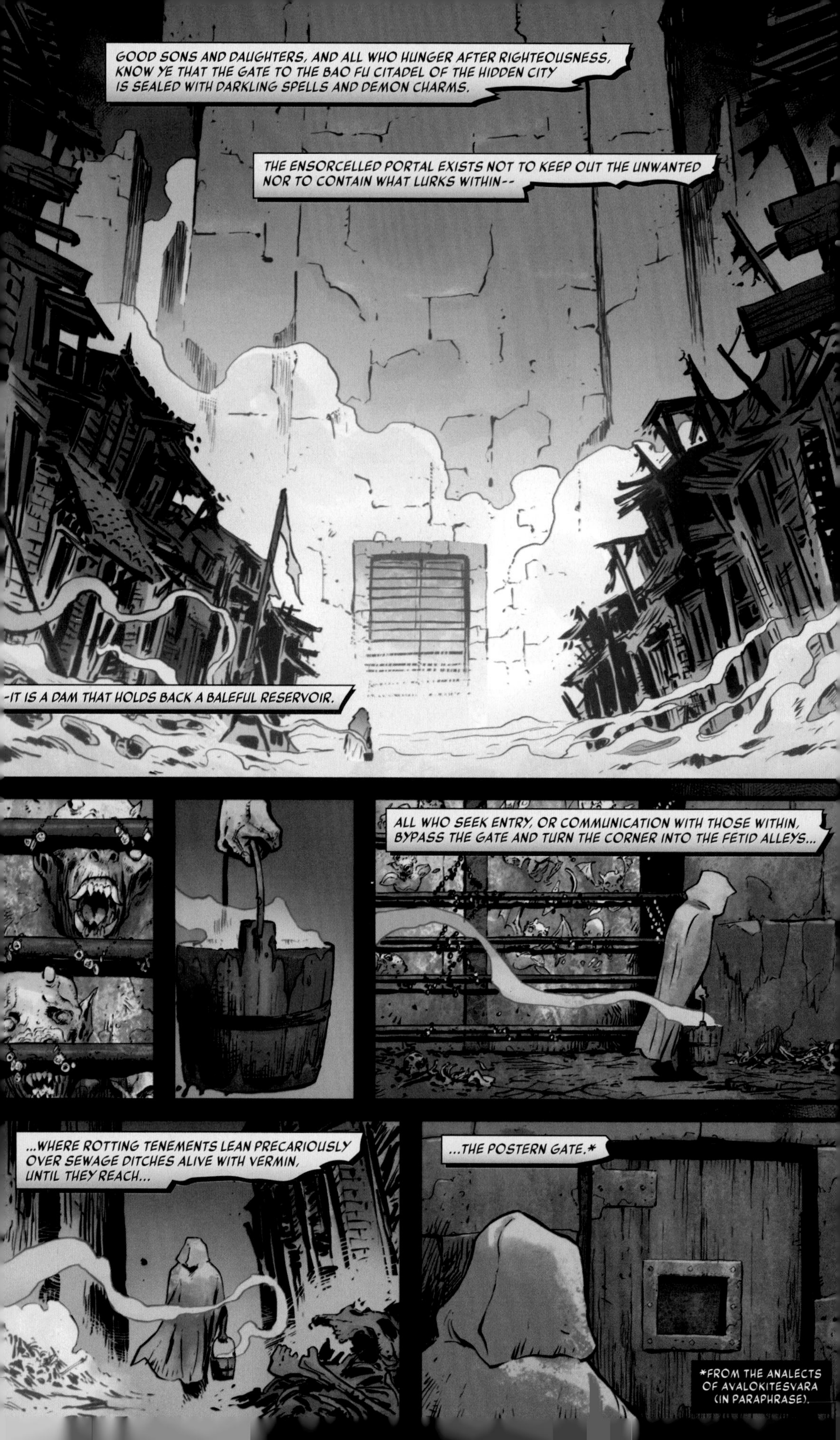
GOOD SONS AND DAUGHTERS, AND ALL WHO HUNGER AFTER RIGHTEOUSNESS, KNOW YE THAT THE GATE TO THE BAO FU CITADEL OF THE HIDDEN CITY IS SEALED WITH DARKLING SPELLS AND DEMON CHARMS.
THE ENSORCELLED PORTAL EXISTS NOT TO KEEP OUT THE UNWANTED NOR TO CONTAIN WHAT LURKS WITHIN--
-IT IS A DAM THAT HOLDS BACK A BALEFUL RESERVOIR.
ALL WHO SEEK ENTRY, OR COMMUNICATION WITH THOSE WITHIN, BYPASS THE GATE AND TURN THE CORNER INTO THE FETID ALLEYS...
...WHERE ROTTING TENEMENTS LEAN PRECARIOUSLY OVER SEWAGE DITCHES ALIVE WITH VERMIN, UNTIL THEY REACH...
...THE POSTERN GATE.*
*FROM THE ANALECTS OF AVALOKITESVARA (IN PARAPHRASE).

I BRING YOU THE HEART OF THE UNDER CITY DRAGON.

YOU HAVE DONE WELL, *TASKMASTER.*

YOU MAY NOW...

...PERFORM THE ABLUTIONS.

AND GIVE US THE DRAGON'S HEART...

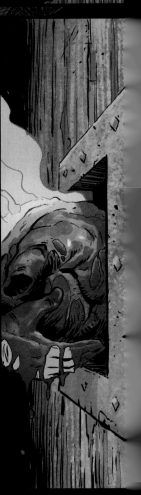

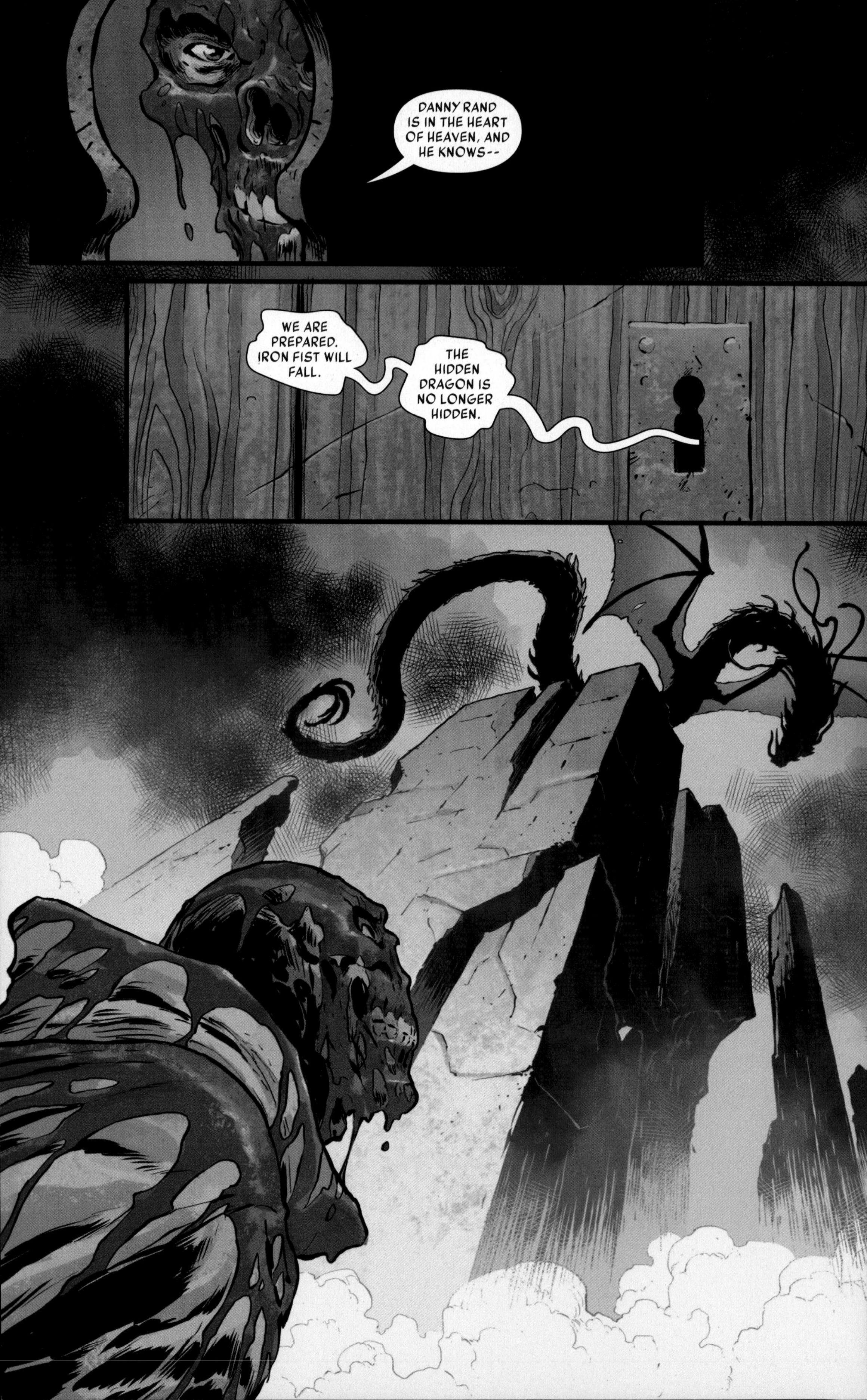
DANNY RAND IS IN THE HEART OF HEAVEN, AND HE KNOWS--
WE ARE PREPARED. IRON FIST WILL FALL.
THE HIDDEN DRAGON IS NO LONGER HIDDEN.

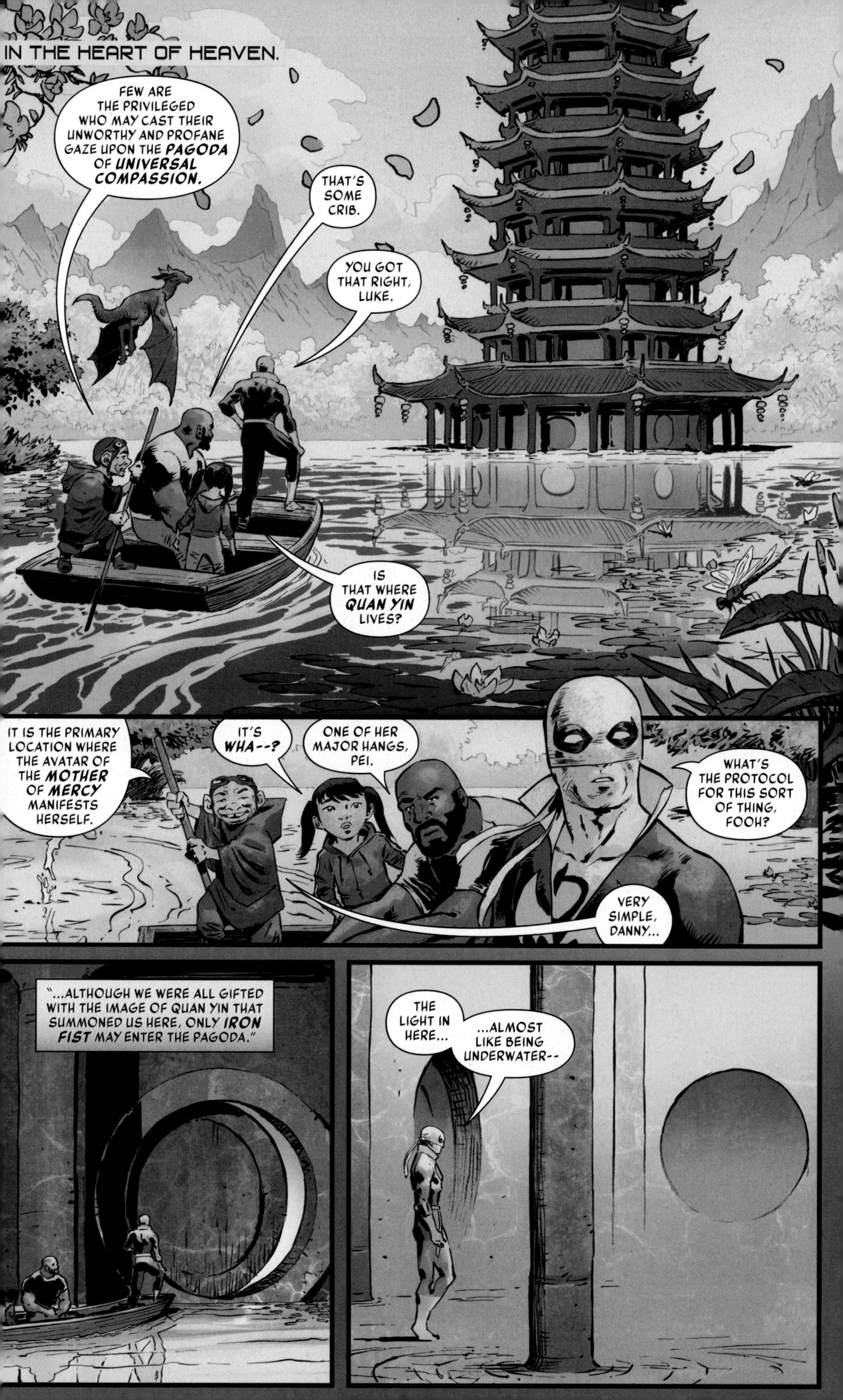
IN THE HEART OF HEAVEN.
FEW ARE THE PRIVILEGED WHO MAY CAST THEIR UNWORTHY AND PROFANE GAZE UPON THE PAGODA OF UNIVERSAL COMPASSION.
THAT'S SOME CRIB.
YOU GOT THAT RIGHT, LUKE.
IS THAT WHERE QUAN YIN LIVES?
IT IS THE PRIMARY LOCATION WHERE THE AVATAR OF THE MOTHER OF MERCY MANIFESTS HERSELF.
IT'S WHA--?
ONE OF HER MAJOR HANGS, PEI.
WHAT'S THE PROTOCOL FOR THIS SORT OF THING, FOOH?
VERY SIMPLE, DANNY...
"...ALTHOUGH WE WERE ALL GIFTED WITH THE IMAGE OF QUAN YIN THAT SUMMONED US HERE, ONLY IRON FIST MAY ENTER THE PAGODA."
THE LIGHT IN HERE...
...ALMOST LIKE BEING UNDERWATER--

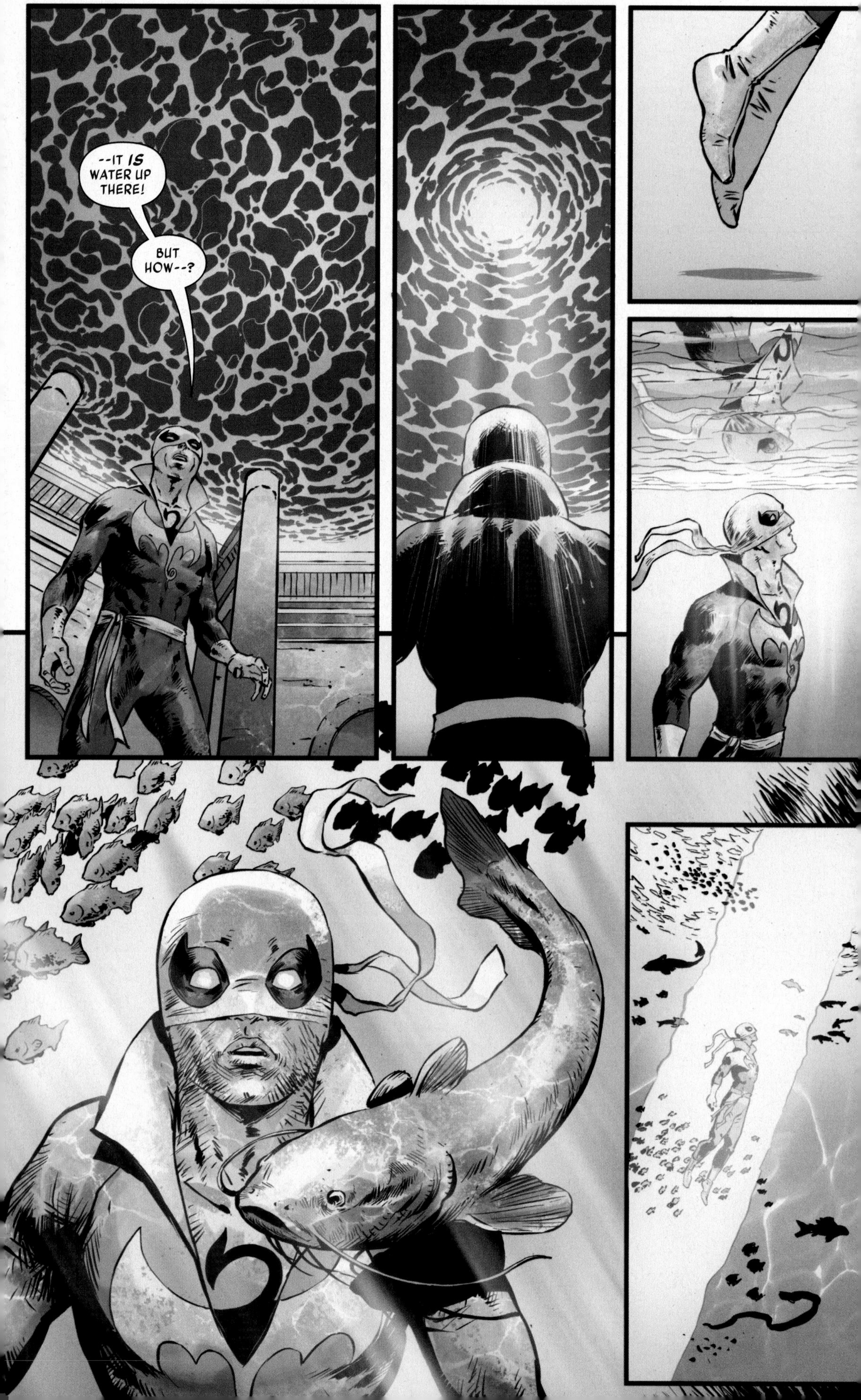
--IT IS WATER UP THERE!
BUT HOW--?

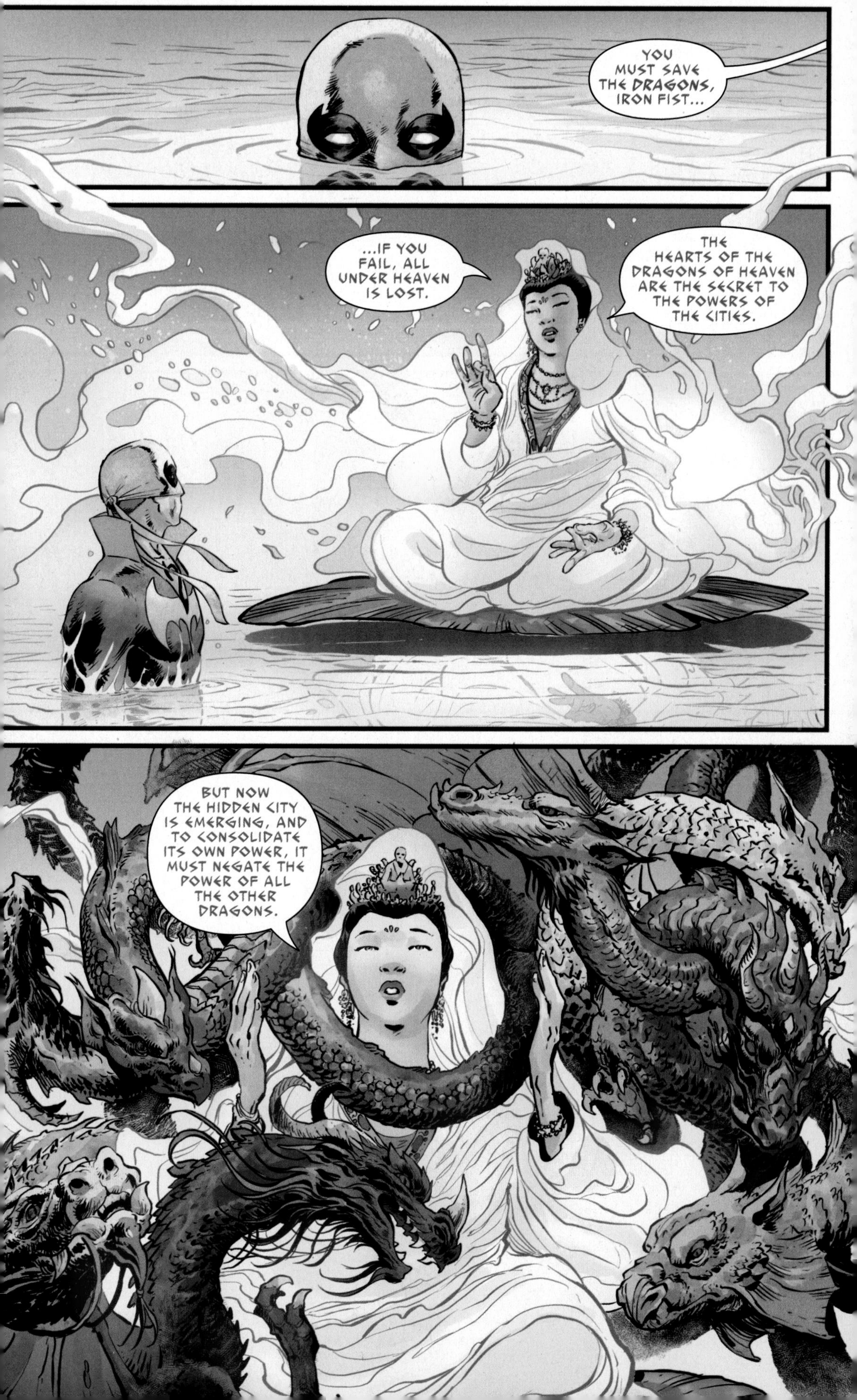

YOU MUST SAVE THE DRAGONS, IRON FIST...
...IF YOU FAIL, ALL UNDER HEAVEN IS LOST.
THE HEARTS OF THE DRAGONS OF HEAVEN ARE THE SECRET TO THE POWERS OF THE CITIES.
BUT NOW THE HIDDEN CITY IS EMERGING, AND TO CONSOLIDATE ITS OWN POWER, IT MUST NEGATE THE POWER OF ALL THE OTHER DRAGONS.

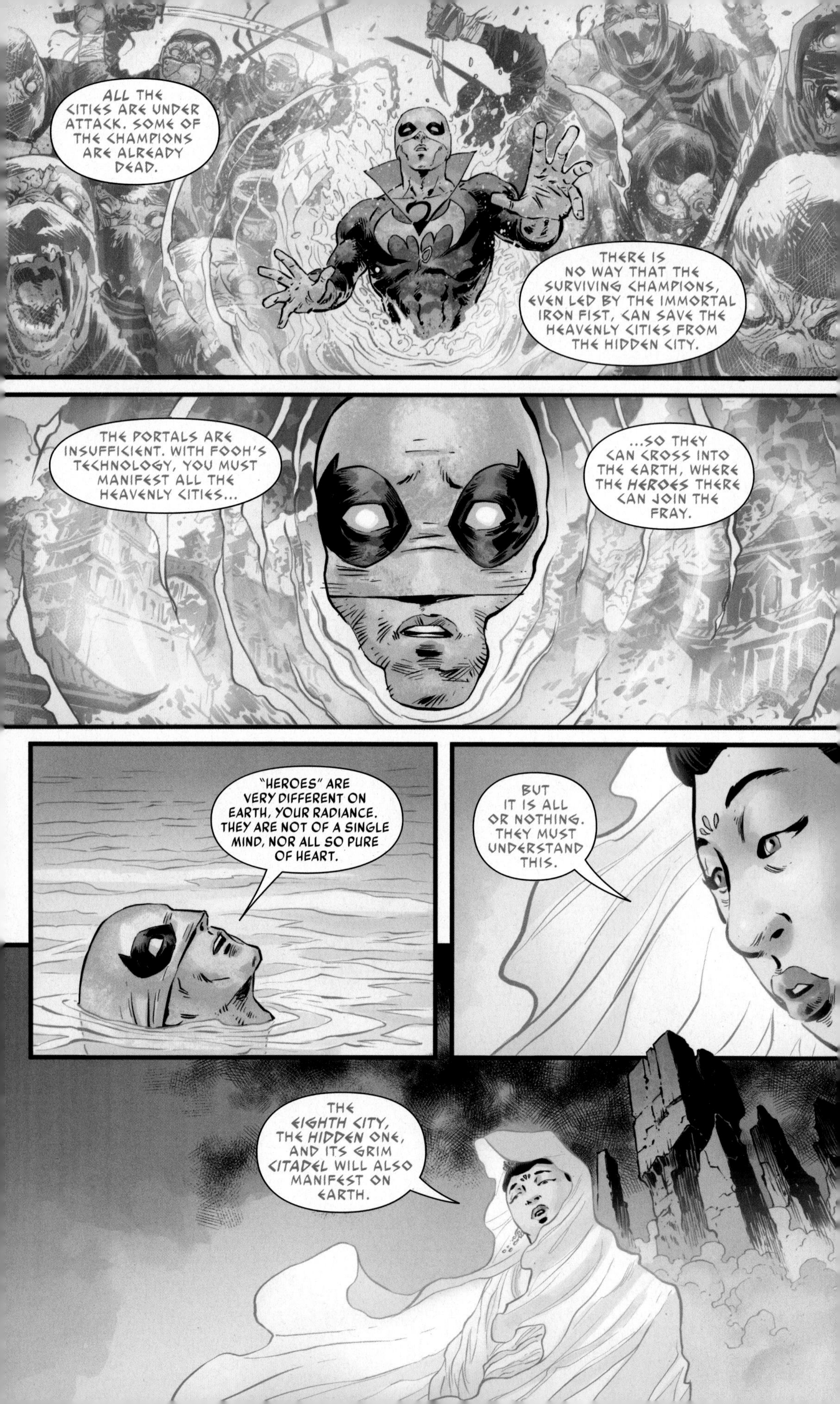
ALL THE CITIES ARE UNDER ATTACK. SOME OF THE CHAMPIONS ARE ALREADY DEAD.
THERE IS NO WAY THAT THE SURVIVING CHAMPIONS, EVEN LED BY THE IMMORTAL IRON FIST, CAN SAVE THE HEAVENLY CITIES FROM THE HIDDEN CITY.
THE PORTALS ARE INSUFFICIENT. WITH FOOH'S TECHNOLOGY, YOU MUST MANIFEST ALL THE HEAVENLY CITIES...
...SO THEY CAN CROSS INTO THE EARTH, WHERE THE HEROES THERE CAN JOIN THE FRAY.
"HEROES" ARE VERY DIFFERENT ON EARTH, YOUR RADIANCE. THEY ARE NOT OF A SINGLE MIND, NOR ALL SO PURE OF HEART.
BUT IT IS ALL OR NOTHING. THEY MUST UNDERSTAND THIS.
THE EIGHTH CITY, THE HIDDEN ONE, AND ITS GRIM CITADEL WILL ALSO MANIFEST ON EARTH.

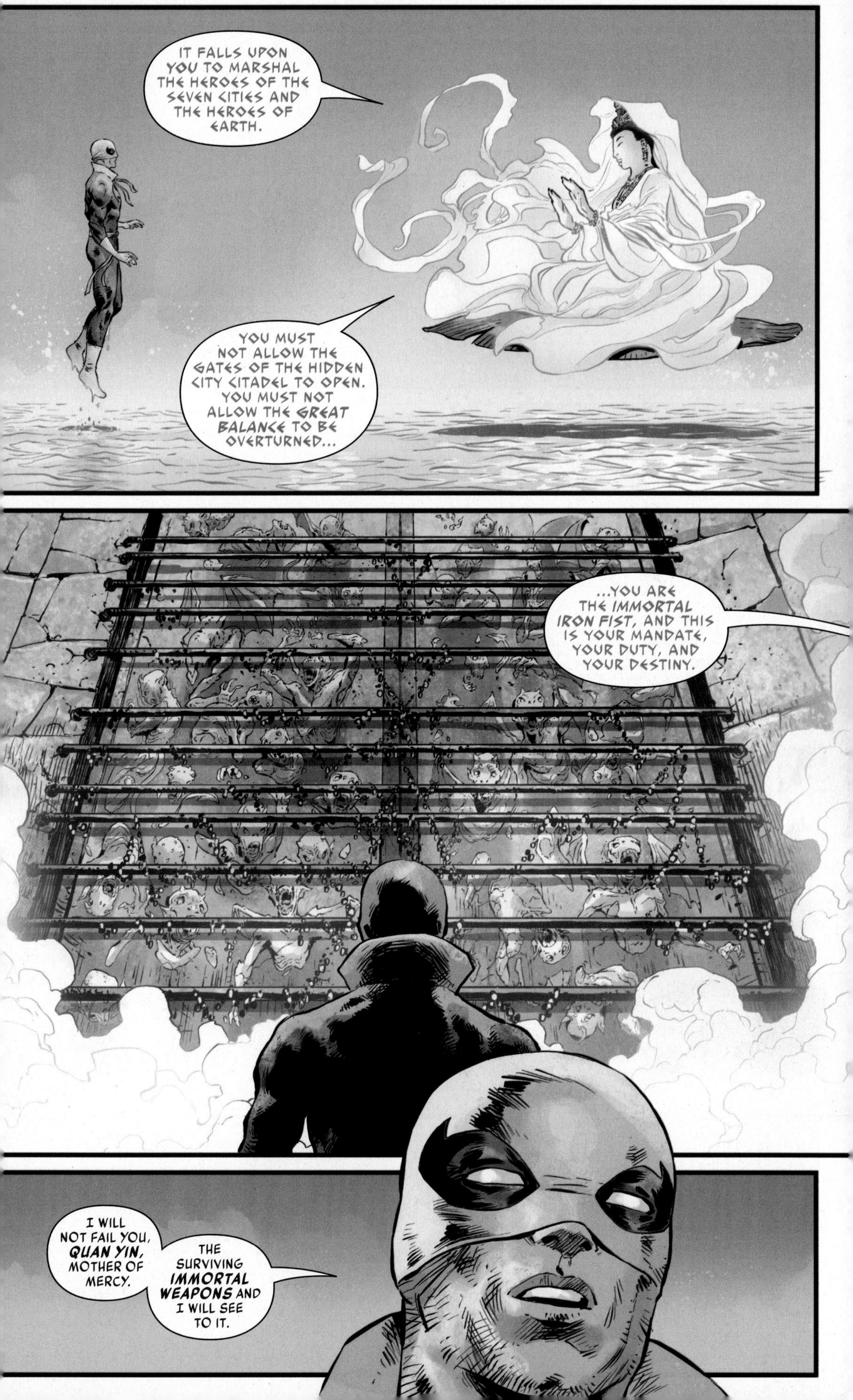
IT FALLS UPON YOU TO MARSHAL THE HEROES OF THE SEVEN CITIES AND THE HEROES OF EARTH.
YOU MUST NOT ALLOW THE GATES OF THE HIDDEN CITY CITADEL TO OPEN. YOU MUST NOT ALLOW THE GREAT BALANCE TO BE OVERTURNED...
...YOU ARE THE IMMORTAL IRON FIST, AND THIS IS YOUR MANDATE, YOUR DUTY, AND YOUR DESTINY.
I WILL NOT FAIL YOU, QUAN YIN, MOTHER OF MERCY.
THE SURVIVING IMMORTAL WEAPONS AND I WILL SEE TO IT.

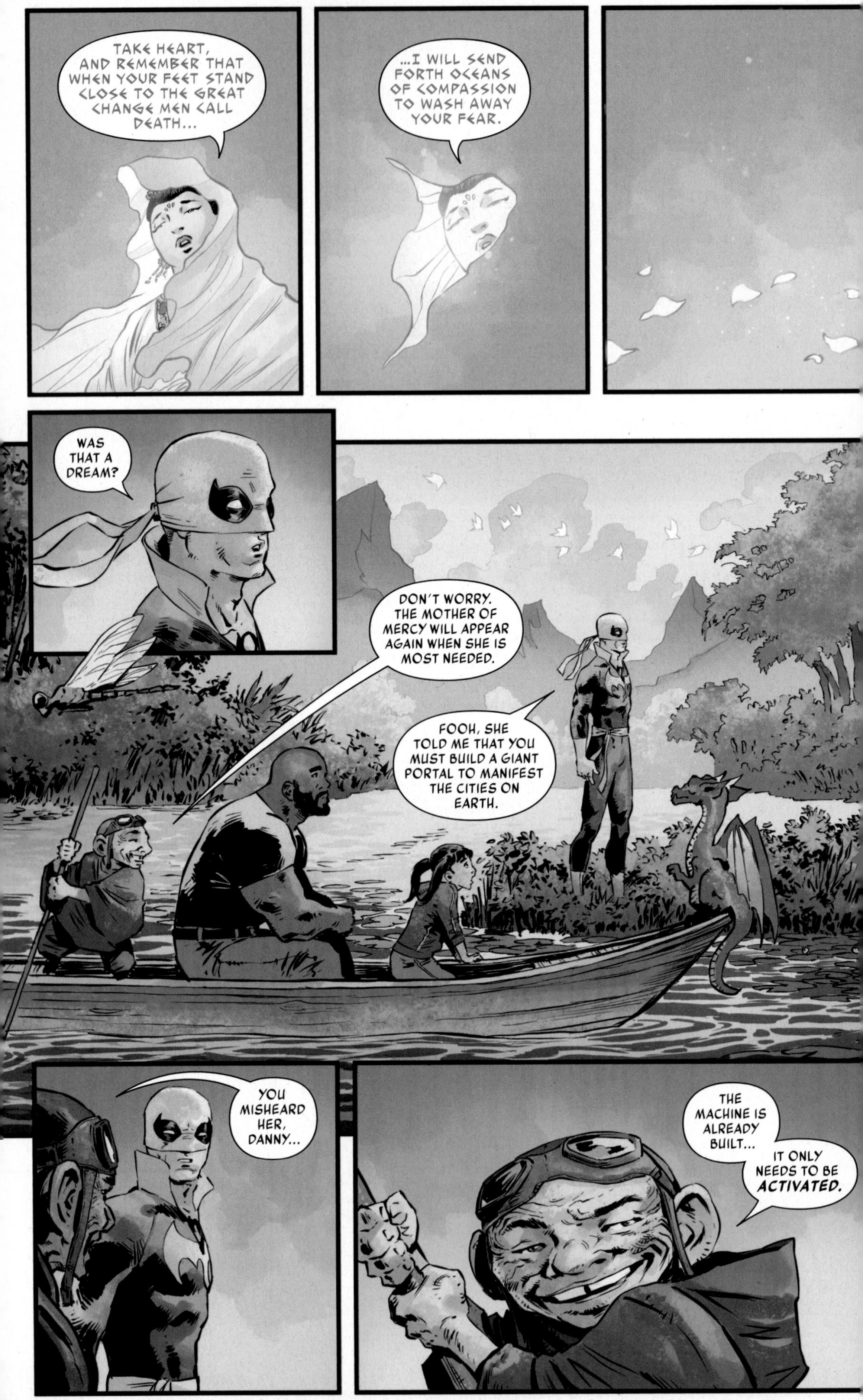
TAKE HEART, AND REMEMBER THAT WHEN YOUR FEET STAND CLOSE TO THE GREAT CHANGE MEN CALL DEATH...
...I WILL SEND FORTH OCEANS OF COMPASSION TO WASH AWAY YOUR FEAR.
WAS THAT A DREAM?
DON'T WORRY. THE MOTHER OF MERCY WILL APPEAR AGAIN WHEN SHE IS MOST NEEDED.
FOOH, SHE TOLD ME THAT YOU MUST BUILD A GIANT PORTAL TO MANIFEST THE CITIES ON EARTH.
YOU MISHEARD HER, DANNY...
THE MACHINE IS ALREADY BUILT...
IT ONLY NEEDS TO BE *ACTIVATED.*

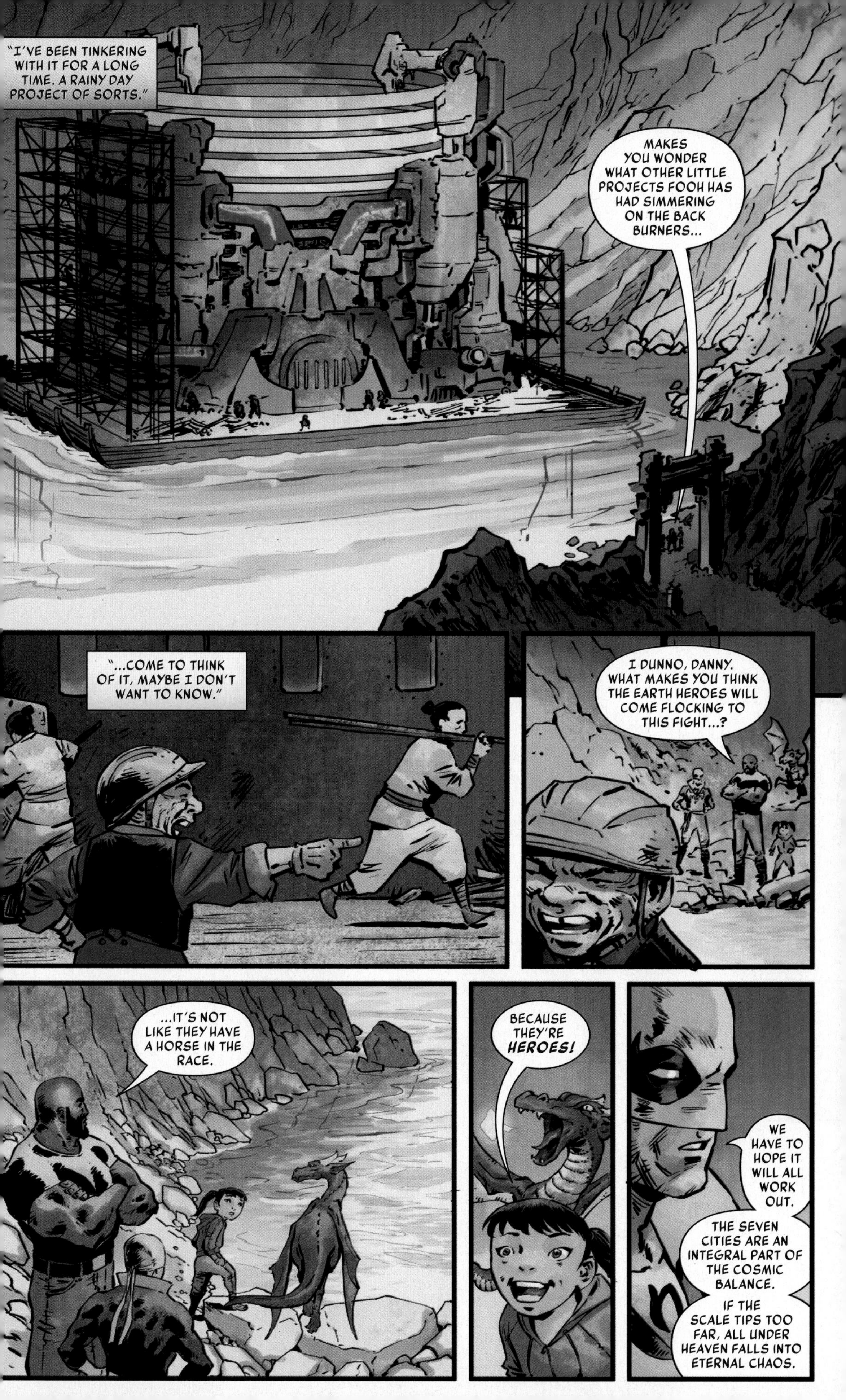
"I'VE BEEN TINKERING WITH IT FOR A LONG TIME. A RAINY DAY PROJECT OF SORTS."
MAKES YOU WONDER WHAT OTHER LITTLE PROJECTS FOOH HAS HAD SIMMERING ON THE BACK BURNERS...
"...COME TO THINK OF IT, MAYBE I DON'T WANT TO KNOW."
I DUNNO, DANNY. WHAT MAKES YOU THINK THE EARTH HEROES WILL COME FLOCKING TO THIS FIGHT...?
...IT'S NOT LIKE THEY HAVE A HORSE IN THE RACE.
BECAUSE THEY'RE ***HEROES!***
WE HAVE TO HOPE IT WILL ALL WORK OUT.
THE SEVEN CITIES ARE AN INTEGRAL PART OF THE COSMIC BALANCE.
IF THE SCALE TIPS TOO FAR, ALL UNDER HEAVEN FALLS INTO ETERNAL CHAOS.

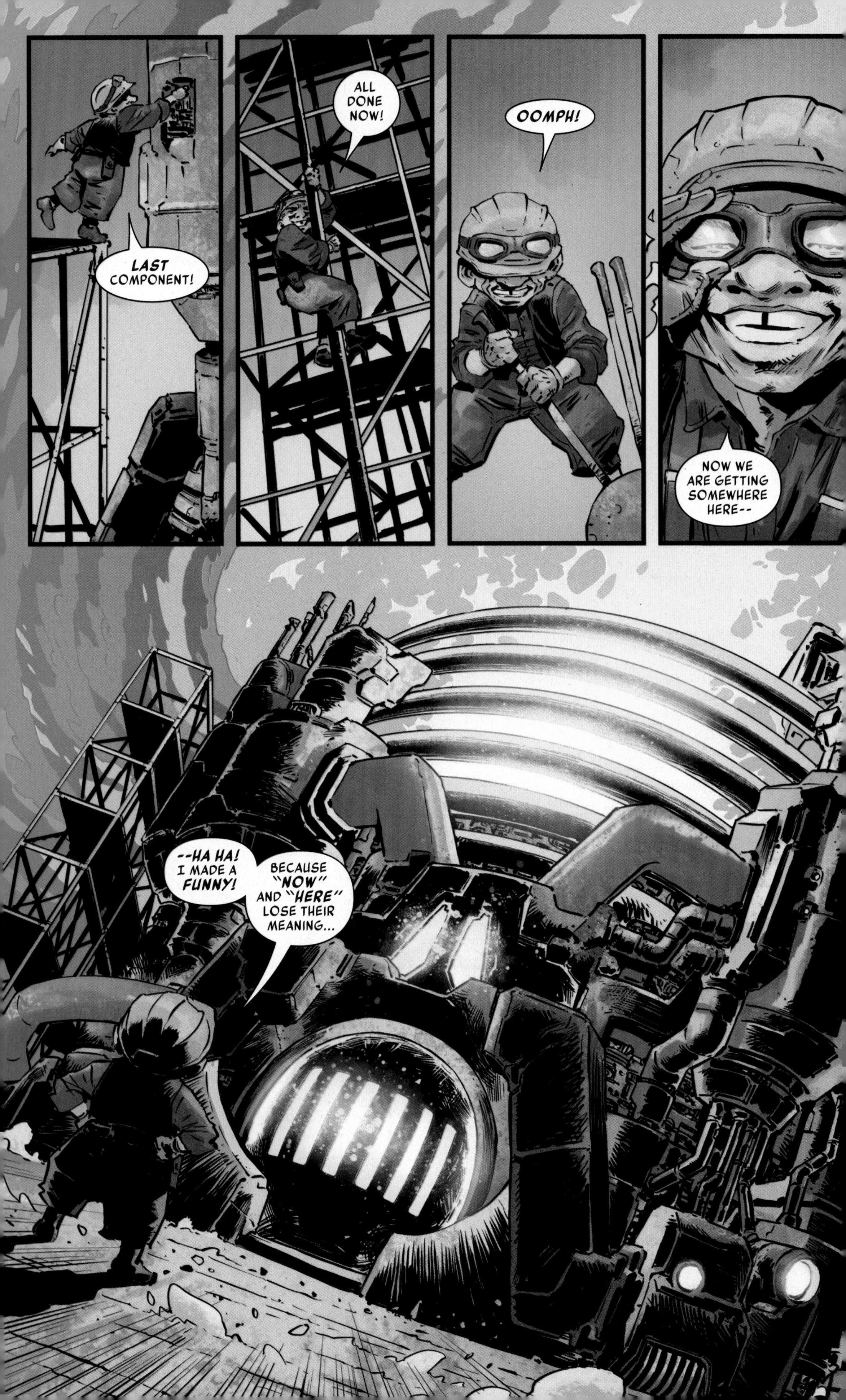
LAST COMPONENT!
ALL DONE NOW!
OOMPH!
NOW WE ARE GETTING SOMEWHERE HERE--
--HA HA! I MADE A FUNNY!
BECAUSE "NOW" AND "HERE" LOSE THEIR MEANING...

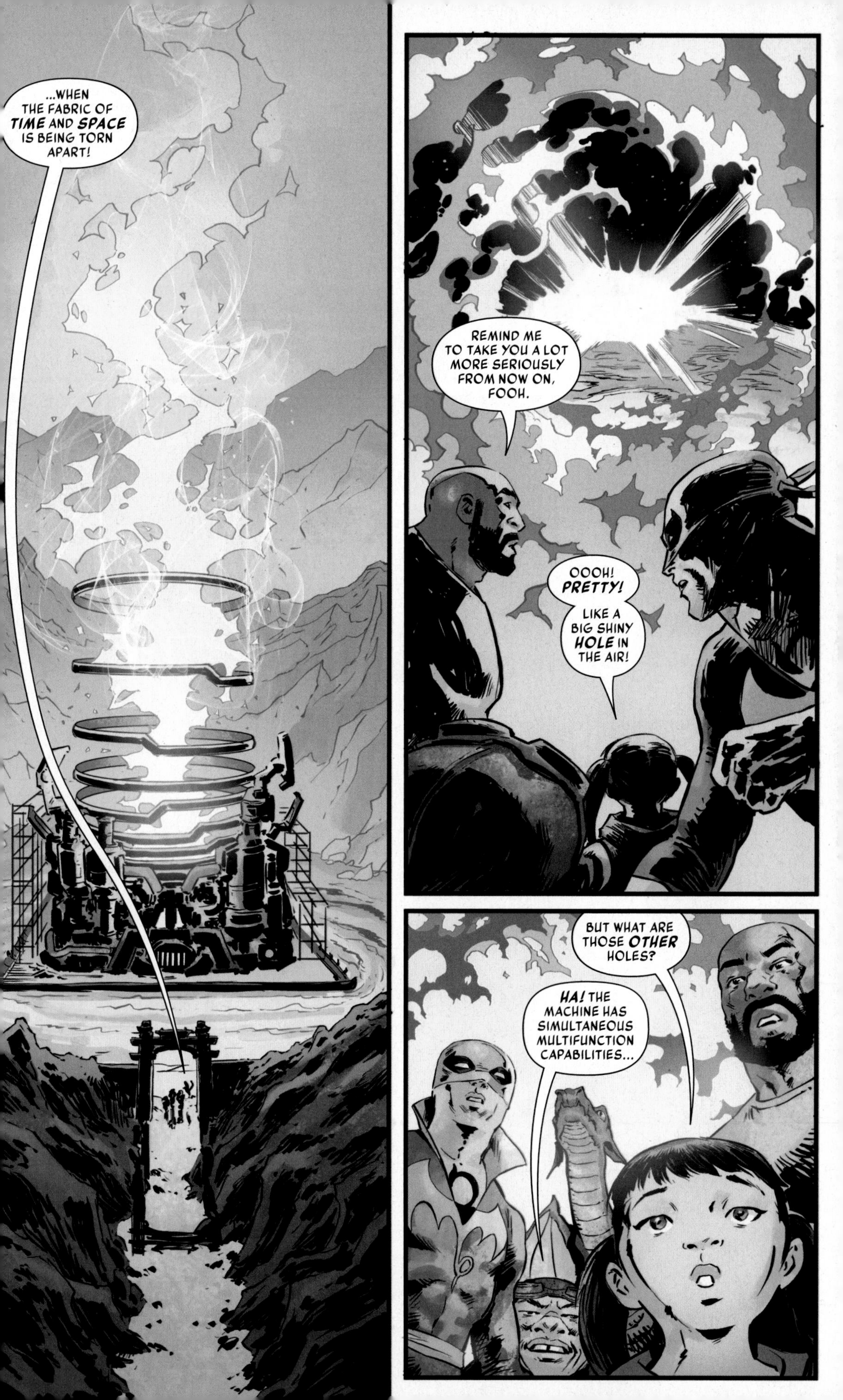

...WHEN THE FABRIC OF TIME AND SPACE IS BEING TORN APART!
REMIND ME TO TAKE YOU A LOT MORE SERIOUSLY FROM NOW ON, FOOH.
OOOH! PRETTY!
LIKE A BIG SHINY HOLE IN THE AIR!
BUT WHAT ARE THOSE OTHER HOLES?
HA! THE MACHINE HAS SIMULTANEOUS MULTIFUNCTION CAPABILITIES...

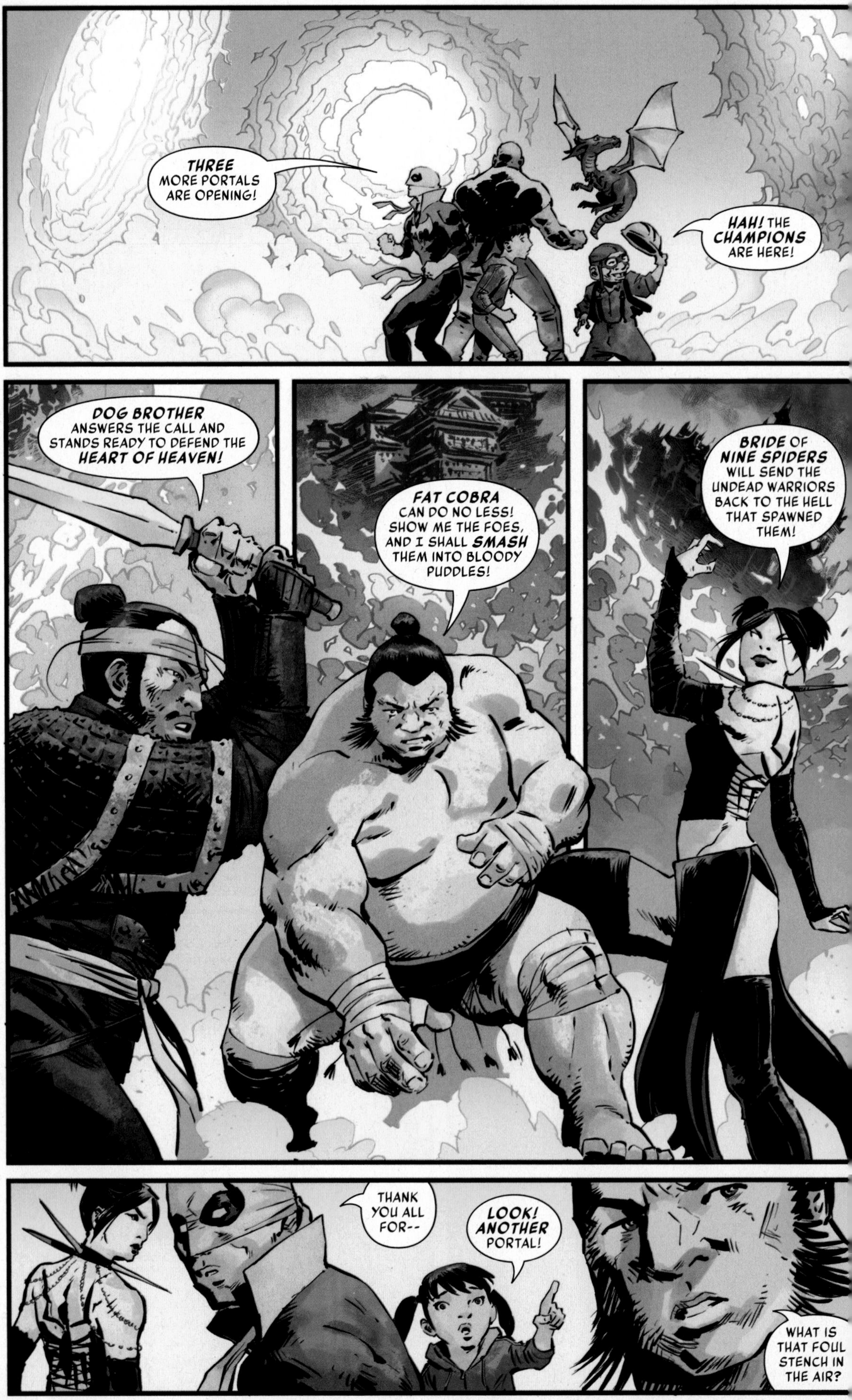
THREE MORE PORTALS ARE OPENING!
HAH! THE CHAMPIONS ARE HERE!
DOG BROTHER ANSWERS THE CALL AND STANDS READY TO DEFEND THE HEART OF HEAVEN!
FAT COBRA CAN DO NO LESS! SHOW ME THE FOES, AND I SHALL SMASH THEM INTO BLOODY PUDDLES!
BRIDE OF NINE SPIDERS WILL SEND THE UNDEAD WARRIORS BACK TO THE HELL THAT SPAWNED THEM!
THANK YOU ALL FOR--
LOOK! ANOTHER PORTAL!
WHAT IS THAT FOUL STENCH IN THE AIR?

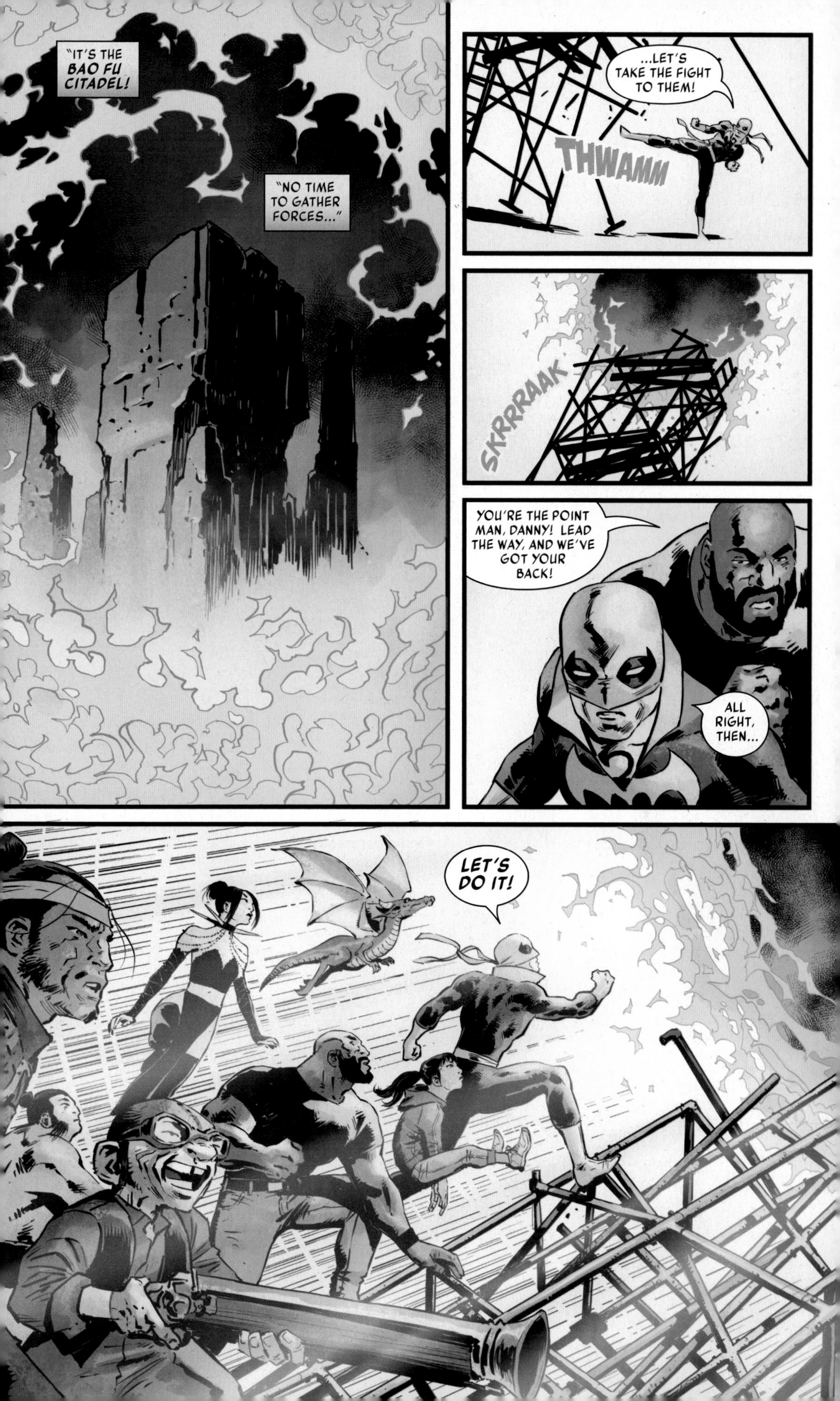
"IT'S THE BAO FU CITADEL!
"NO TIME TO GATHER FORCES..."
...LET'S TAKE THE FIGHT TO THEM!
THWAMM
SKRRRAAK
YOU'RE THE POINT MAN, DANNY! LEAD THE WAY, AND WE'VE GOT YOUR BACK!
ALL RIGHT, THEN...
LET'S DO IT!

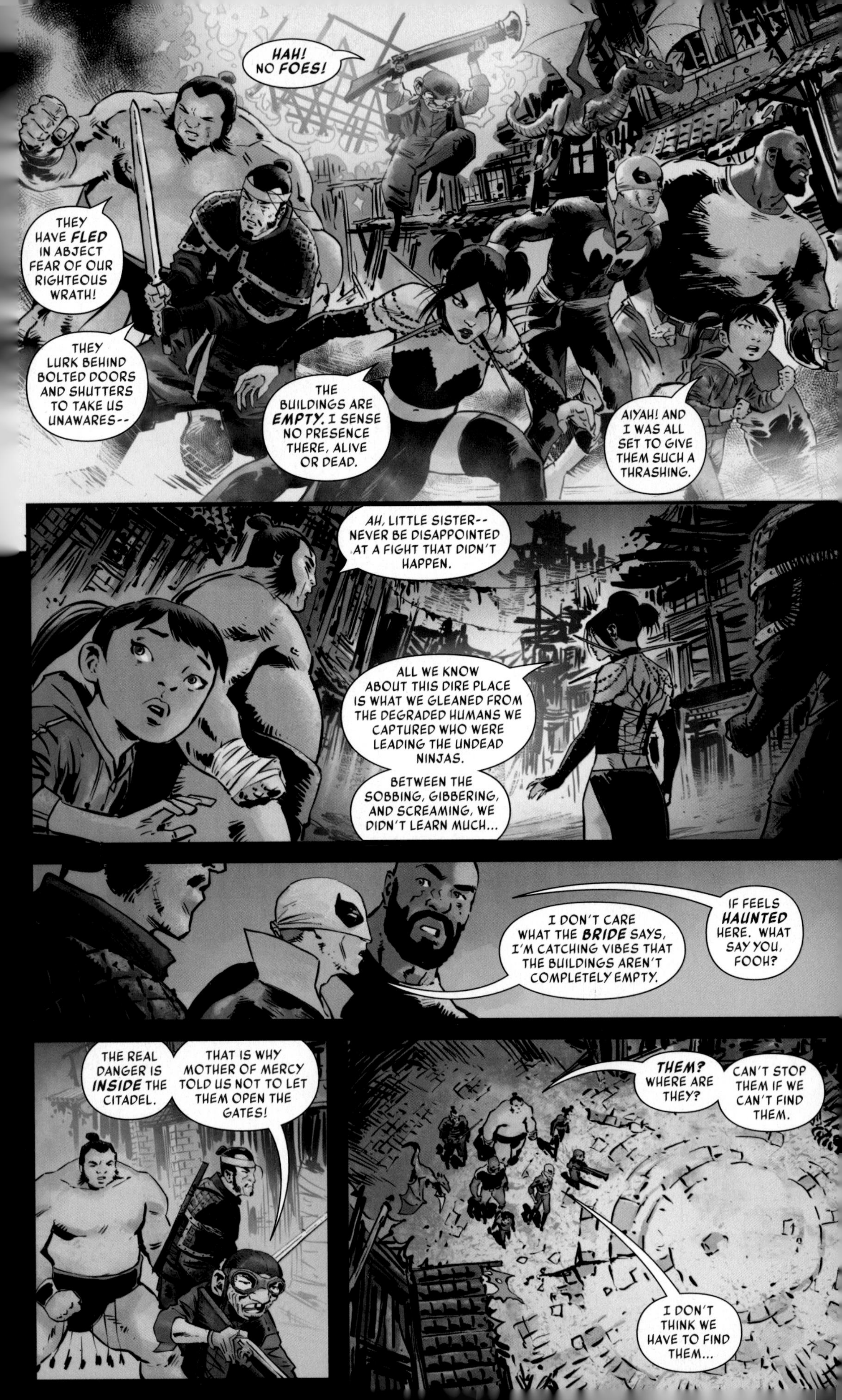

HAH! NO FOES!
THEY HAVE FLED IN ABJECT FEAR OF OUR RIGHTEOUS WRATH!
THEY LURK BEHIND BOLTED DOORS AND SHUTTERS TO TAKE US UNAWARES--
THE BUILDINGS ARE EMPTY. I SENSE NO PRESENCE THERE, ALIVE OR DEAD.
AIYAH! AND I WAS ALL SET TO GIVE THEM SUCH A THRASHING.
AH, LITTLE SISTER-- NEVER BE DISAPPOINTED AT A FIGHT THAT DIDN'T HAPPEN.
ALL WE KNOW ABOUT THIS DIRE PLACE IS WHAT WE GLEANED FROM THE DEGRADED HUMANS WE CAPTURED WHO WERE LEADING THE UNDEAD NINJAS.
BETWEEN THE SOBBING, GIBBERING, AND SCREAMING, WE DIDN'T LEARN MUCH...
IF FEELS HAUNTED HERE. WHAT SAY YOU, FOOH?
I DON'T CARE WHAT THE BRIDE SAYS, I'M CATCHING VIBES THAT THE BUILDINGS AREN'T COMPLETELY EMPTY.
THE REAL DANGER IS INSIDE THE CITADEL.
THAT IS WHY MOTHER OF MERCY TOLD US NOT TO LET THEM OPEN THE GATES!
THEM? WHERE ARE THEY?
CAN'T STOP THEM IF WE CAN'T FIND THEM.
I DON'T THINK WE HAVE TO FIND THEM...

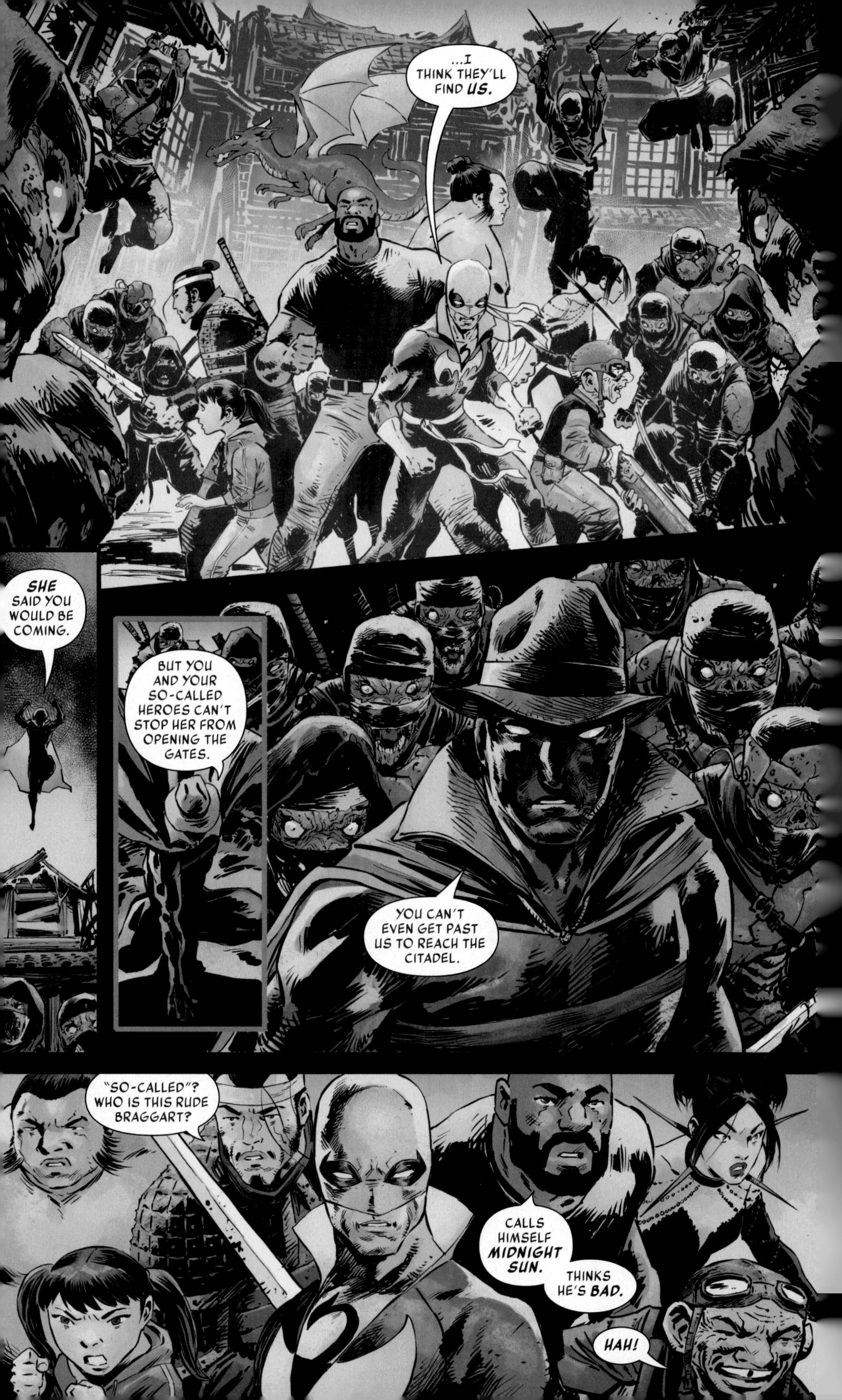
...I THINK THEY'LL FIND US.
SHE SAID YOU WOULD BE COMING.
BUT YOU AND YOUR SO-CALLED HEROES CAN'T STOP HER FROM OPENING THE GATES.
YOU CAN'T EVEN GET PAST US TO REACH THE CITADEL.
"SO-CALLED"? WHO IS THIS RUDE BRAGGART?
CALLS HIMSELF MIDNIGHT SUN.
THINKS HE'S BAD.
HAH!

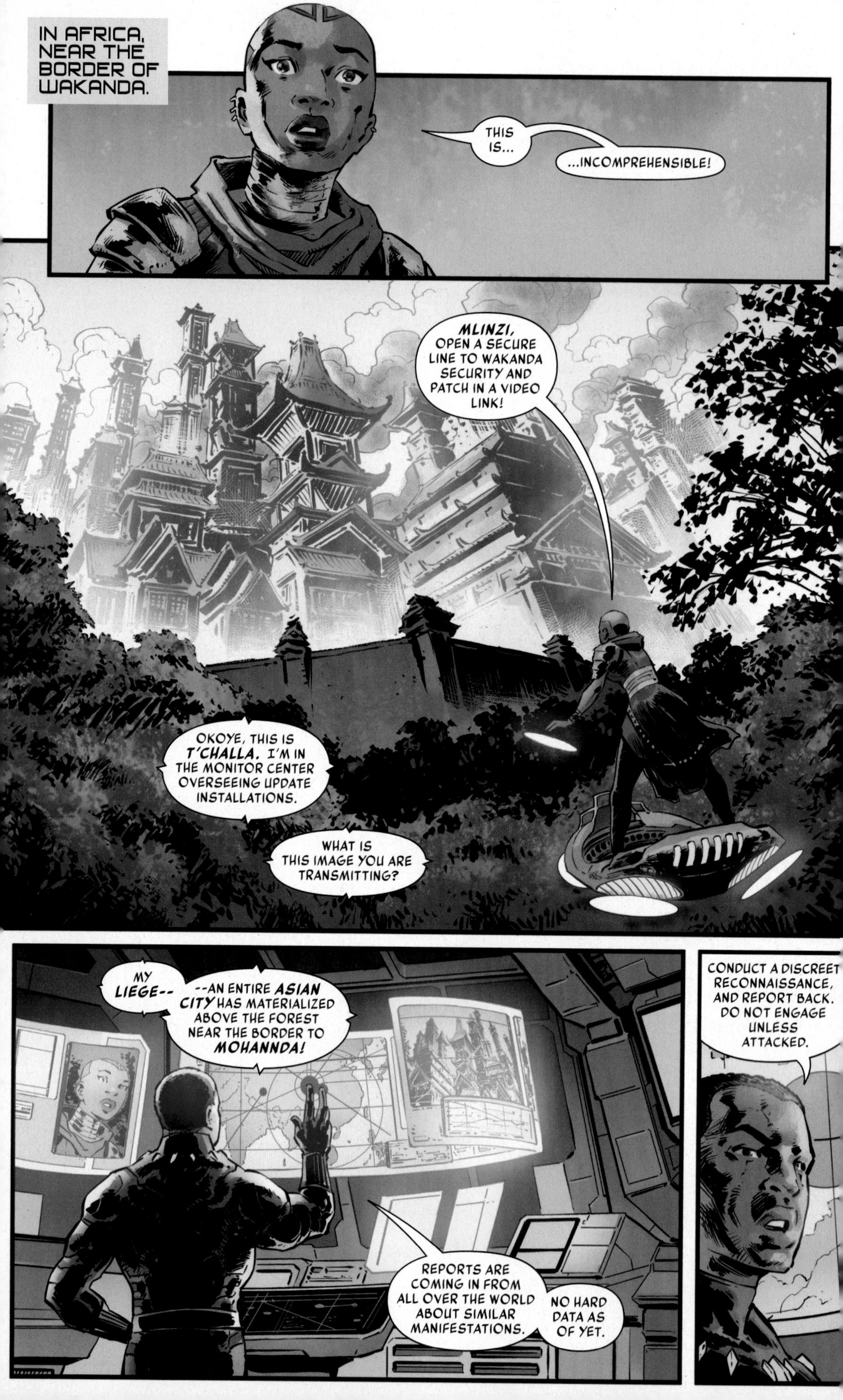
IN AFRICA, NEAR THE BORDER OF WAKANDA.
THIS IS...
...INCOMPREHENSIBLE!
MLINZI, OPEN A SECURE LINE TO WAKANDA SECURITY AND PATCH IN A VIDEO LINK!
OKOYE, THIS IS T'CHALLA. I'M IN THE MONITOR CENTER OVERSEEING UPDATE INSTALLATIONS.
WHAT IS THIS IMAGE YOU ARE TRANSMITTING?
MY LIEGE--
--AN ENTIRE ASIAN CITY HAS MATERIALIZED ABOVE THE FOREST NEAR THE BORDER TO MOHANNDA!
REPORTS ARE COMING IN FROM ALL OVER THE WORLD ABOUT SIMILAR MANIFESTATIONS.
NO HARD DATA AS OF YET.
CONDUCT A DISCREET RECONNAISSANCE, AND REPORT BACK. DO NOT ENGAGE UNLESS ATTACKED.

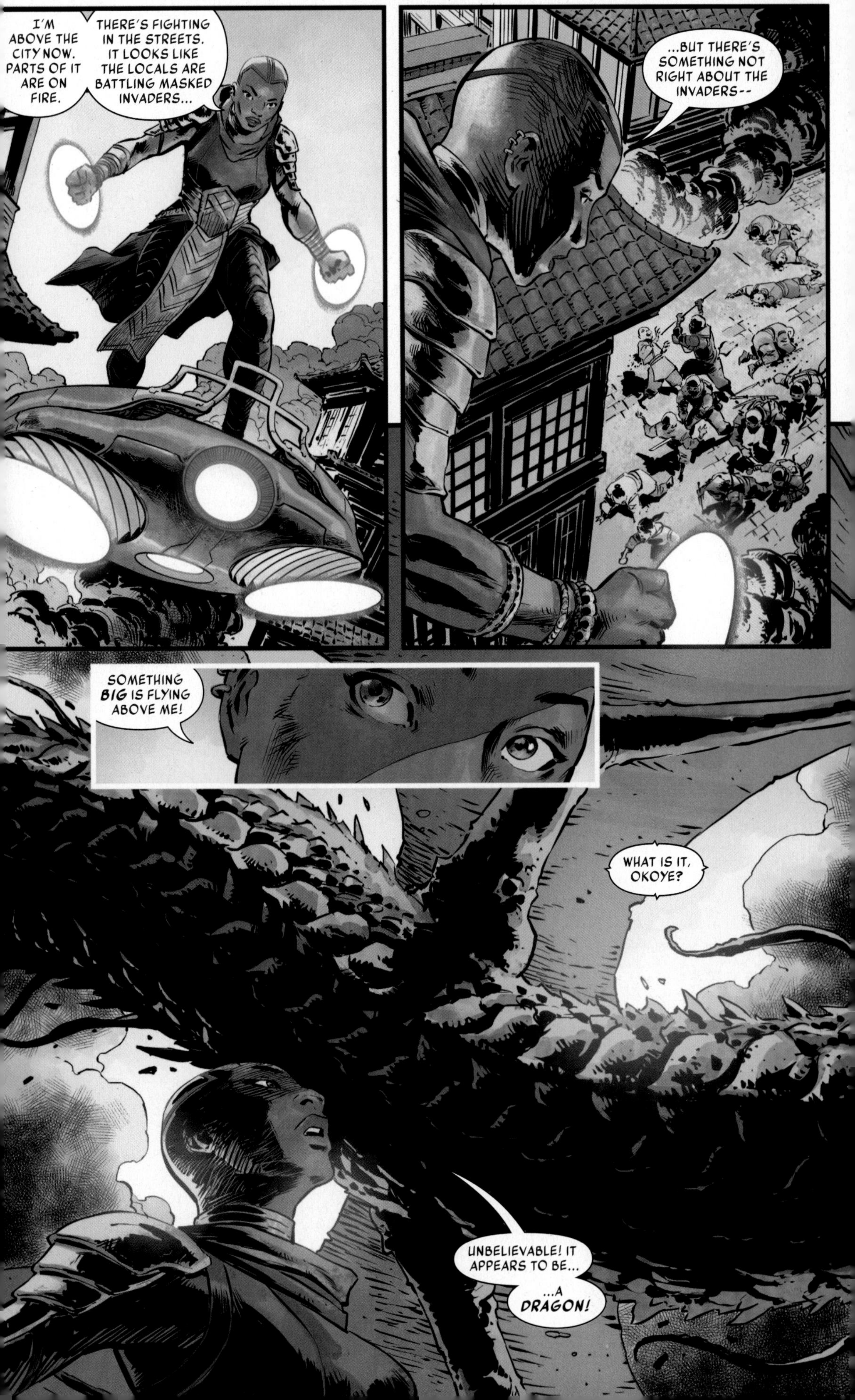
I'M ABOVE THE CITY NOW. PARTS OF IT ARE ON FIRE.
THERE'S FIGHTING IN THE STREETS. IT LOOKS LIKE THE LOCALS ARE BATTLING MASKED INVADERS...
...BUT THERE'S SOMETHING NOT RIGHT ABOUT THE INVADERS--
SOMETHING *BIG* IS FLYING ABOVE ME!
WHAT IS IT, OKOYE?
UNBELIEVABLE! IT APPEARS TO BE...
...A *DRAGON!*

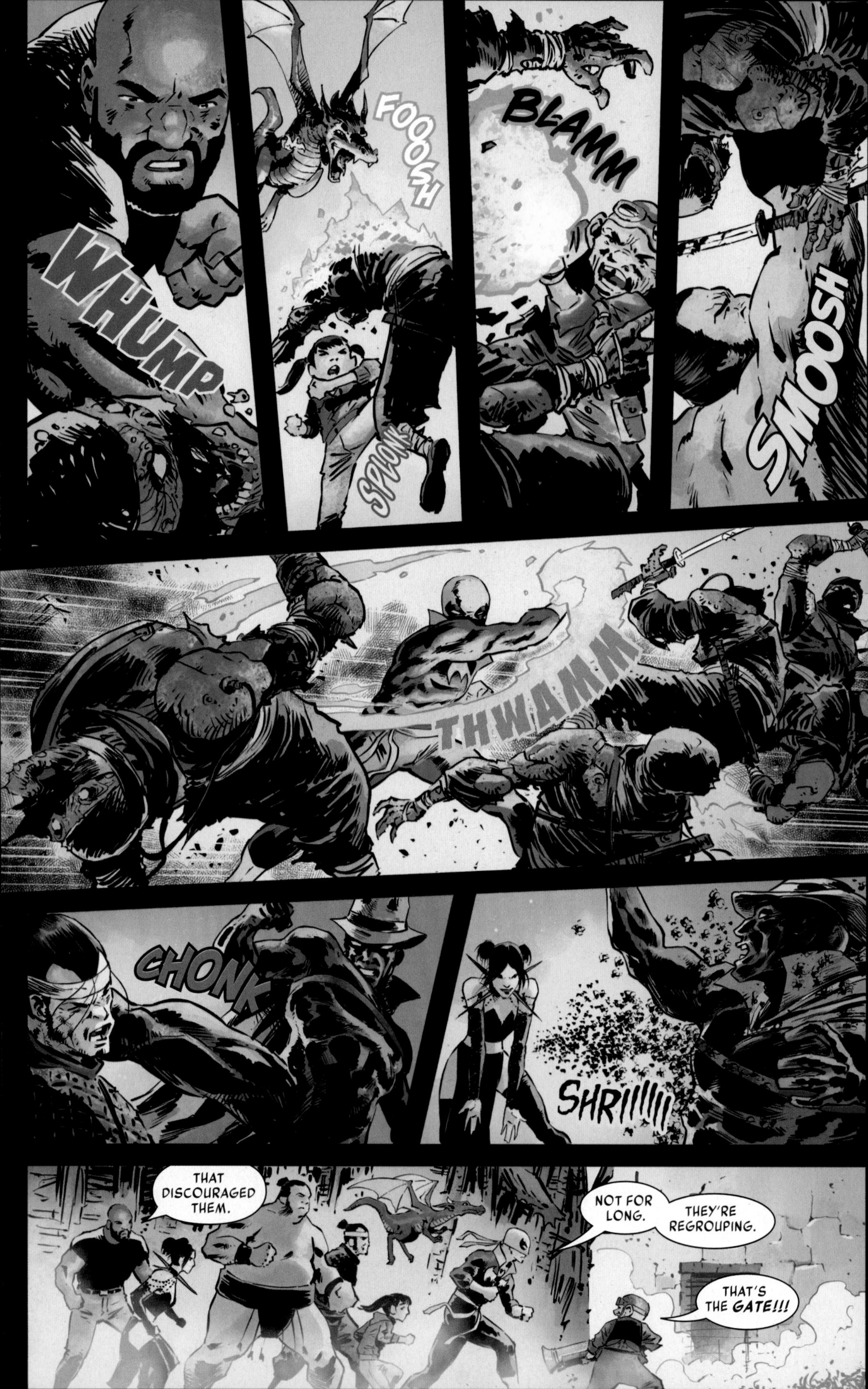
WHUMP
FOOOSH
SPLONK
BLAMM
SMOOSH
THWAMM
CHONK
SHRIIIIII
THAT DISCOURAGED THEM.
NOT FOR LONG.
THEY'RE REGROUPING.
THAT'S THE GATE!!!

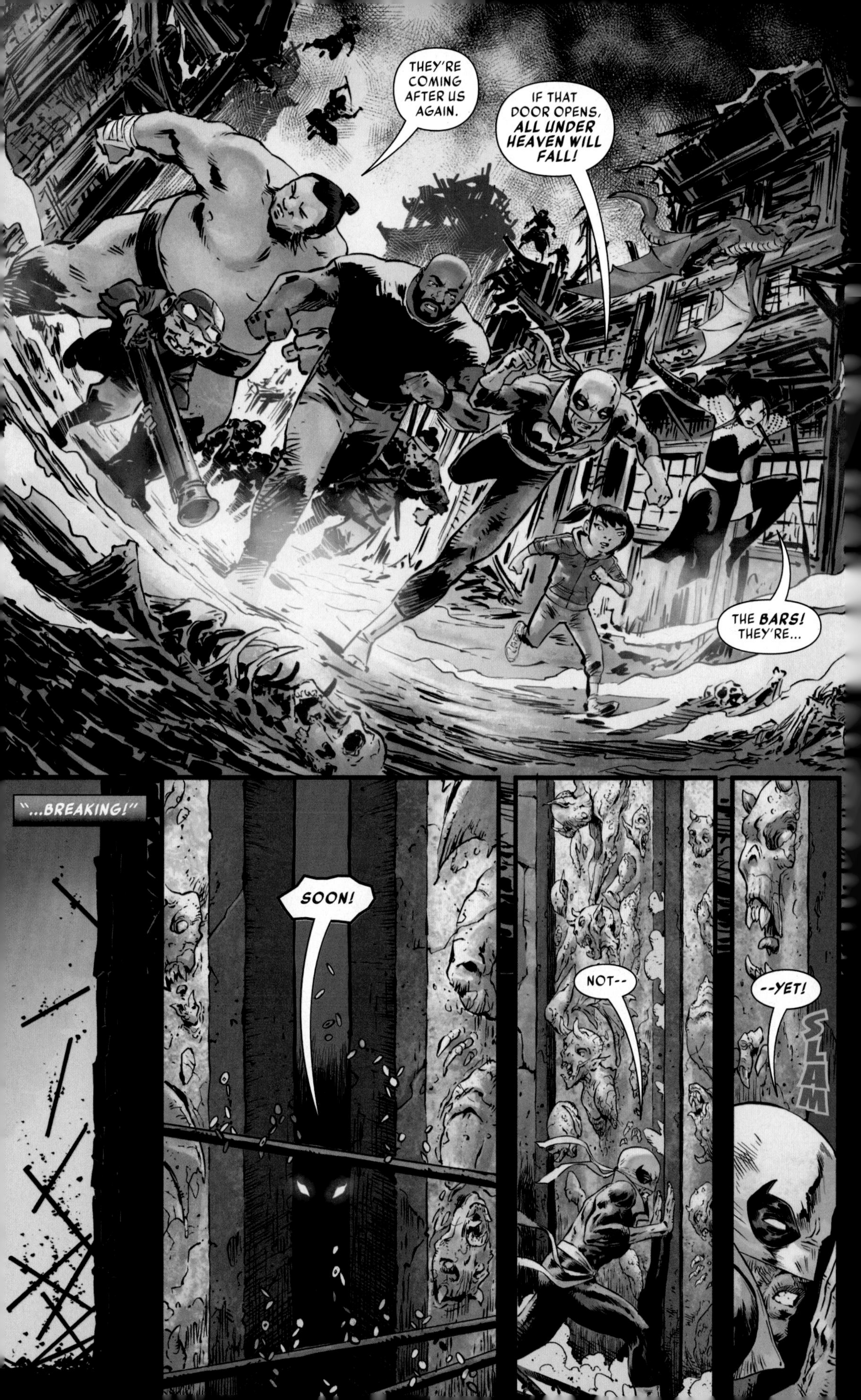
THEY'RE COMING AFTER US AGAIN.
IF THAT DOOR OPENS, ALL UNDER HEAVEN WILL FALL!
THE BARS! THEY'RE...
"...BREAKING!"
SOON!
NOT--
--YET!
SLAM

# THREE

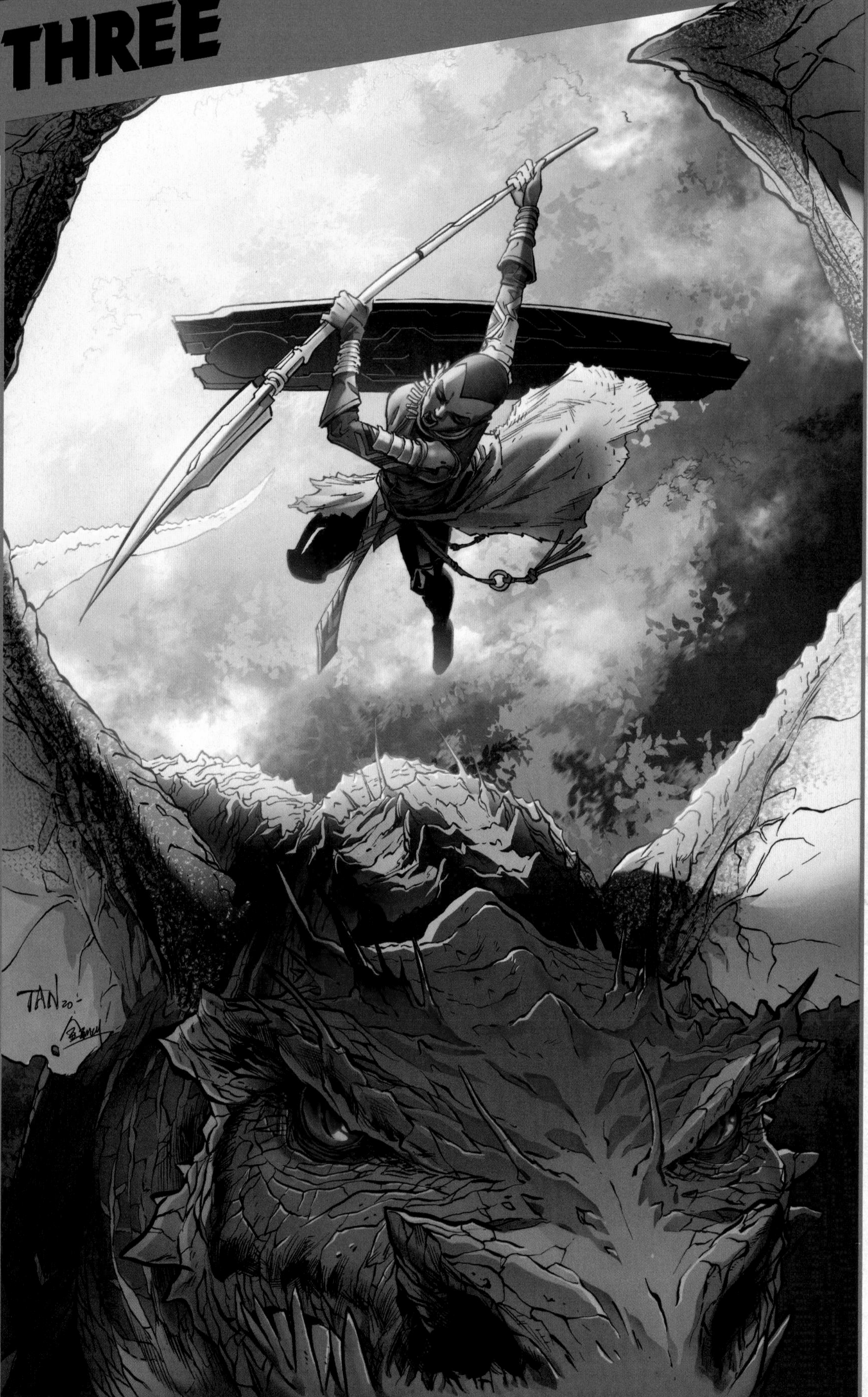

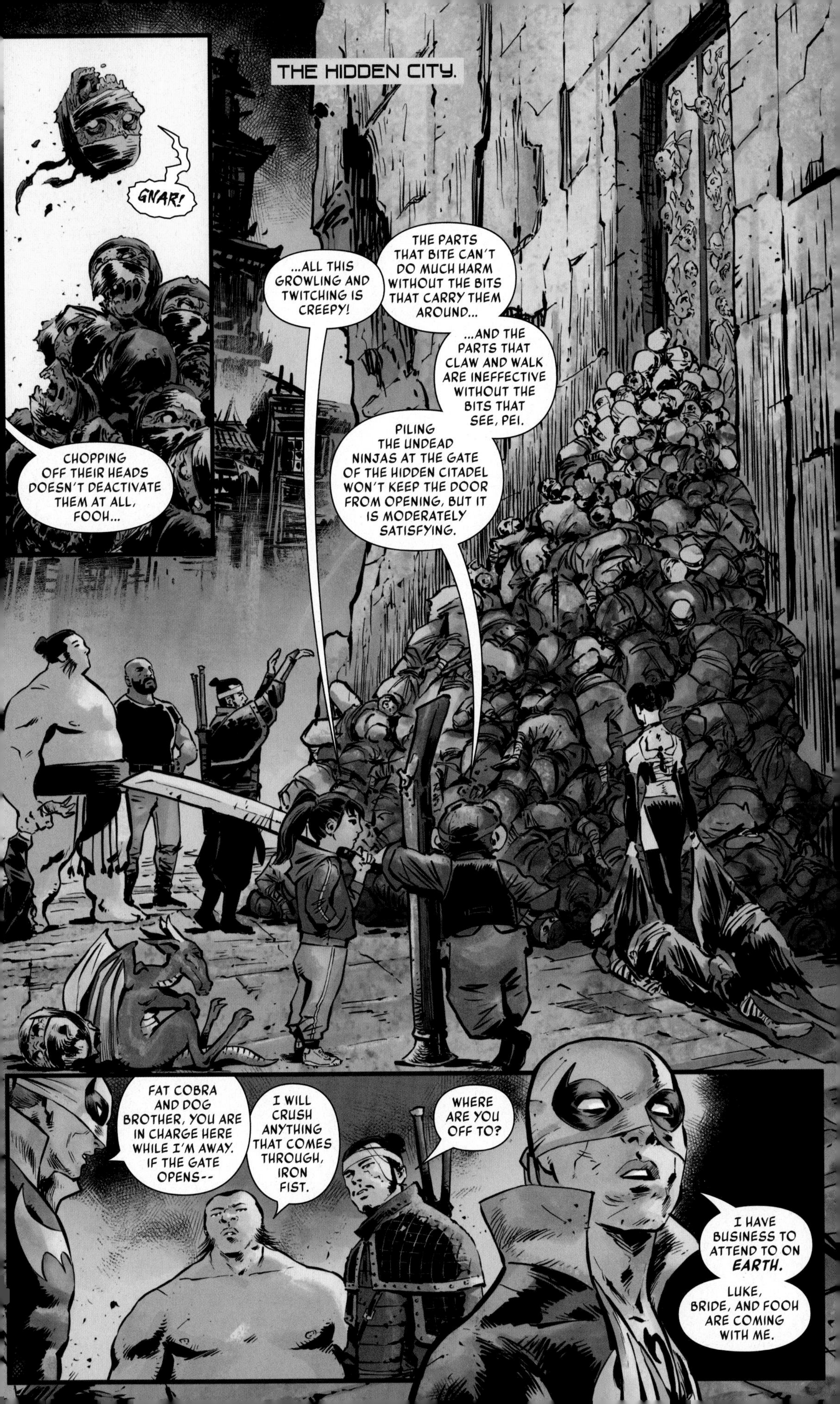
THE HIDDEN CITY.
GNAR!
CHOPPING OFF THEIR HEADS DOESN'T DEACTIVATE THEM AT ALL, FOOH...
...ALL THIS GROWLING AND TWITCHING IS CREEPY!
THE PARTS THAT BITE CAN'T DO MUCH HARM WITHOUT THE BITS THAT CARRY THEM AROUND...
...AND THE PARTS THAT CLAW AND WALK ARE INEFFECTIVE WITHOUT THE BITS THAT SEE, PEI.
PILING THE UNDEAD NINJAS AT THE GATE OF THE HIDDEN CITADEL WON'T KEEP THE DOOR FROM OPENING, BUT IT IS MODERATELY SATISFYING.
FAT COBRA AND DOG BROTHER, YOU ARE IN CHARGE HERE WHILE I'M AWAY. IF THE GATE OPENS--
I WILL CRUSH ANYTHING THAT COMES THROUGH, IRON FIST.
WHERE ARE YOU OFF TO?
I HAVE BUSINESS TO ATTEND TO ON EARTH.
LUKE, BRIDE, AND FOOH ARE COMING WITH ME.

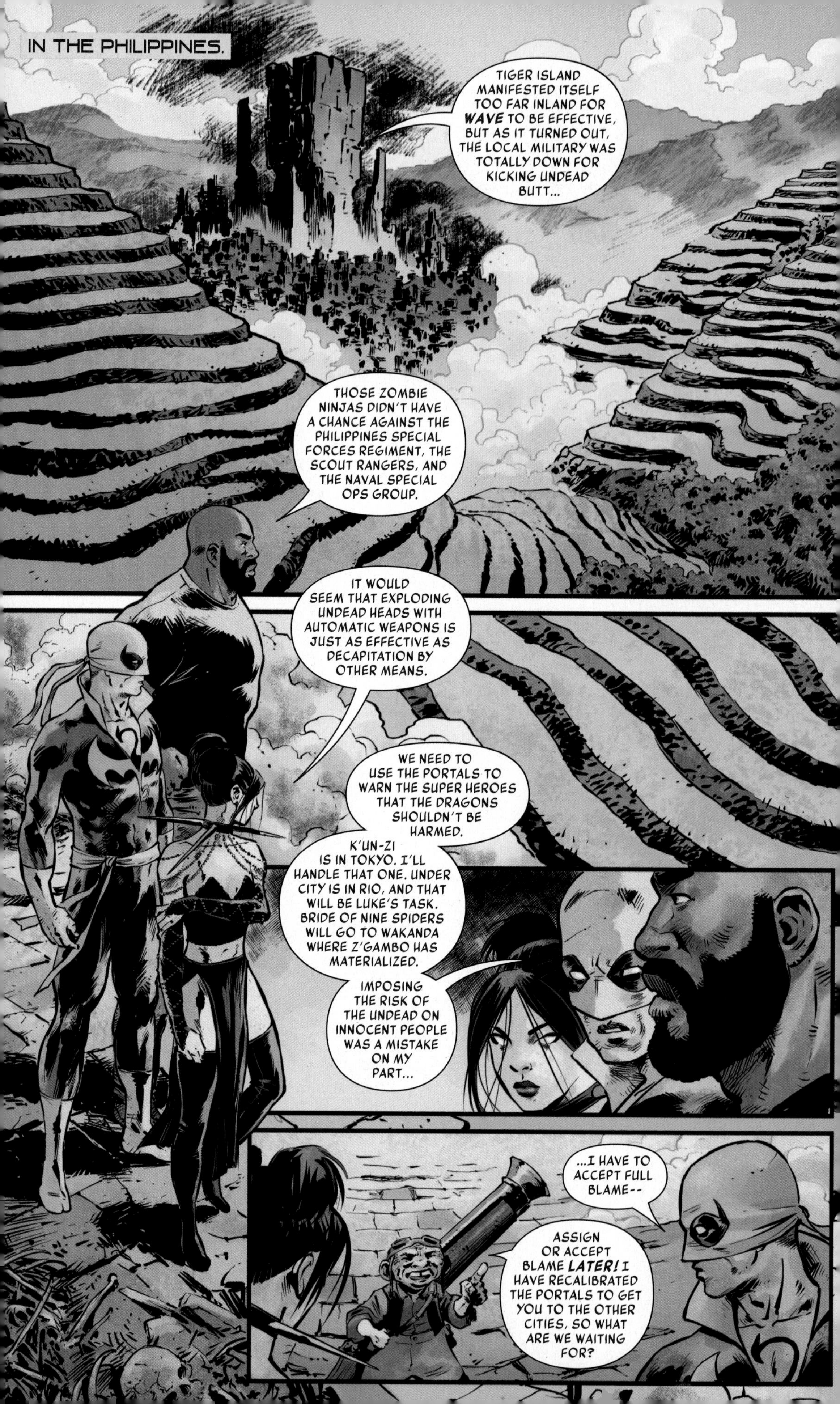

IN THE PHILIPPINES.
TIGER ISLAND MANIFESTED ITSELF TOO FAR INLAND FOR WAVE TO BE EFFECTIVE, BUT AS IT TURNED OUT, THE LOCAL MILITARY WAS TOTALLY DOWN FOR KICKING UNDEAD BUTT...
THOSE ZOMBIE NINJAS DIDN'T HAVE A CHANCE AGAINST THE PHILIPPINES SPECIAL FORCES REGIMENT, THE SCOUT RANGERS, AND THE NAVAL SPECIAL OPS GROUP.
IT WOULD SEEM THAT EXPLODING UNDEAD HEADS WITH AUTOMATIC WEAPONS IS JUST AS EFFECTIVE AS DECAPITATION BY OTHER MEANS.
WE NEED TO USE THE PORTALS TO WARN THE SUPER HEROES THAT THE DRAGONS SHOULDN'T BE HARMED.
K'UN-ZI IS IN TOKYO. I'LL HANDLE THAT ONE. UNDER CITY IS IN RIO, AND THAT WILL BE LUKE'S TASK. BRIDE OF NINE SPIDERS WILL GO TO WAKANDA WHERE Z'GAMBO HAS MATERIALIZED.
IMPOSING THE RISK OF THE UNDEAD ON INNOCENT PEOPLE WAS A MISTAKE ON MY PART...
...I HAVE TO ACCEPT FULL BLAME--
ASSIGN OR ACCEPT BLAME LATER! I HAVE RECALIBRATED THE PORTALS TO GET YOU TO THE OTHER CITIES, SO WHAT ARE WE WAITING FOR?

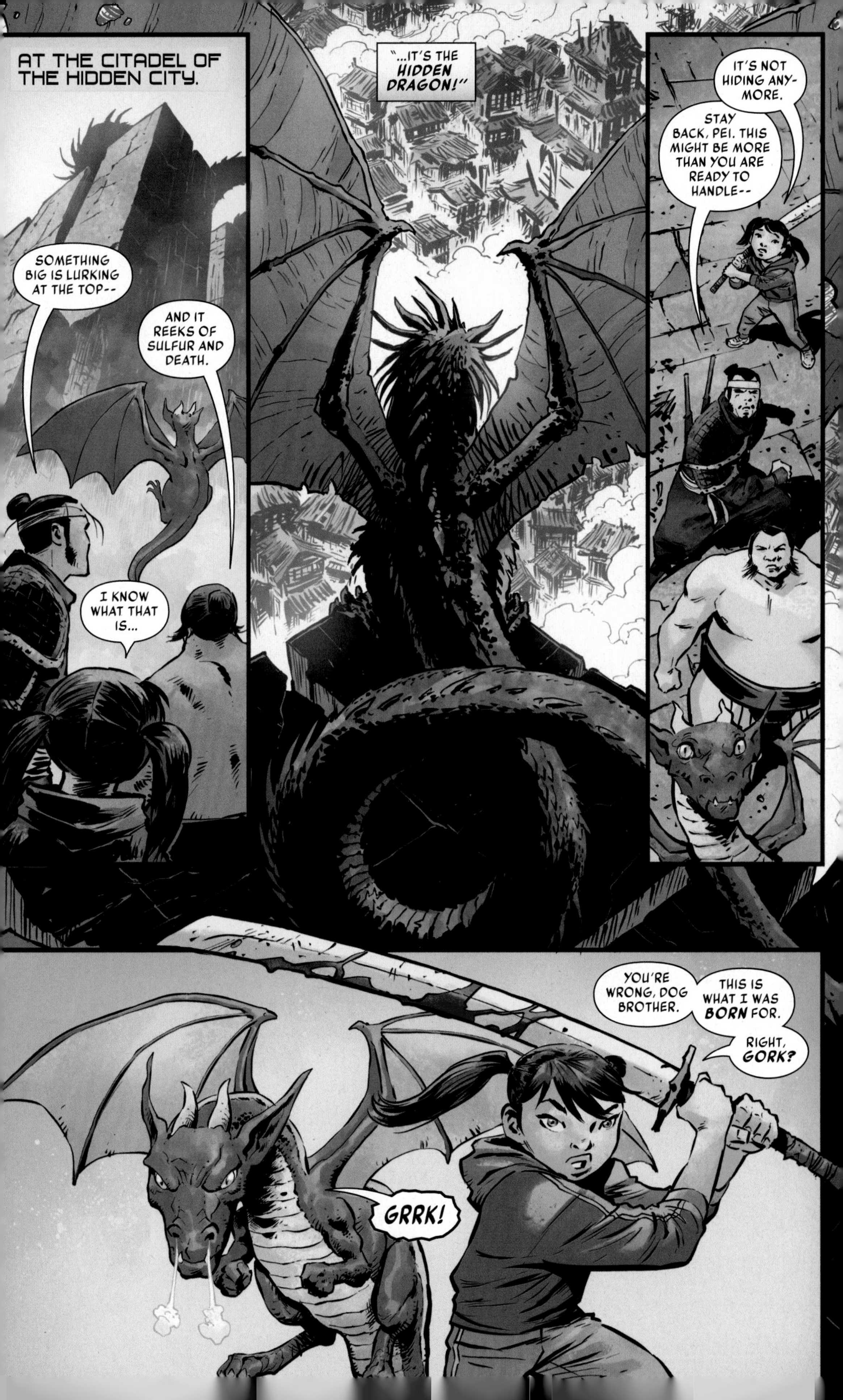
AT THE CITADEL OF THE HIDDEN CITY.
SOMETHING BIG IS LURKING AT THE TOP--
AND IT REEKS OF SULFUR AND DEATH.
I KNOW WHAT THAT IS...
"...IT'S THE HIDDEN DRAGON!"
IT'S NOT HIDING ANY-MORE.
STAY BACK, PEI. THIS MIGHT BE MORE THAN YOU ARE READY TO HANDLE--
YOU'RE WRONG, DOG BROTHER.
THIS IS WHAT I WAS BORN FOR.
RIGHT, GORK?
GRRK!

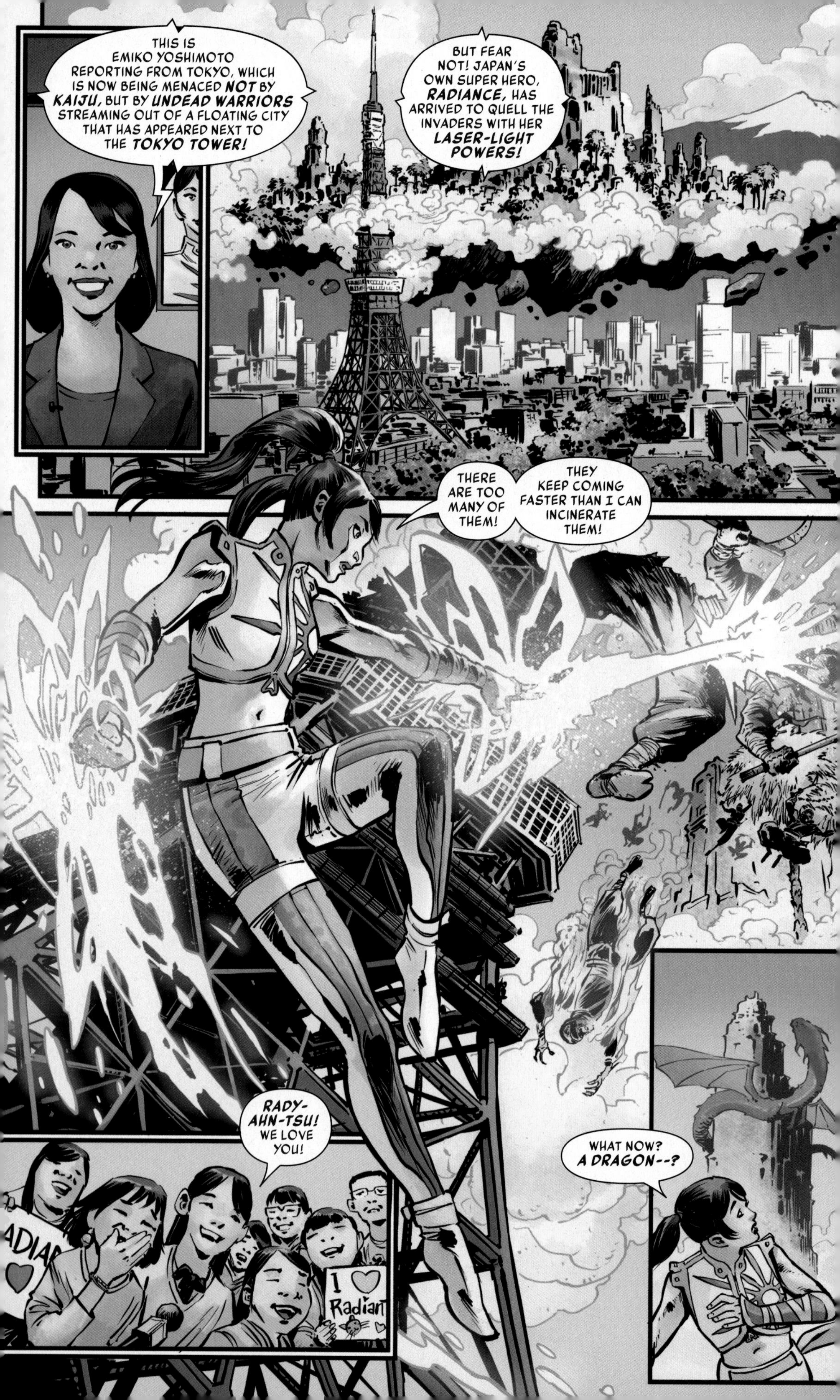

THIS IS EMIKO YOSHIMOTO REPORTING FROM TOKYO, WHICH IS NOW BEING MENACED **NOT** BY ***KAIJU,*** BUT BY ***UNDEAD WARRIORS*** STREAMING OUT OF A FLOATING CITY THAT HAS APPEARED NEXT TO THE ***TOKYO TOWER!***
BUT FEAR NOT! JAPAN'S OWN SUPER HERO, ***RADIANCE,*** HAS ARRIVED TO QUELL THE INVADERS WITH HER ***LASER-LIGHT POWERS!***
THERE ARE TOO MANY OF THEM!
THEY KEEP COMING FASTER THAN I CAN INCINERATE THEM!
***RADY-AHN-TSU!*** WE LOVE YOU!
RADIAN
I ♥ Radiant
WHAT NOW? ***A DRAGON--?***

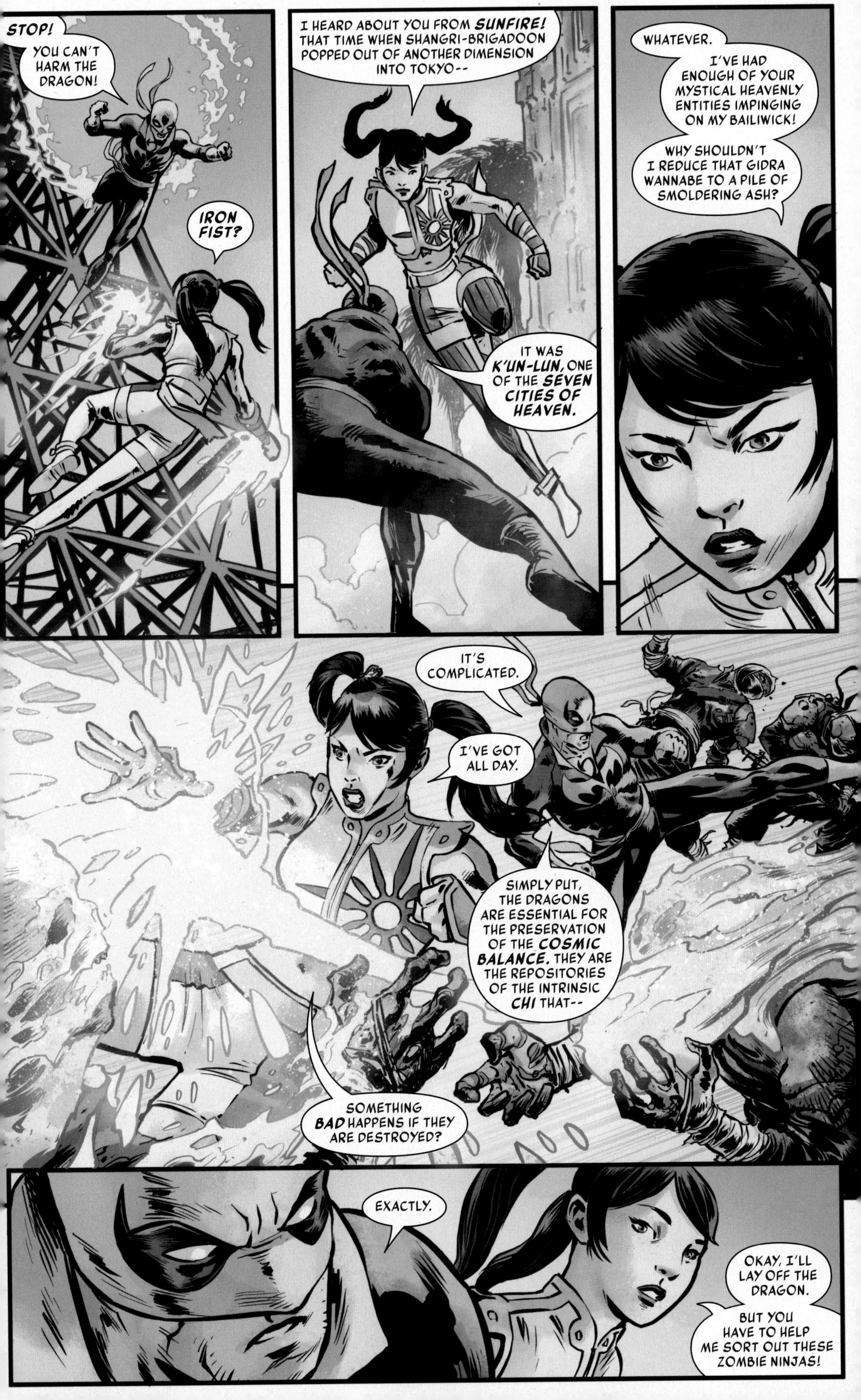

STOP!
YOU CAN'T HARM THE DRAGON!
IRON FIST?
I HEARD ABOUT YOU FROM SUNFIRE! THAT TIME WHEN SHANGRI-BRIGADOON POPPED OUT OF ANOTHER DIMENSION INTO TOKYO--
IT WAS K'UN-LUN, ONE OF THE SEVEN CITIES OF HEAVEN.
WHATEVER.
I'VE HAD ENOUGH OF YOUR MYSTICAL HEAVENLY ENTITIES IMPINGING ON MY BAILIWICK!
WHY SHOULDN'T I REDUCE THAT GIDRA WANNABE TO A PILE OF SMOLDERING ASH?
IT'S COMPLICATED.
I'VE GOT ALL DAY.
SIMPLY PUT, THE DRAGONS ARE ESSENTIAL FOR THE PRESERVATION OF THE COSMIC BALANCE. THEY ARE THE REPOSITORIES OF THE INTRINSIC CHI THAT--
SOMETHING BAD HAPPENS IF THEY ARE DESTROYED?
EXACTLY.
OKAY, I'LL LAY OFF THE DRAGON.
BUT YOU HAVE TO HELP ME SORT OUT THESE ZOMBIE NINJAS!

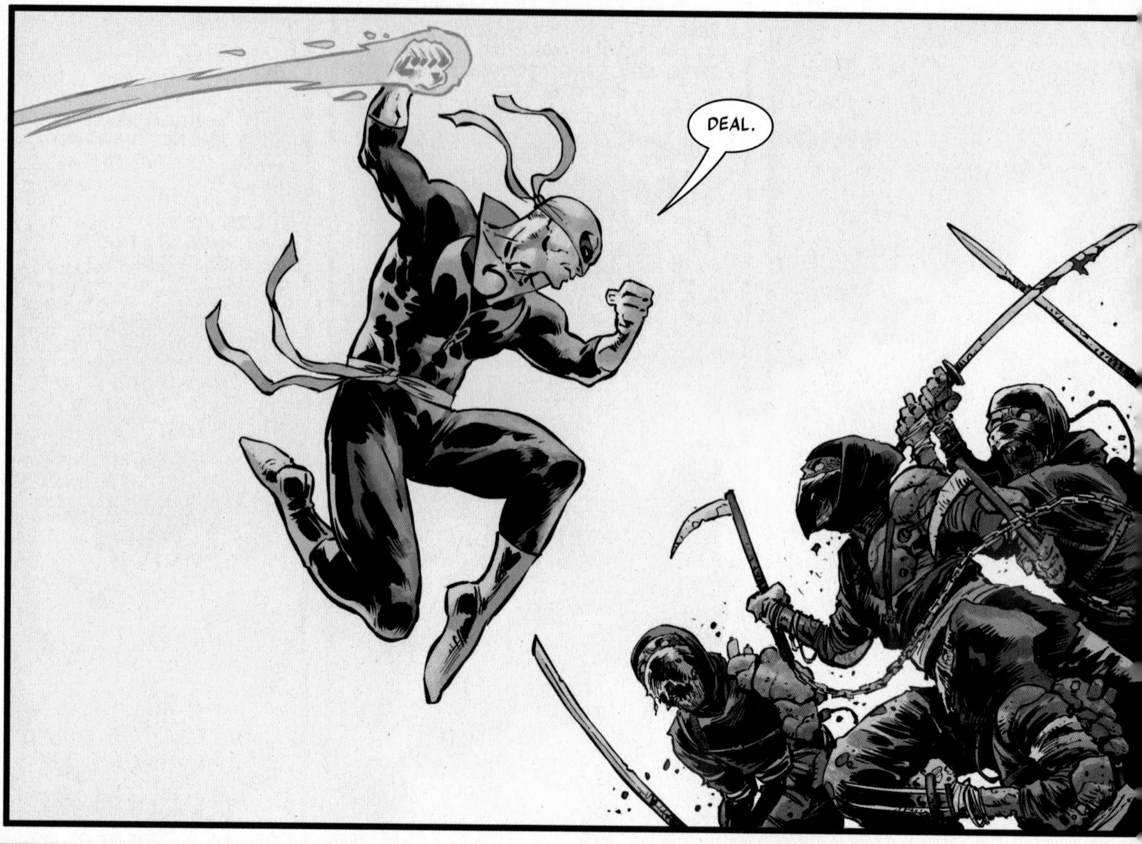
DEAL.

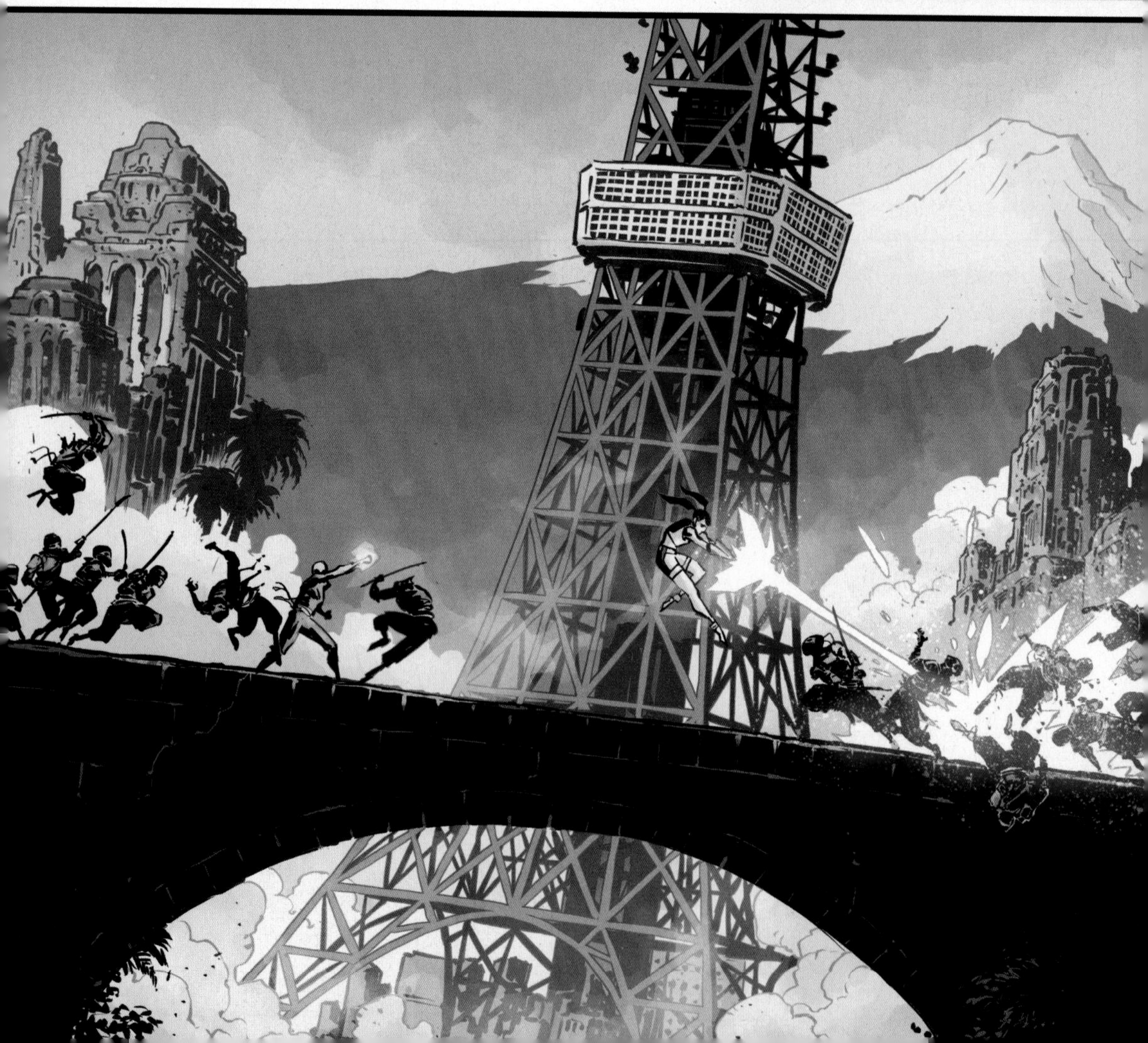

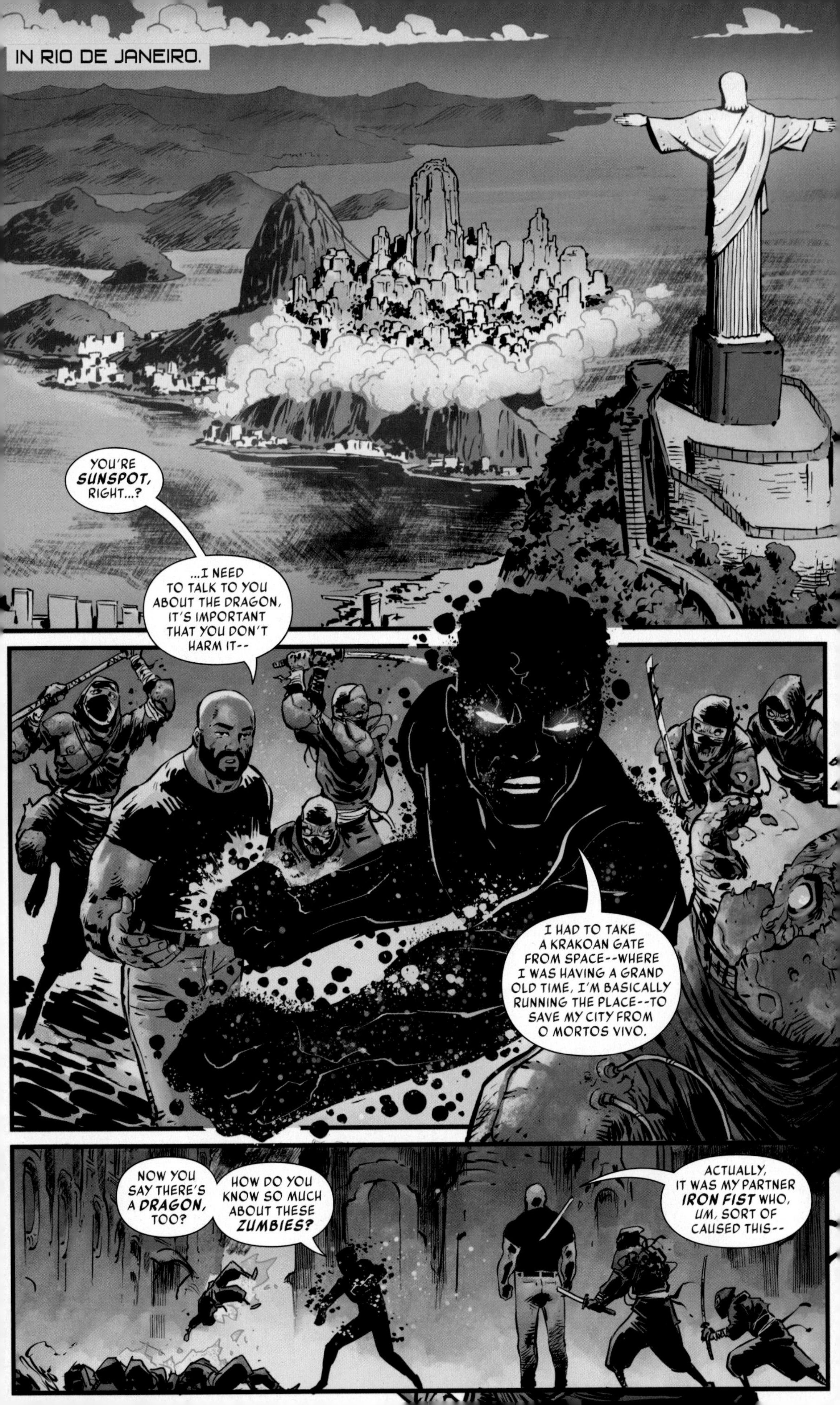
IN RIO DE JANEIRO.
YOU'RE SUNSPOT, RIGHT...?
...I NEED TO TALK TO YOU ABOUT THE DRAGON, IT'S IMPORTANT THAT YOU DON'T HARM IT--
I HAD TO TAKE A KRAKOAN GATE FROM SPACE--WHERE I WAS HAVING A GRAND OLD TIME, I'M BASICALLY RUNNING THE PLACE--TO SAVE MY CITY FROM O MORTOS VIVO.
NOW YOU SAY THERE'S A DRAGON, TOO?
HOW DO YOU KNOW SO MUCH ABOUT THESE ZUMBIES?
ACTUALLY, IT WAS MY PARTNER IRON FIST WHO, UM, SORT OF CAUSED THIS--

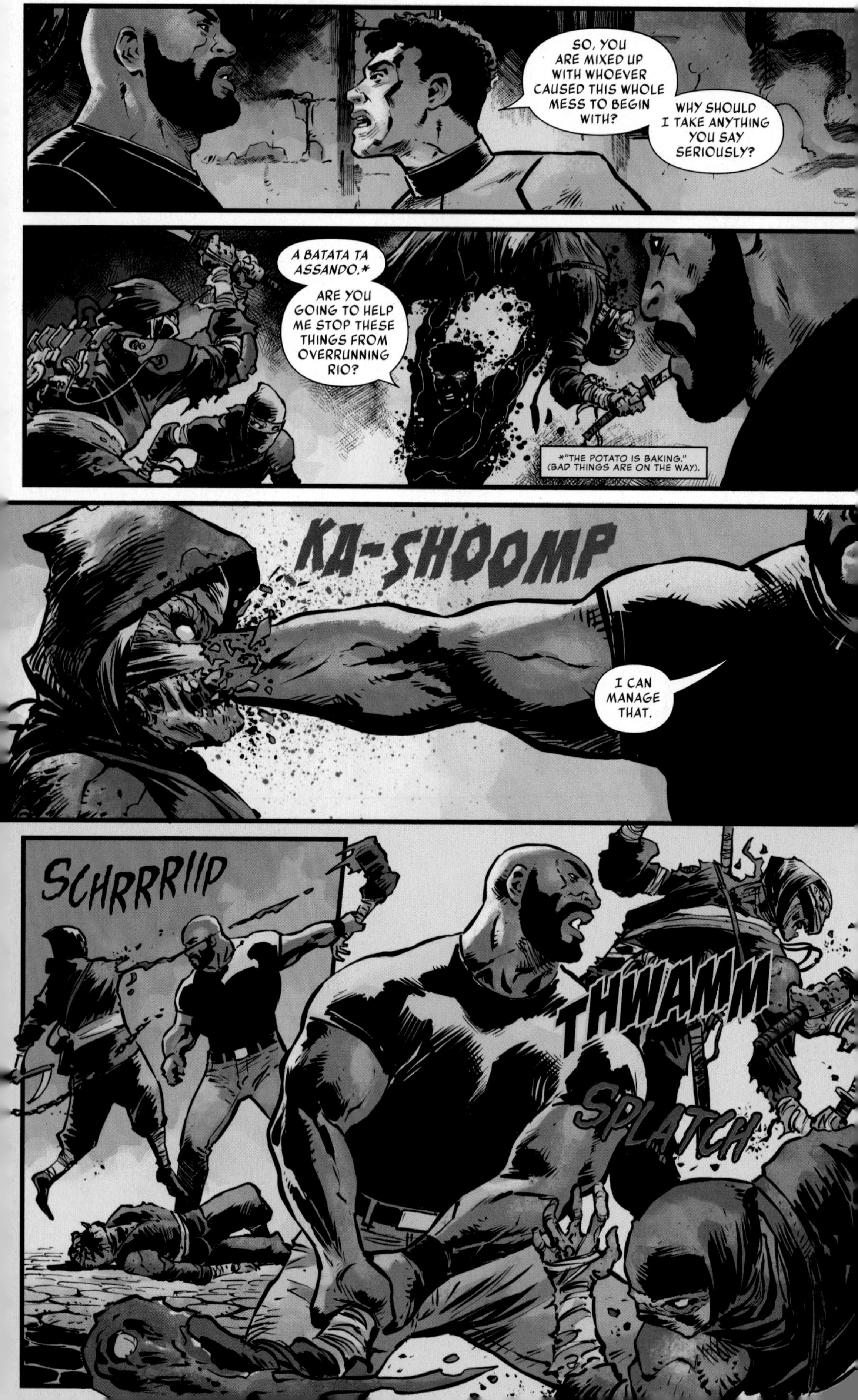

SO, YOU ARE MIXED UP WITH WHOEVER CAUSED THIS WHOLE MESS TO BEGIN WITH?
WHY SHOULD I TAKE ANYTHING YOU SAY SERIOUSLY?
A BATATA TA ASSANDO.*
ARE YOU GOING TO HELP ME STOP THESE THINGS FROM OVERRUNNING RIO?
*"THE POTATO IS BAKING." (BAD THINGS ARE ON THE WAY).
KA-SHOOMP
I CAN MANAGE THAT.
SCHRRRIIP
THWAMM
SPLATCH

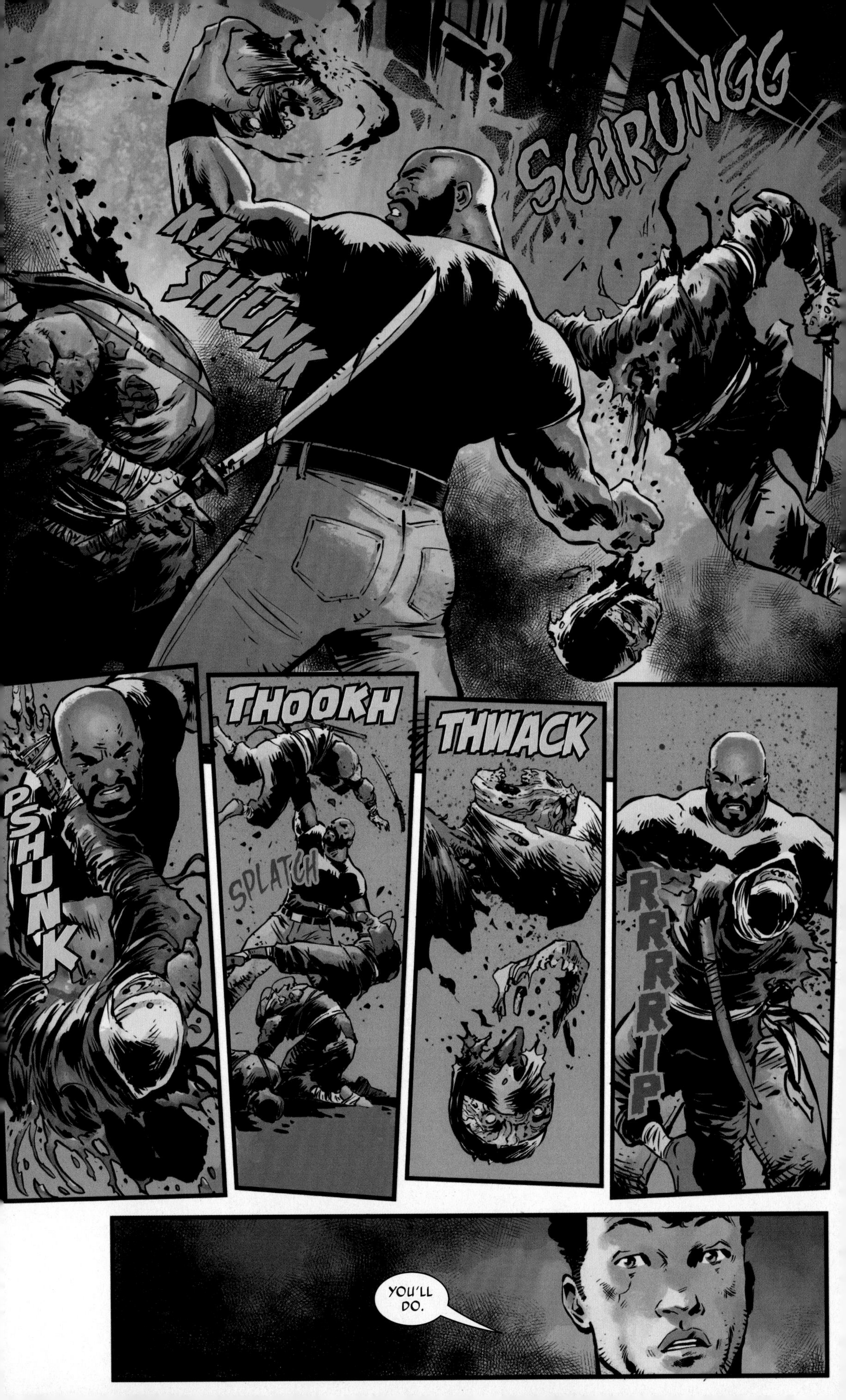
KA-SHUNK
SCHRUNGG
PSHUNK
THOOKH
SPLATCH
THWACK
RRRRRIP
YOU'LL DO.

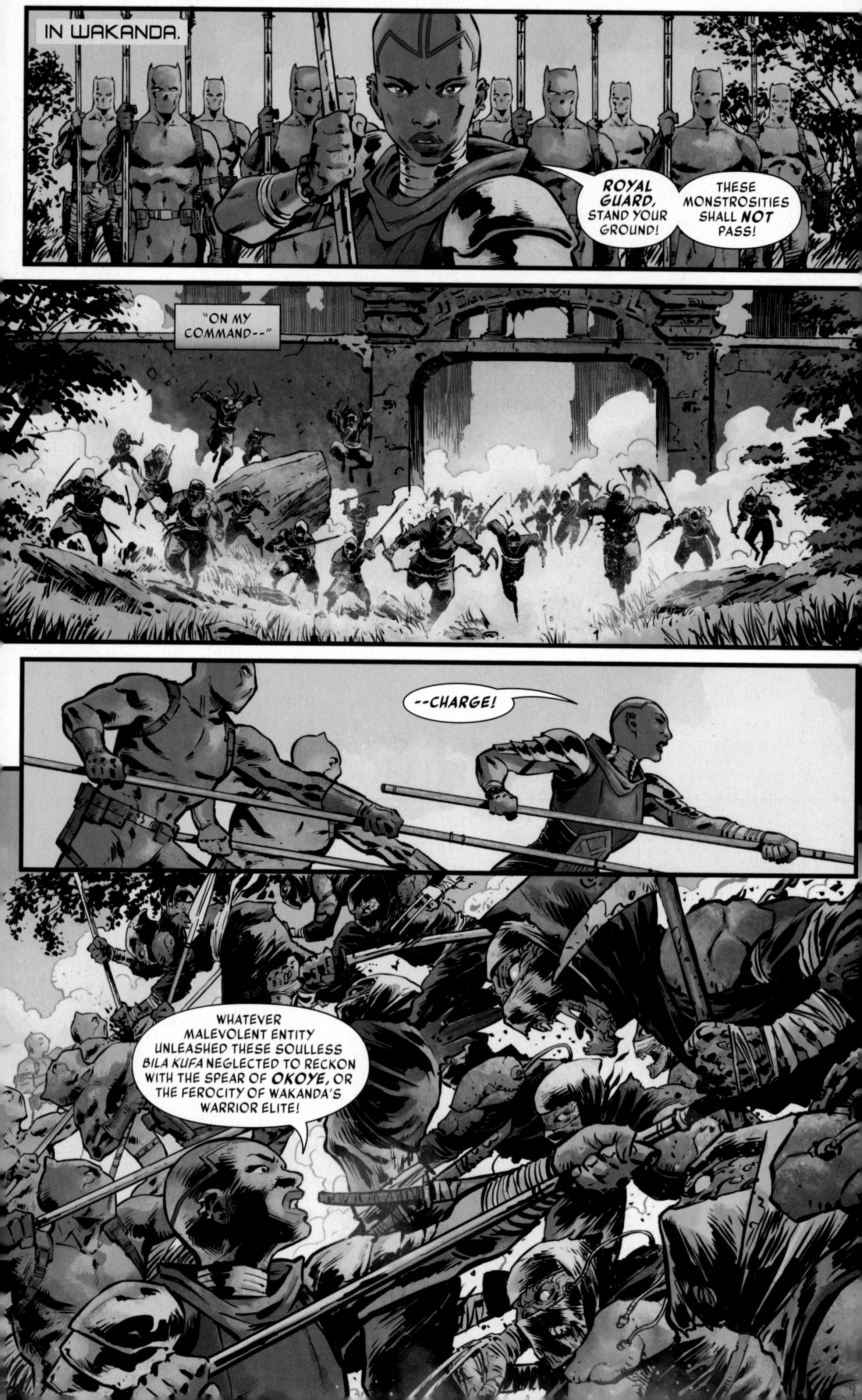
IN WAKANDA.
ROYAL GUARD, STAND YOUR GROUND!
THESE MONSTROSITIES SHALL NOT PASS!
"ON MY COMMAND--"
--CHARGE!
WHATEVER MALEVOLENT ENTITY UNLEASHED THESE SOULLESS BILA KUFA NEGLECTED TO RECKON WITH THE SPEAR OF OKOYE, OR THE FEROCITY OF WAKANDA'S WARRIOR ELITE!

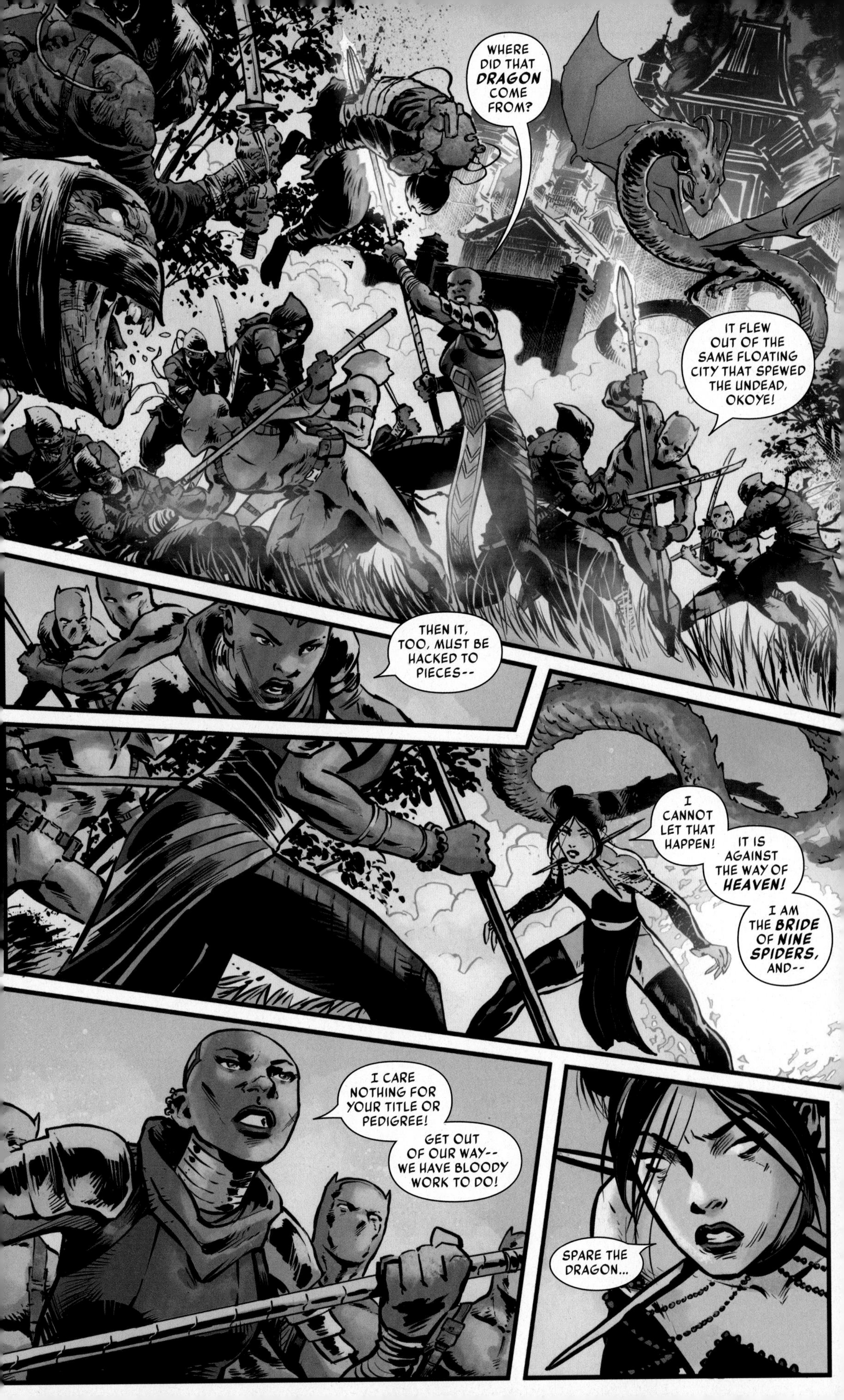
WHERE DID THAT DRAGON COME FROM?
IT FLEW OUT OF THE SAME FLOATING CITY THAT SPEWED THE UNDEAD, OKOYE!
THEN IT, TOO, MUST BE HACKED TO PIECES--
I CANNOT LET THAT HAPPEN!
IT IS AGAINST THE WAY OF HEAVEN!
I AM THE BRIDE OF NINE SPIDERS, AND--
I CARE NOTHING FOR YOUR TITLE OR PEDIGREE!
GET OUT OF OUR WAY-- WE HAVE BLOODY WORK TO DO!
SPARE THE DRAGON...

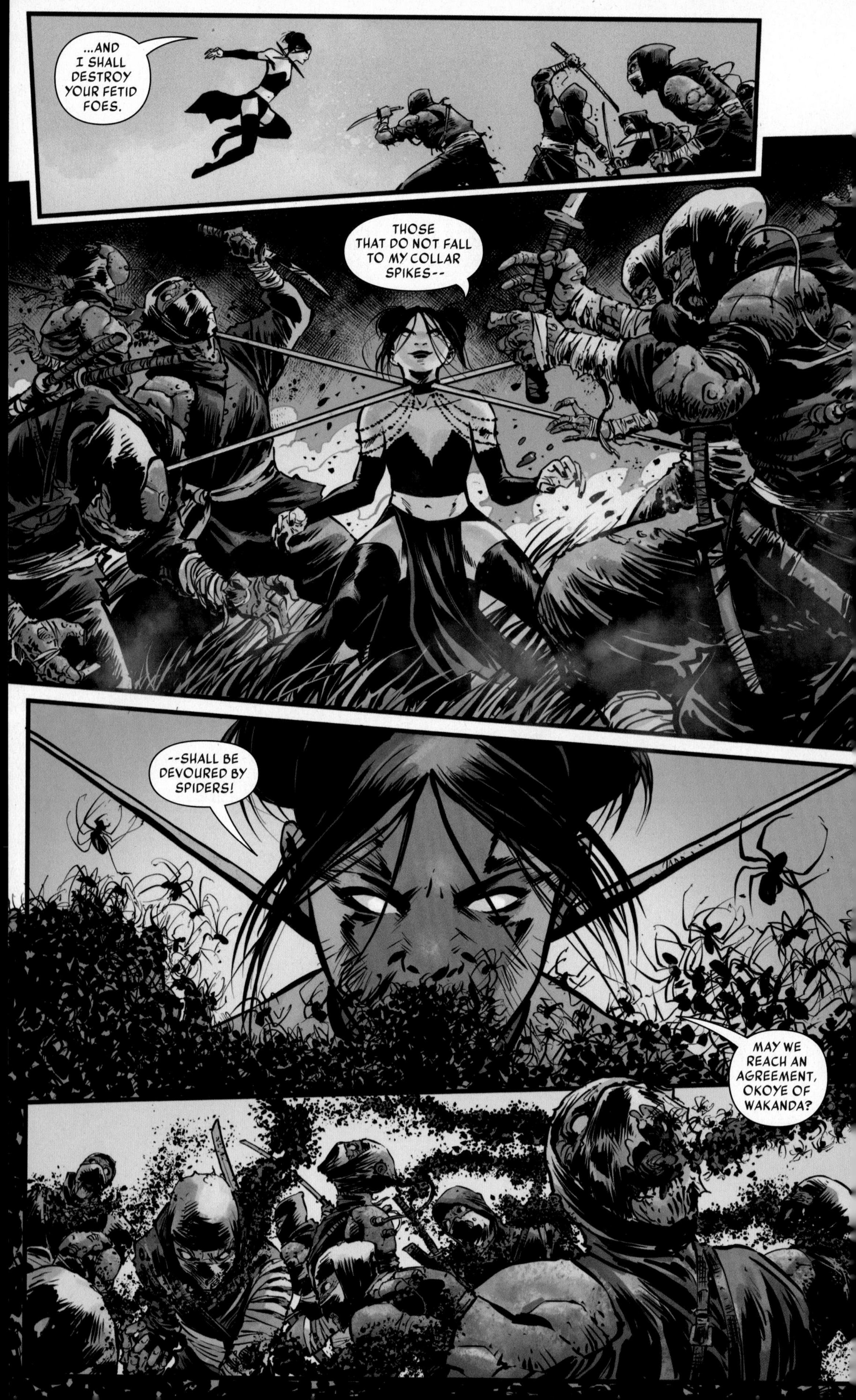
...AND I SHALL DESTROY YOUR FETID FOES.
THOSE THAT DO NOT FALL TO MY COLLAR SPIKES--
--SHALL BE DEVOURED BY SPIDERS!
MAY WE REACH AN AGREEMENT, OKOYE OF WAKANDA?

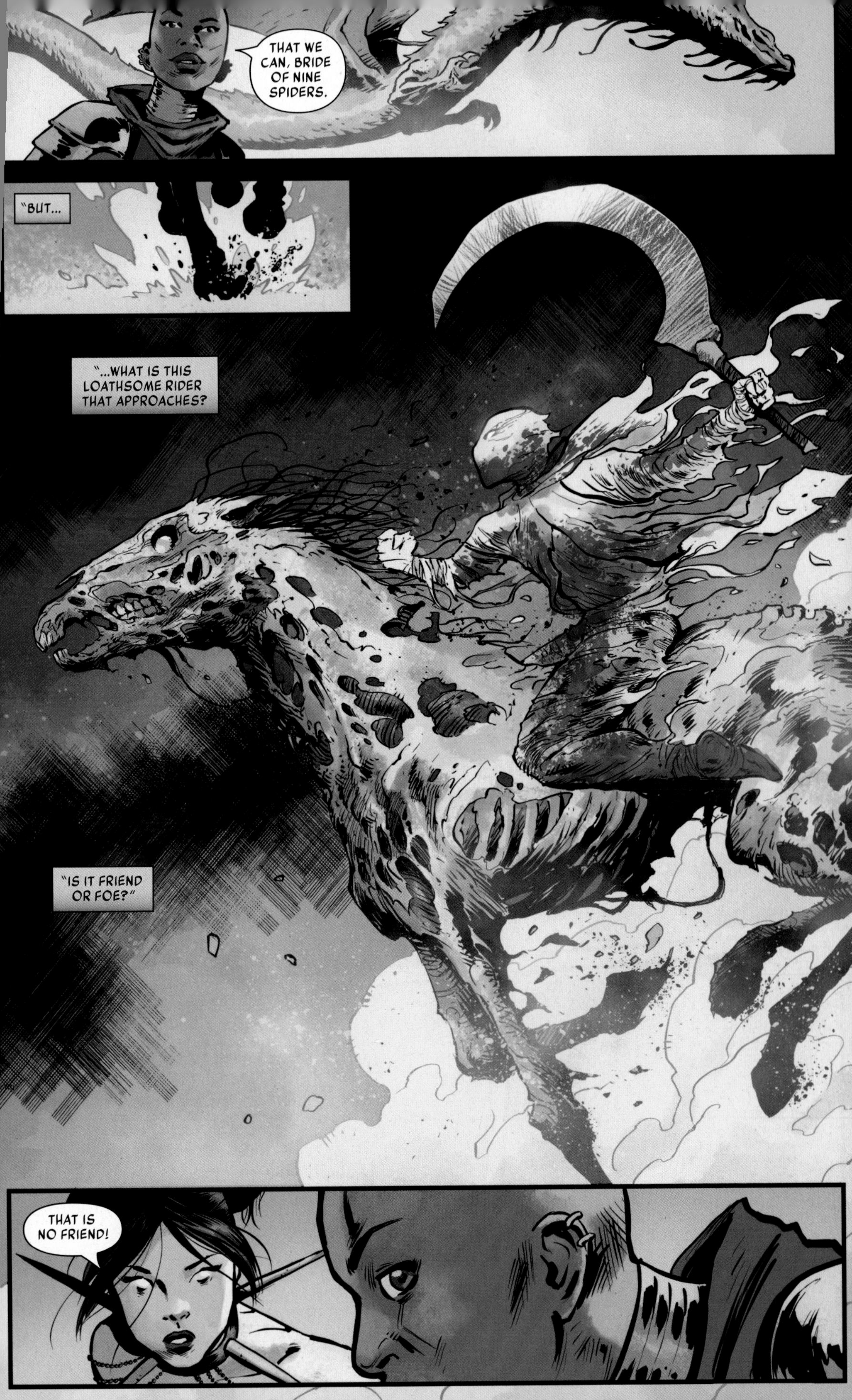

THAT WE CAN, BRIDE OF NINE SPIDERS.
"BUT...
"...WHAT IS THIS LOATHSOME RIDER THAT APPROACHES?
"IS IT FRIEND OR FOE?"
THAT IS NO FRIEND!

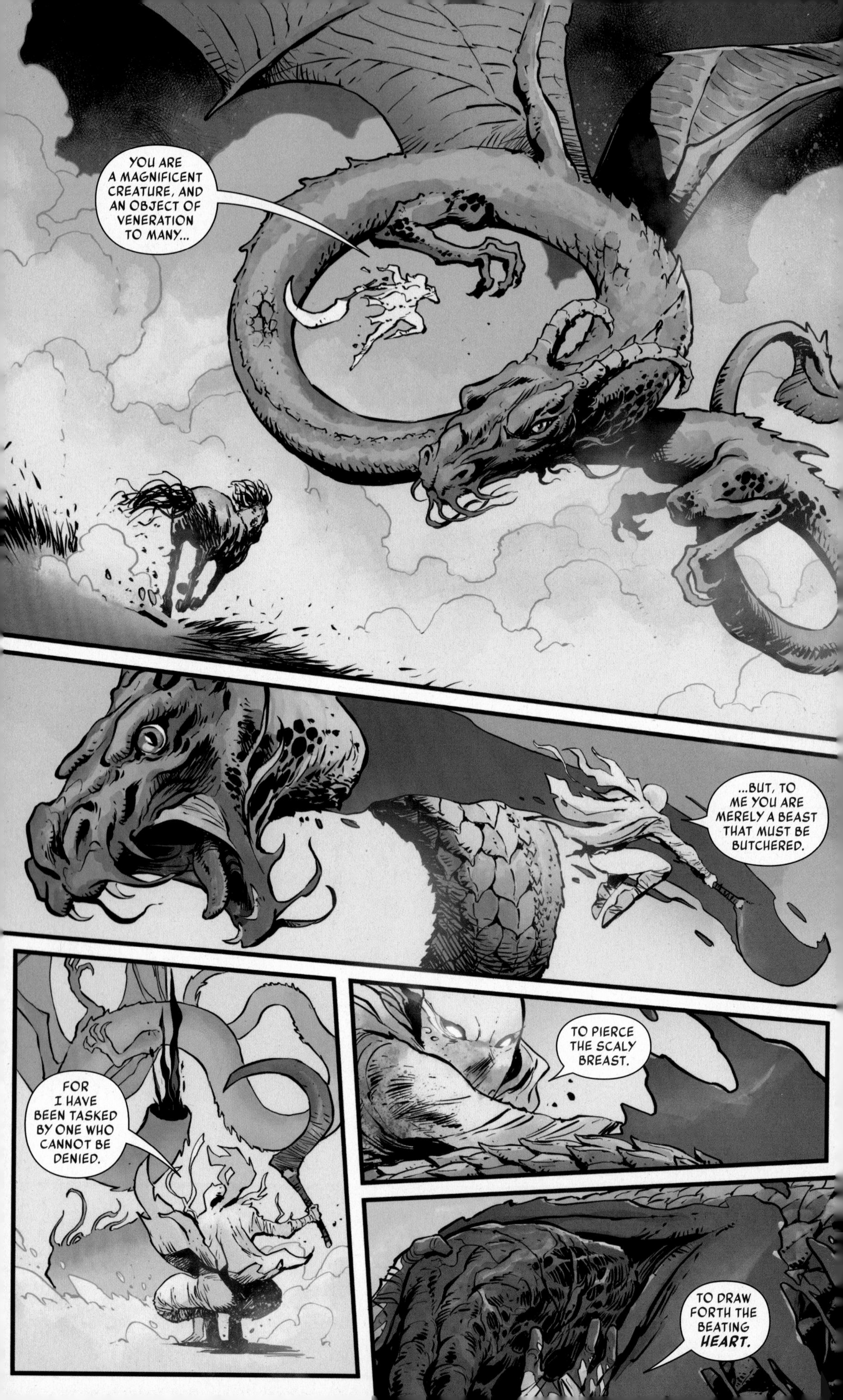
YOU ARE A MAGNIFICENT CREATURE, AND AN OBJECT OF VENERATION TO MANY...
...BUT, TO ME YOU ARE MERELY A BEAST THAT MUST BE BUTCHERED.
FOR I HAVE BEEN TASKED BY ONE WHO CANNOT BE DENIED.
TO PIERCE THE SCALY BREAST.
TO DRAW FORTH THE BEATING HEART.

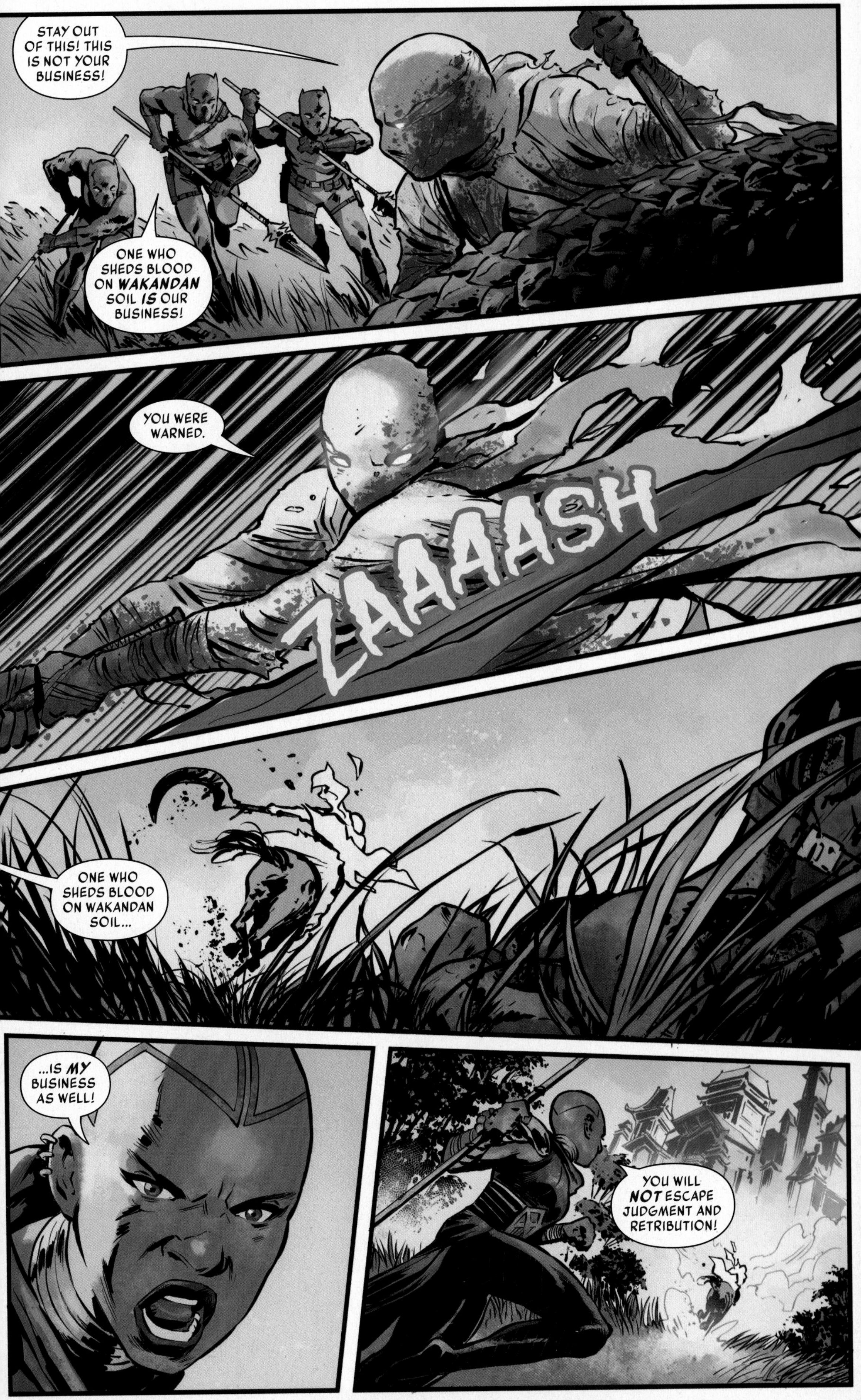
STAY OUT OF THIS! THIS IS NOT YOUR BUSINESS!
ONE WHO SHEDS BLOOD ON **WAKANDAN** SOIL **IS** OUR BUSINESS!
YOU WERE WARNED.
ZAAAASH
ONE WHO SHEDS BLOOD ON WAKANDAN SOIL...
...IS **MY** BUSINESS AS WELL!
YOU WILL **NOT** ESCAPE JUDGMENT AND RETRIBUTION!

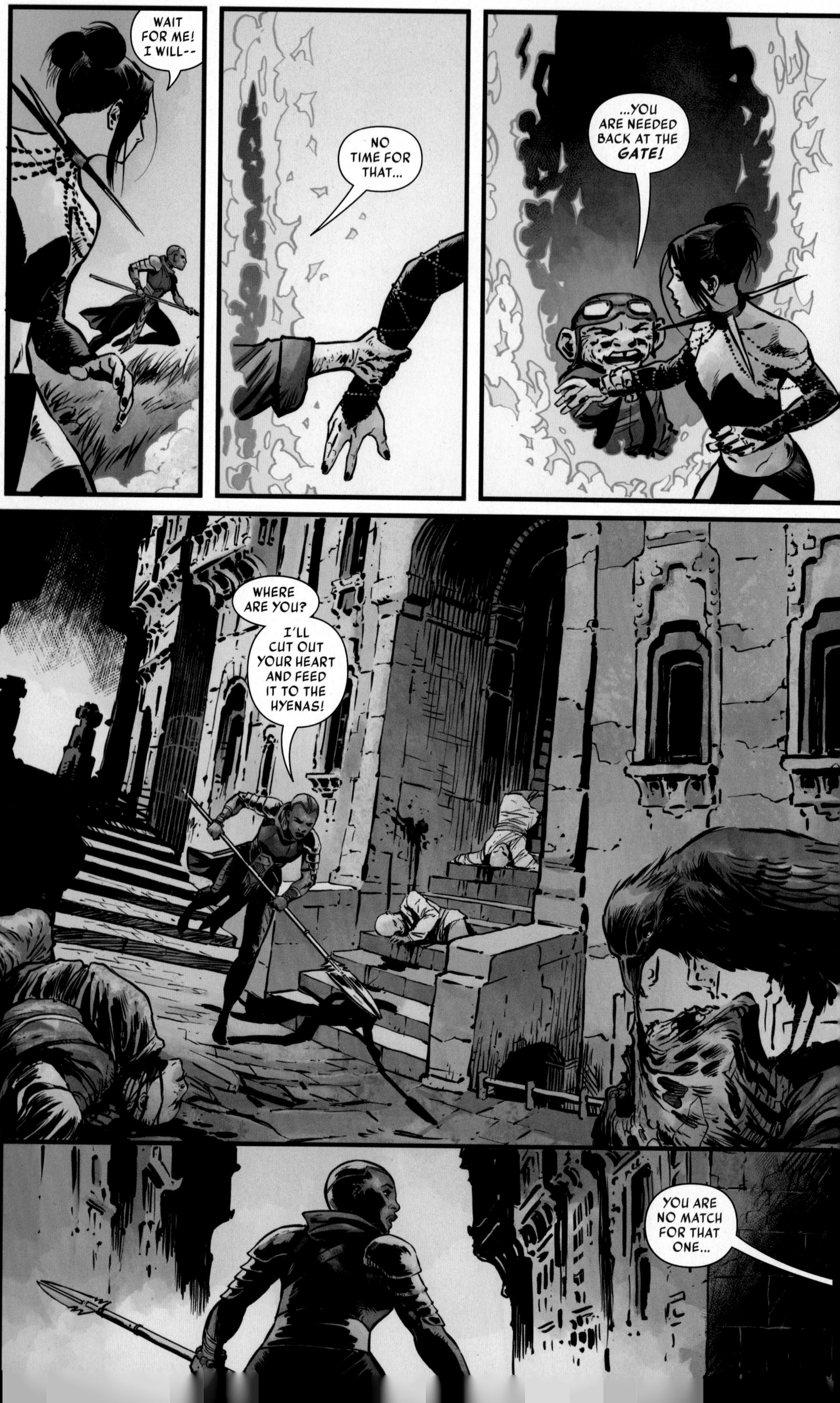
WAIT FOR ME! I WILL--
NO TIME FOR THAT...
...YOU ARE NEEDED BACK AT THE GATE!
WHERE ARE YOU?
I'LL CUT OUT YOUR HEART AND FEED IT TO THE HYENAS!
YOU ARE NO MATCH FOR THAT ONE...

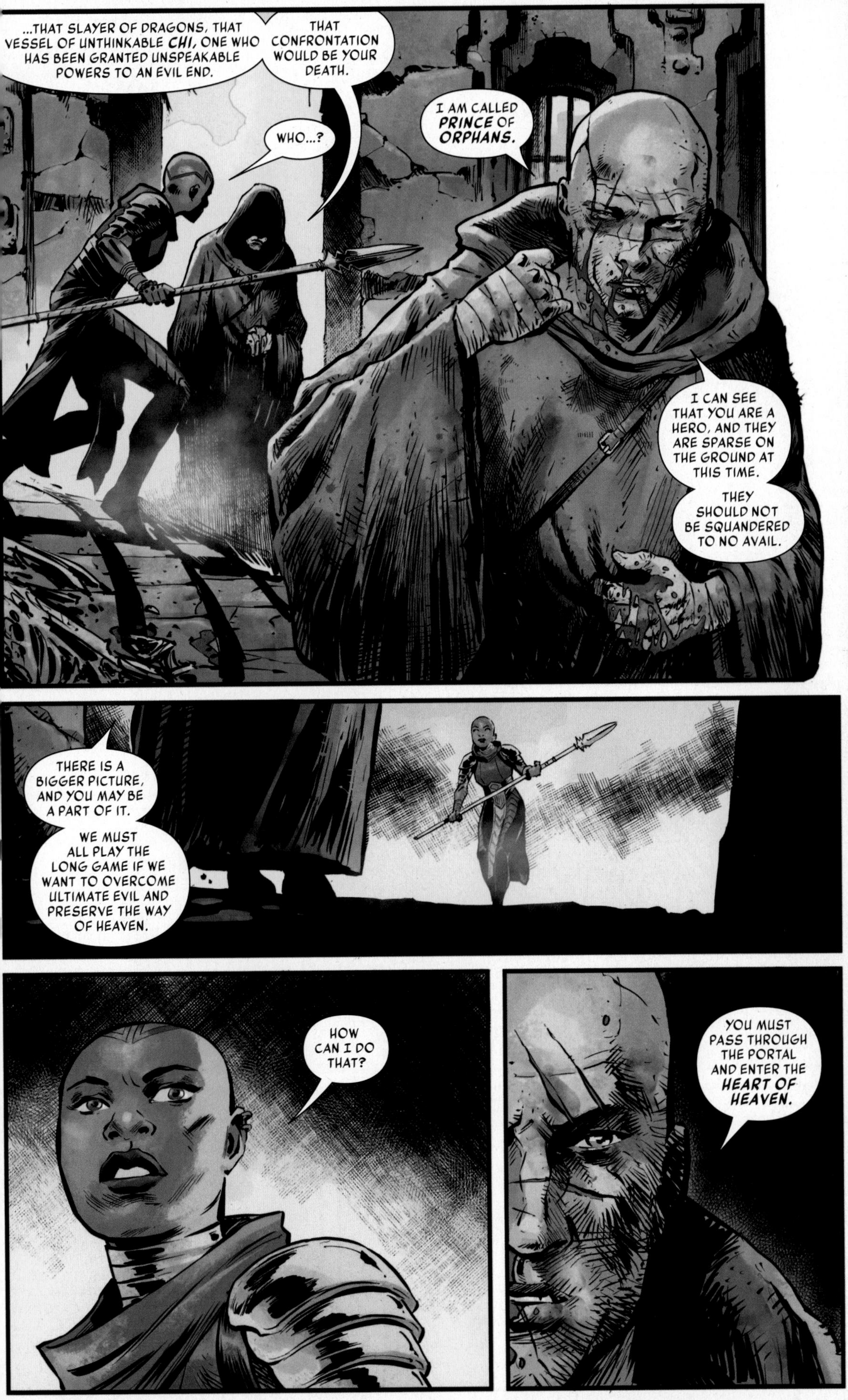
...THAT SLAYER OF DRAGONS, THAT VESSEL OF UNTHINKABLE CHI, ONE WHO HAS BEEN GRANTED UNSPEAKABLE POWERS TO AN EVIL END.
THAT CONFRONTATION WOULD BE YOUR DEATH.
WHO...?
I AM CALLED PRINCE OF ORPHANS.
I CAN SEE THAT YOU ARE A HERO, AND THEY ARE SPARSE ON THE GROUND AT THIS TIME.
THEY SHOULD NOT BE SQUANDERED TO NO AVAIL.
THERE IS A BIGGER PICTURE, AND YOU MAY BE A PART OF IT.
WE MUST ALL PLAY THE LONG GAME IF WE WANT TO OVERCOME ULTIMATE EVIL AND PRESERVE THE WAY OF HEAVEN.
HOW CAN I DO THAT?
YOU MUST PASS THROUGH THE PORTAL AND ENTER THE HEART OF HEAVEN.

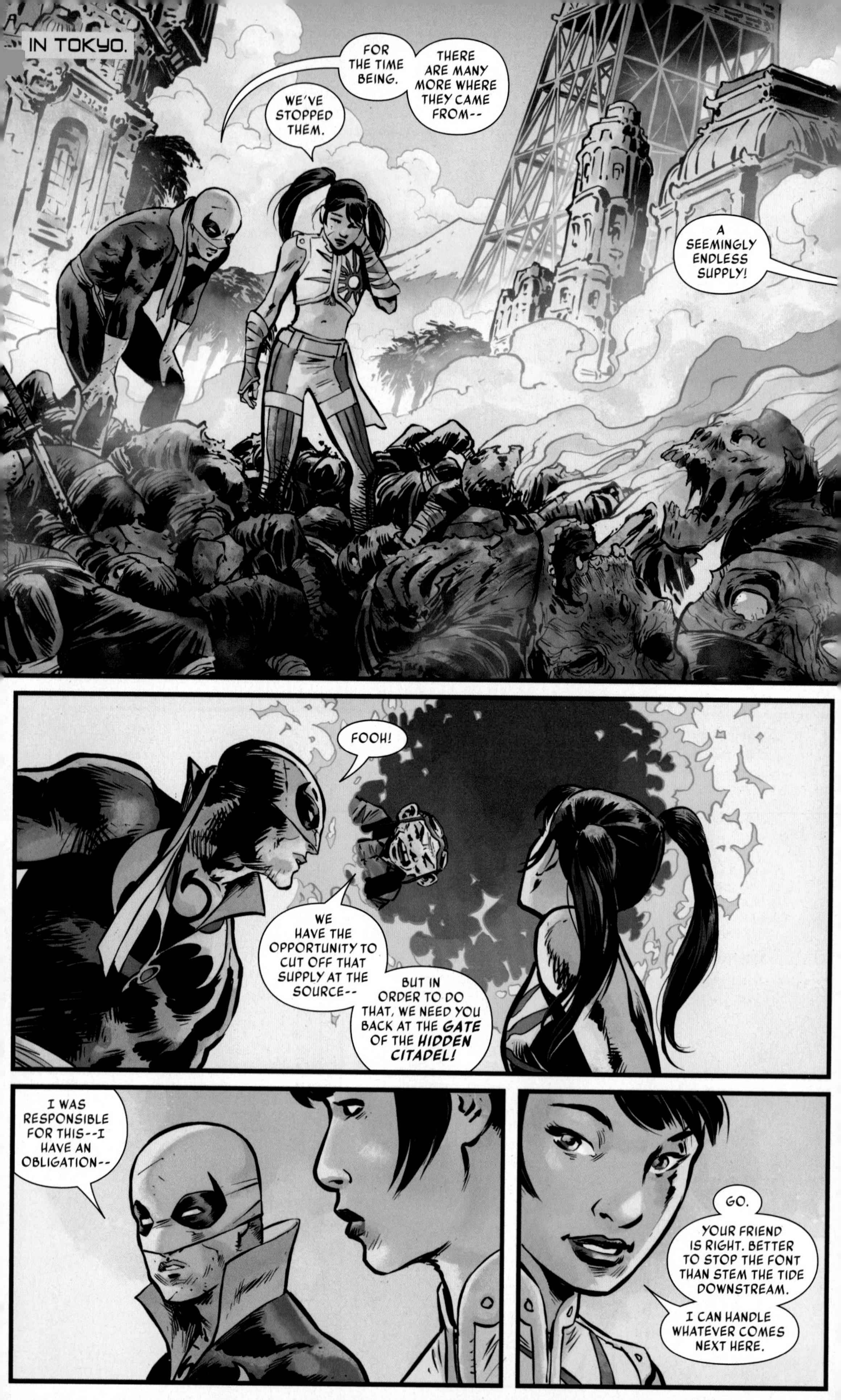
IN TOKYO.
WE'VE STOPPED THEM.
FOR THE TIME BEING.
THERE ARE MANY MORE WHERE THEY CAME FROM--
A SEEMINGLY ENDLESS SUPPLY!
FOOH!
WE HAVE THE OPPORTUNITY TO CUT OFF THAT SUPPLY AT THE SOURCE--
BUT IN ORDER TO DO THAT, WE NEED YOU BACK AT THE GATE OF THE HIDDEN CITADEL!
I WAS RESPONSIBLE FOR THIS--I HAVE AN OBLIGATION--
GO.
YOUR FRIEND IS RIGHT. BETTER TO STOP THE FONT THAN STEM THE TIDE DOWNSTREAM.
I CAN HANDLE WHATEVER COMES NEXT HERE.

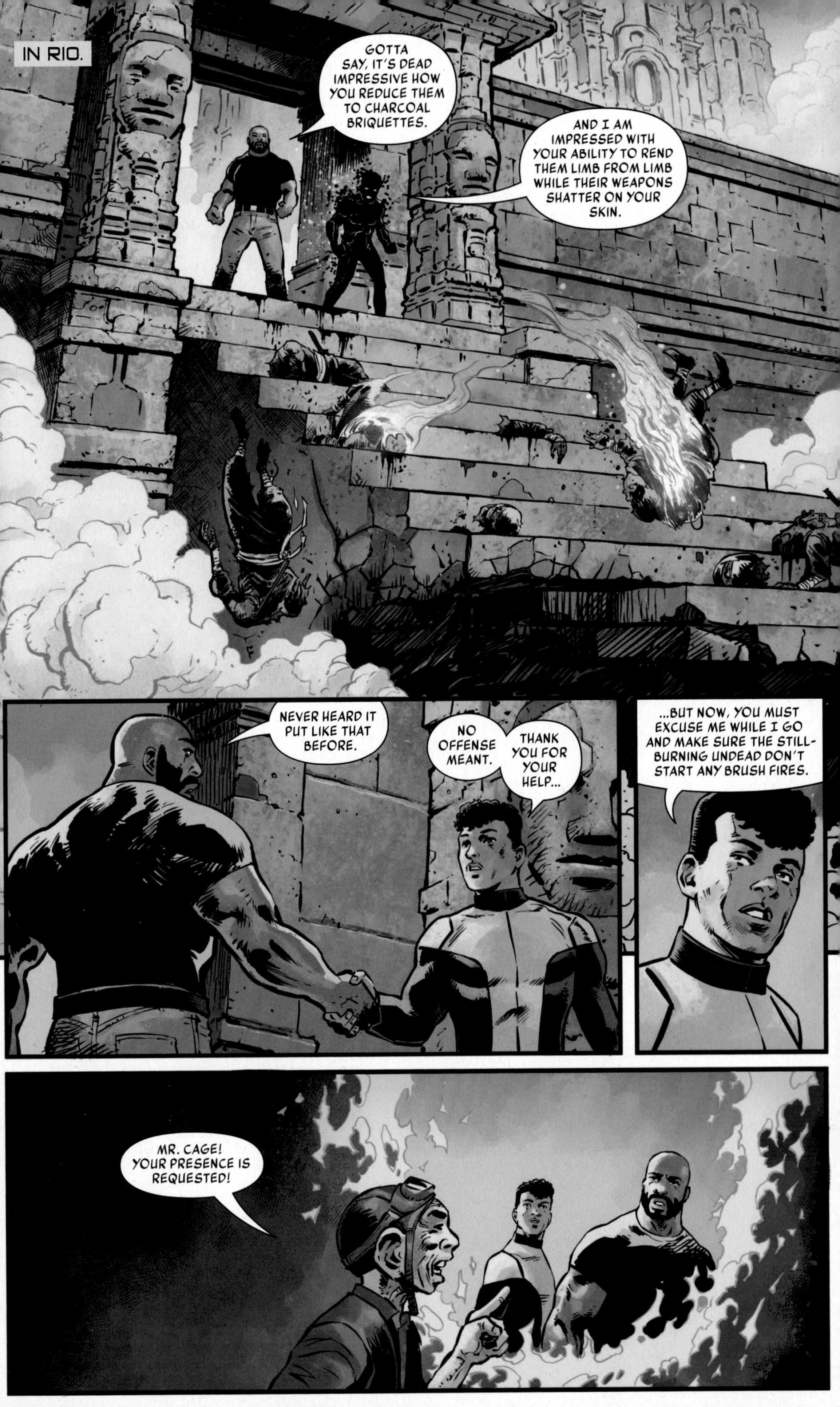
IN RIO.
GOTTA SAY, IT'S DEAD IMPRESSIVE HOW YOU REDUCE THEM TO CHARCOAL BRIQUETTES.
AND I AM IMPRESSED WITH YOUR ABILITY TO REND THEM LIMB FROM LIMB WHILE THEIR WEAPONS SHATTER ON YOUR SKIN.
NEVER HEARD IT PUT LIKE THAT BEFORE.
NO OFFENSE MEANT.
THANK YOU FOR YOUR HELP...
...BUT NOW, YOU MUST EXCUSE ME WHILE I GO AND MAKE SURE THE STILL-BURNING UNDEAD DON'T START ANY BRUSH FIRES.
MR. CAGE! YOUR PRESENCE IS REQUESTED!

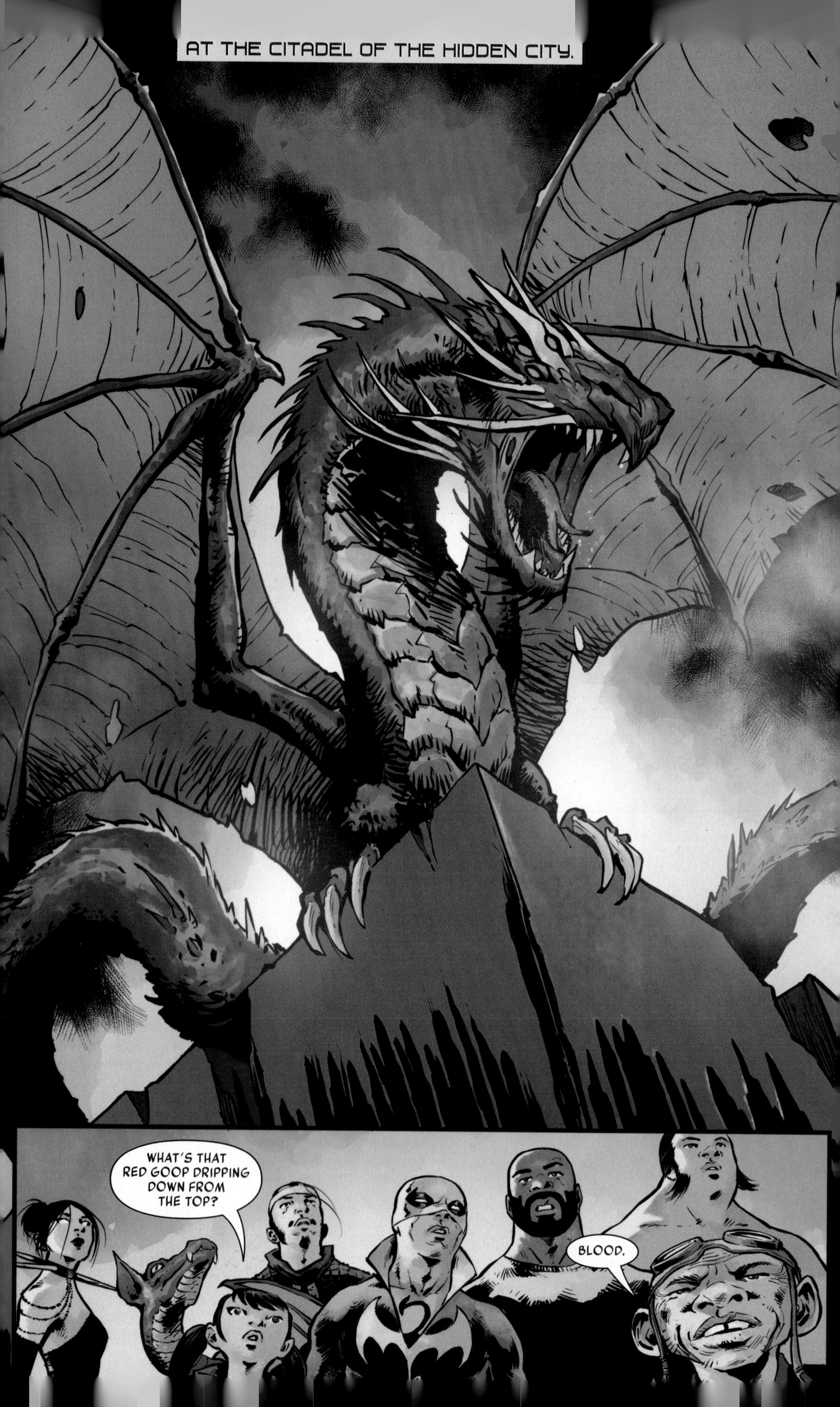
AT THE CITADEL OF THE HIDDEN CITY.
WHAT'S THAT RED GOOP DRIPPING DOWN FROM THE TOP?
BLOOD.

# FOUR

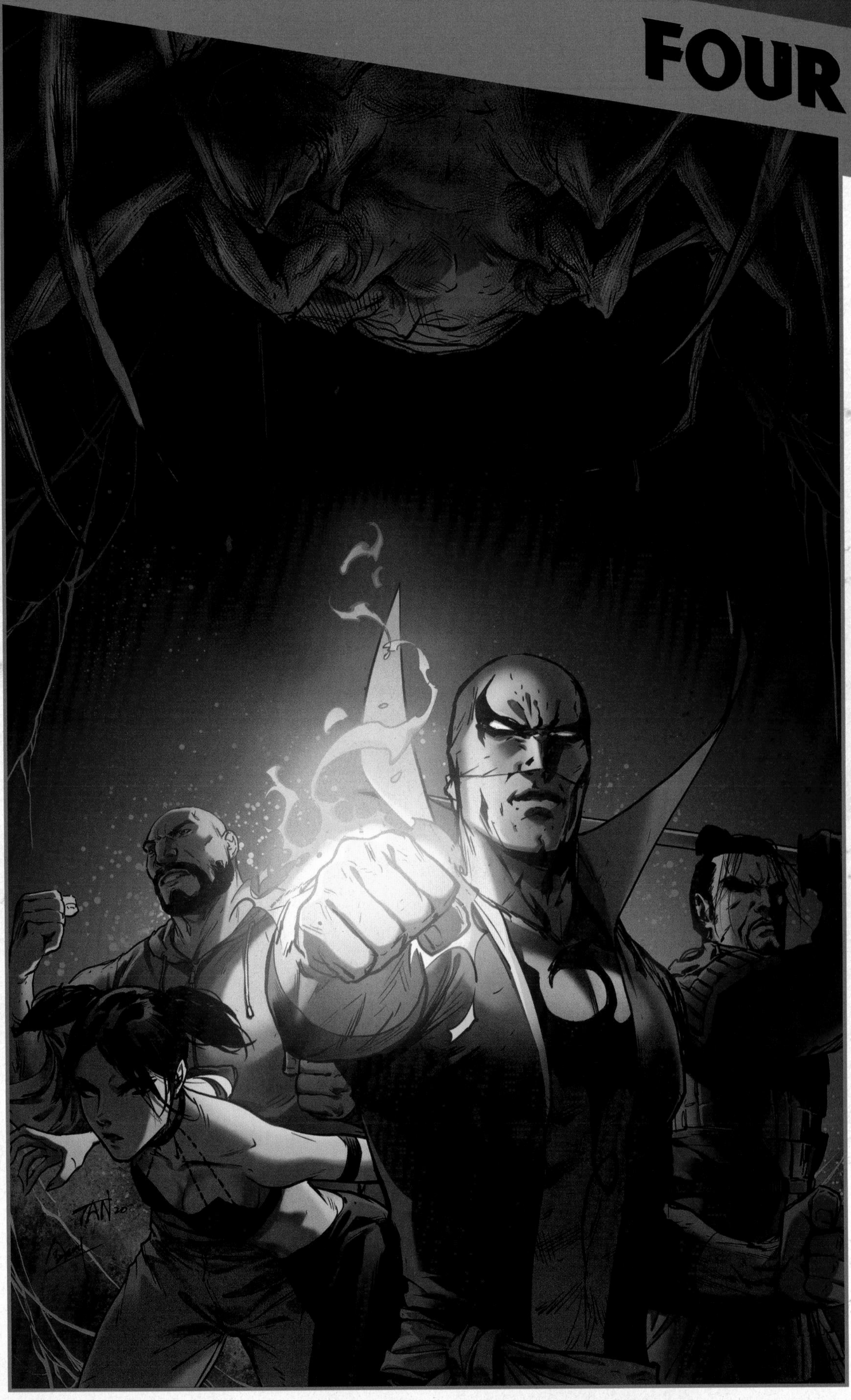

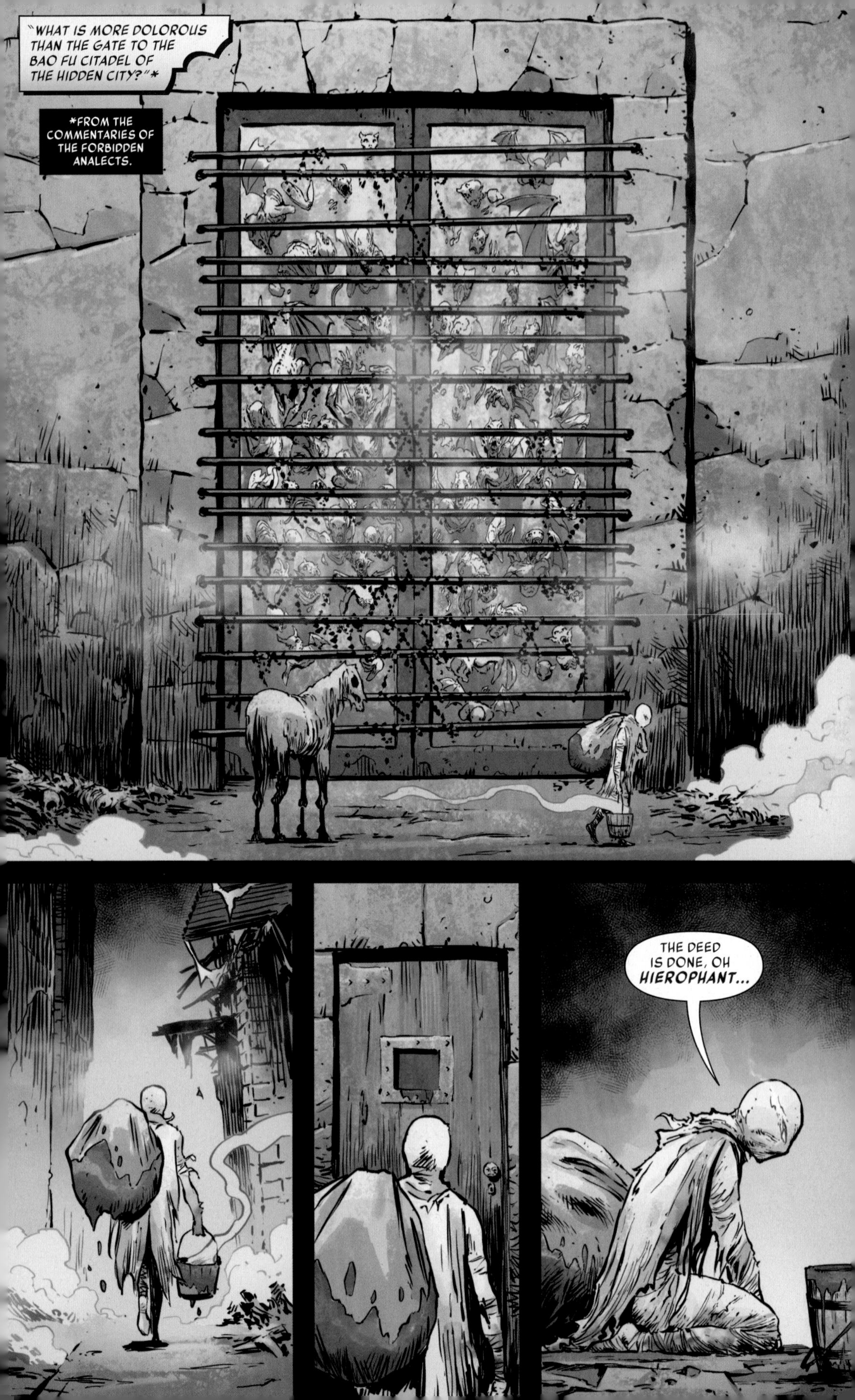
"WHAT IS MORE DOLOROUS THAN THE GATE TO THE BAO FU CITADEL OF THE HIDDEN CITY?"*
*FROM THE COMMENTARIES OF THE FORBIDDEN ANALECTS.
THE DEED IS DONE, OH HIEROPHANT...

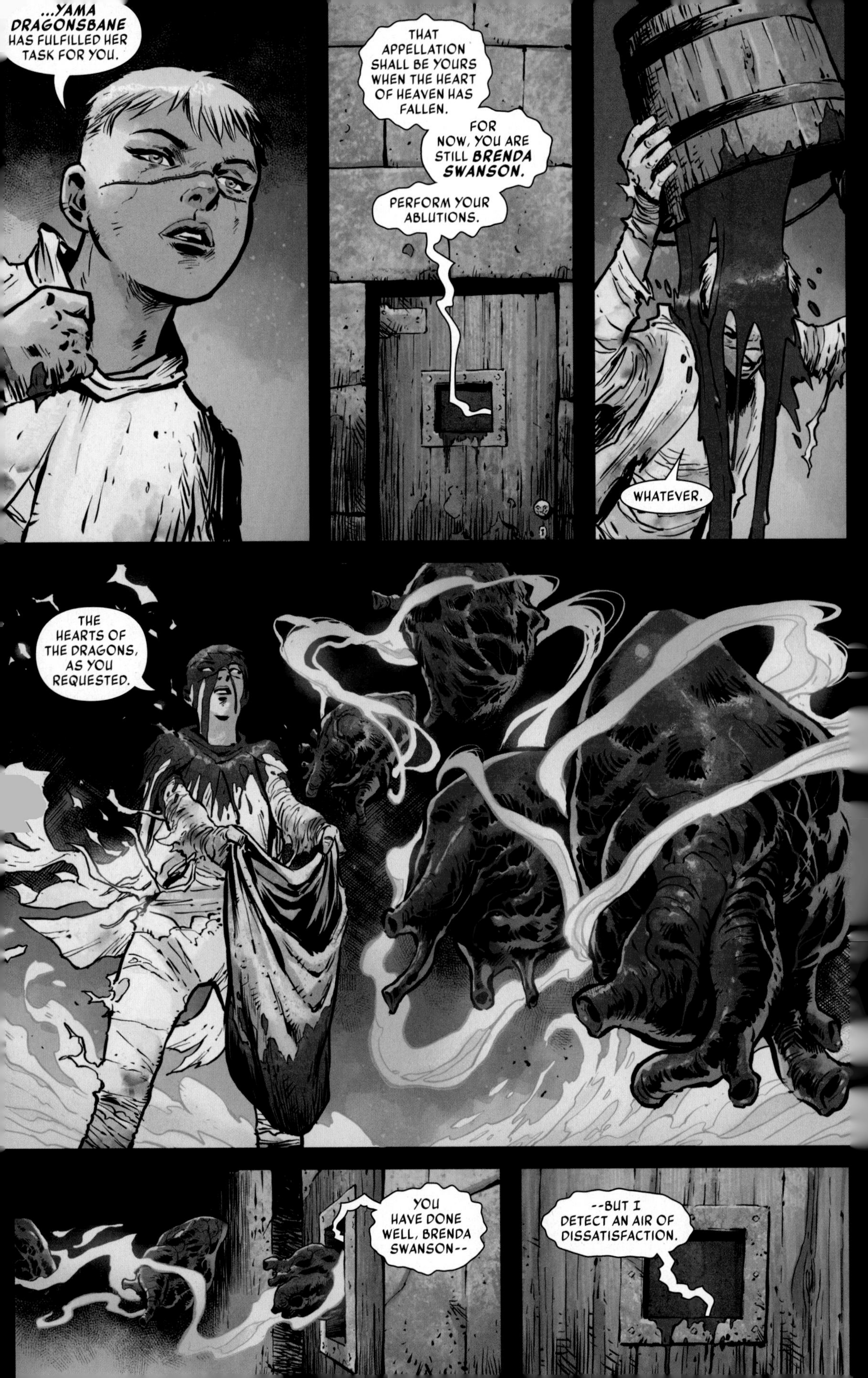
...YAMA DRAGONSBANE HAS FULFILLED HER TASK FOR YOU.
THAT APPELLATION SHALL BE YOURS WHEN THE HEART OF HEAVEN HAS FALLEN.
FOR NOW, YOU ARE STILL BRENDA SWANSON.
PERFORM YOUR ABLUTIONS.
WHATEVER.
THE HEARTS OF THE DRAGONS, AS YOU REQUESTED.
YOU HAVE DONE WELL, BRENDA SWANSON--
--BUT I DETECT AN AIR OF DISSATISFACTION.

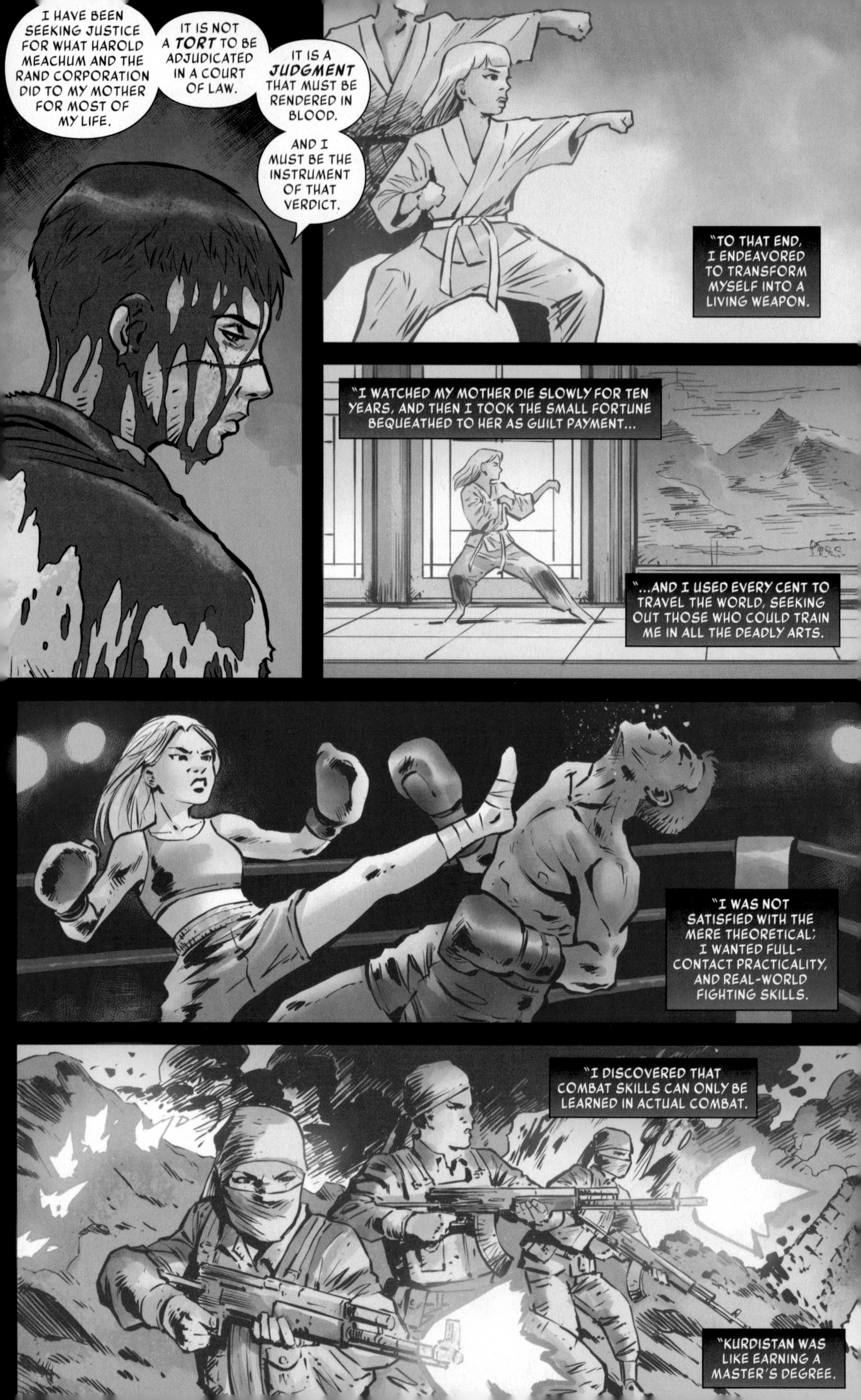
I HAVE BEEN SEEKING JUSTICE FOR WHAT HAROLD MEACHUM AND THE RAND CORPORATION DID TO MY MOTHER FOR MOST OF MY LIFE.
IT IS NOT A **TORT** TO BE ADJUDICATED IN A COURT OF LAW.
IT IS A **JUDGMENT** THAT MUST BE RENDERED IN BLOOD.
AND I MUST BE THE INSTRUMENT OF THAT VERDICT.
"TO THAT END, I ENDEAVORED TO TRANSFORM MYSELF INTO A LIVING WEAPON.
"I WATCHED MY MOTHER DIE SLOWLY FOR TEN YEARS, AND THEN I TOOK THE SMALL FORTUNE BEQUEATHED TO HER AS GUILT PAYMENT...
"...AND I USED EVERY CENT TO TRAVEL THE WORLD, SEEKING OUT THOSE WHO COULD TRAIN ME IN ALL THE DEADLY ARTS.
"I WAS NOT SATISFIED WITH THE MERE THEORETICAL; I WANTED FULL-CONTACT PRACTICALITY, AND REAL-WORLD FIGHTING SKILLS.
"I DISCOVERED THAT COMBAT SKILLS CAN ONLY BE LEARNED IN ACTUAL COMBAT.
"KURDISTAN WAS LIKE EARNING A MASTER'S DEGREE.

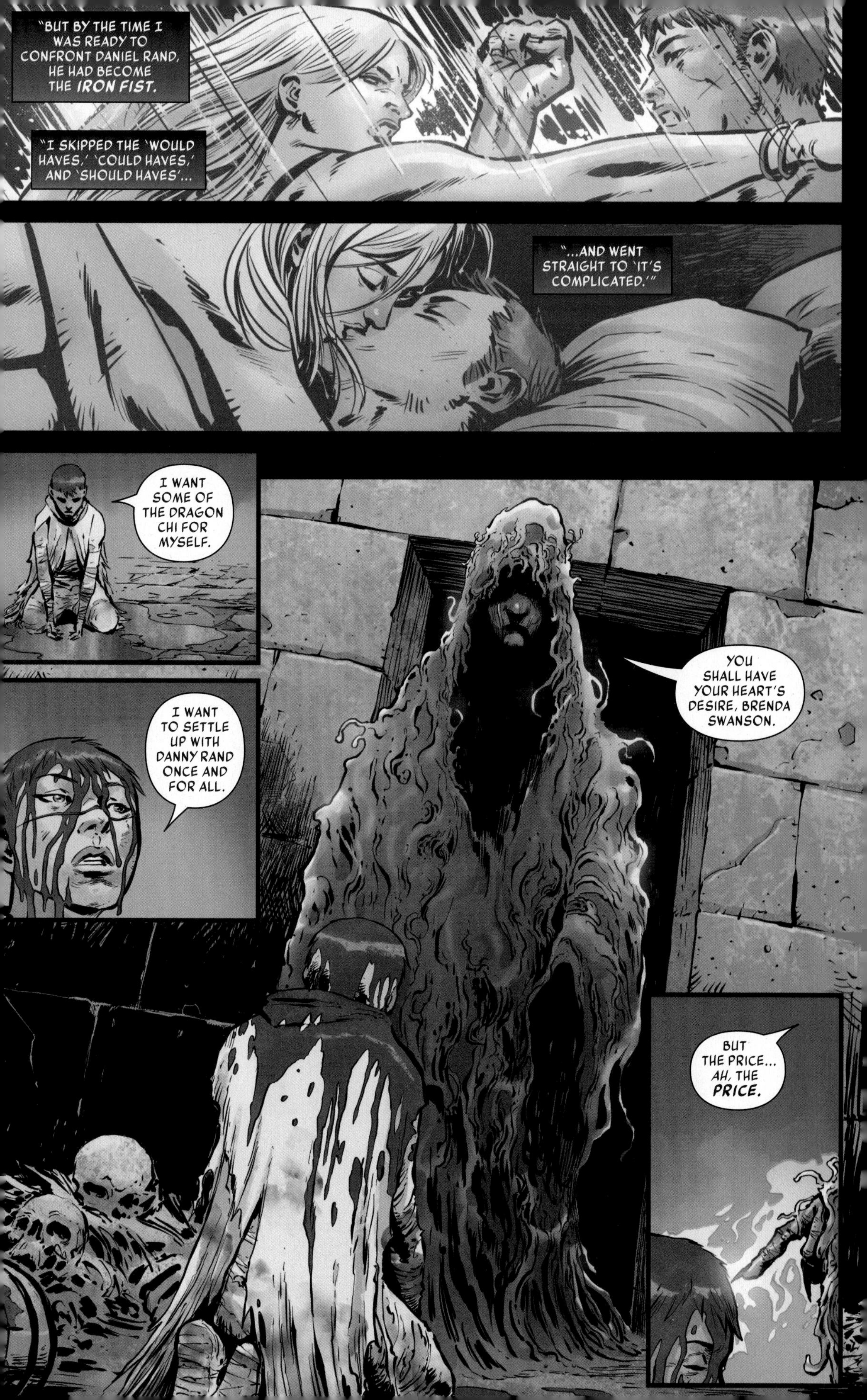
"BUT BY THE TIME I WAS READY TO CONFRONT DANIEL RAND, HE HAD BECOME THE IRON FIST.
"I SKIPPED THE 'WOULD HAVES,' 'COULD HAVES,' AND 'SHOULD HAVES'...
"...AND WENT STRAIGHT TO 'IT'S COMPLICATED.'"
I WANT SOME OF THE DRAGON CHI FOR MYSELF.
I WANT TO SETTLE UP WITH DANNY RAND ONCE AND FOR ALL.
YOU SHALL HAVE YOUR HEART'S DESIRE, BRENDA SWANSON.
BUT THE PRICE... AH, THE PRICE.

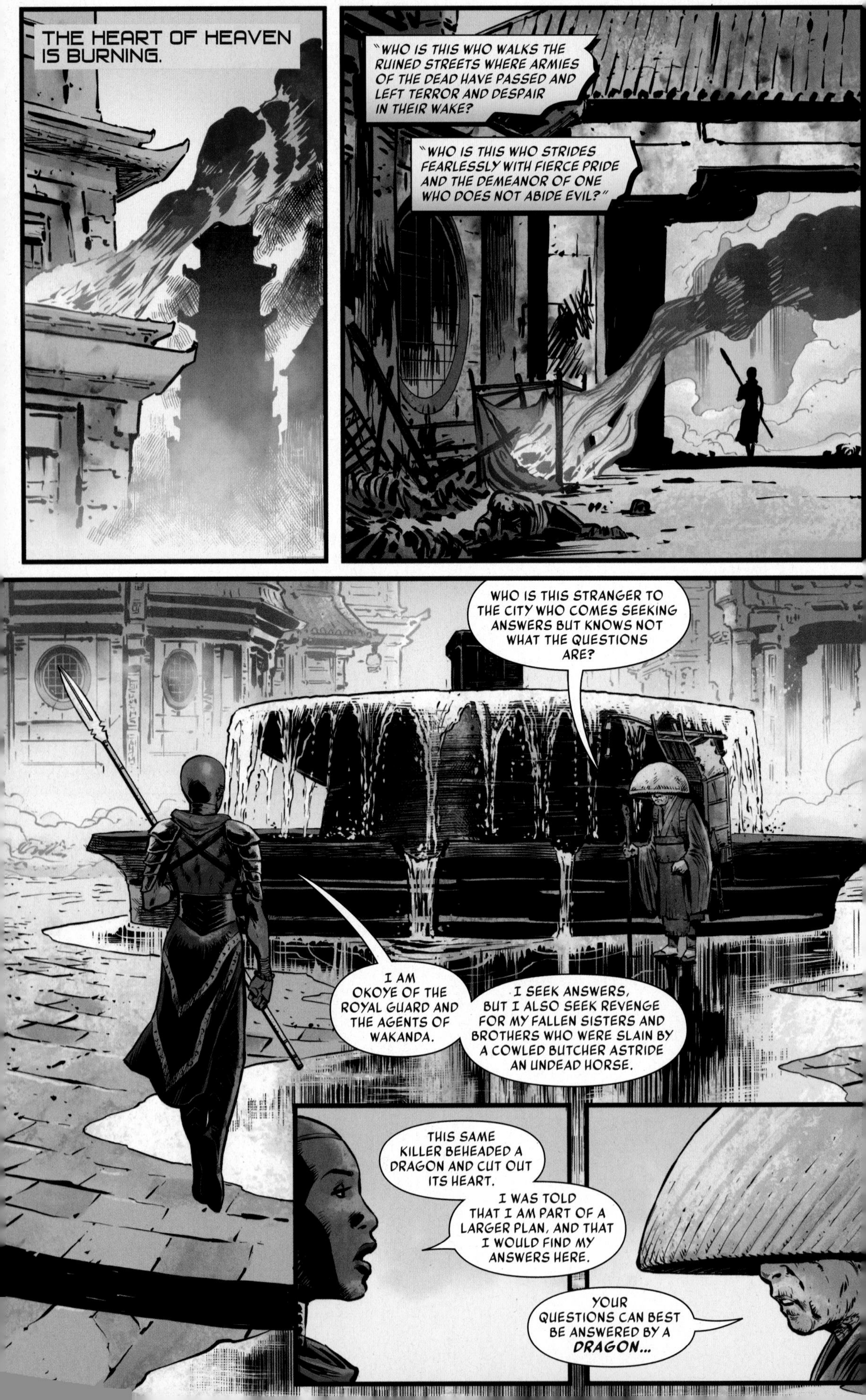
THE HEART OF HEAVEN IS BURNING.
"WHO IS THIS WHO WALKS THE RUINED STREETS WHERE ARMIES OF THE DEAD HAVE PASSED AND LEFT TERROR AND DESPAIR IN THEIR WAKE?
"WHO IS THIS WHO STRIDES FEARLESSLY WITH FIERCE PRIDE AND THE DEMEANOR OF ONE WHO DOES NOT ABIDE EVIL?"
WHO IS THIS STRANGER TO THE CITY WHO COMES SEEKING ANSWERS BUT KNOWS NOT WHAT THE QUESTIONS ARE?
I AM OKOYE OF THE ROYAL GUARD AND THE AGENTS OF WAKANDA.
I SEEK ANSWERS, BUT I ALSO SEEK REVENGE FOR MY FALLEN SISTERS AND BROTHERS WHO WERE SLAIN BY A COWLED BUTCHER ASTRIDE AN UNDEAD HORSE.
THIS SAME KILLER BEHEADED A DRAGON AND CUT OUT ITS HEART.
I WAS TOLD THAT I AM PART OF A LARGER PLAN, AND THAT I WOULD FIND MY ANSWERS HERE.
YOUR QUESTIONS CAN BEST BE ANSWERED BY A DRAGON...

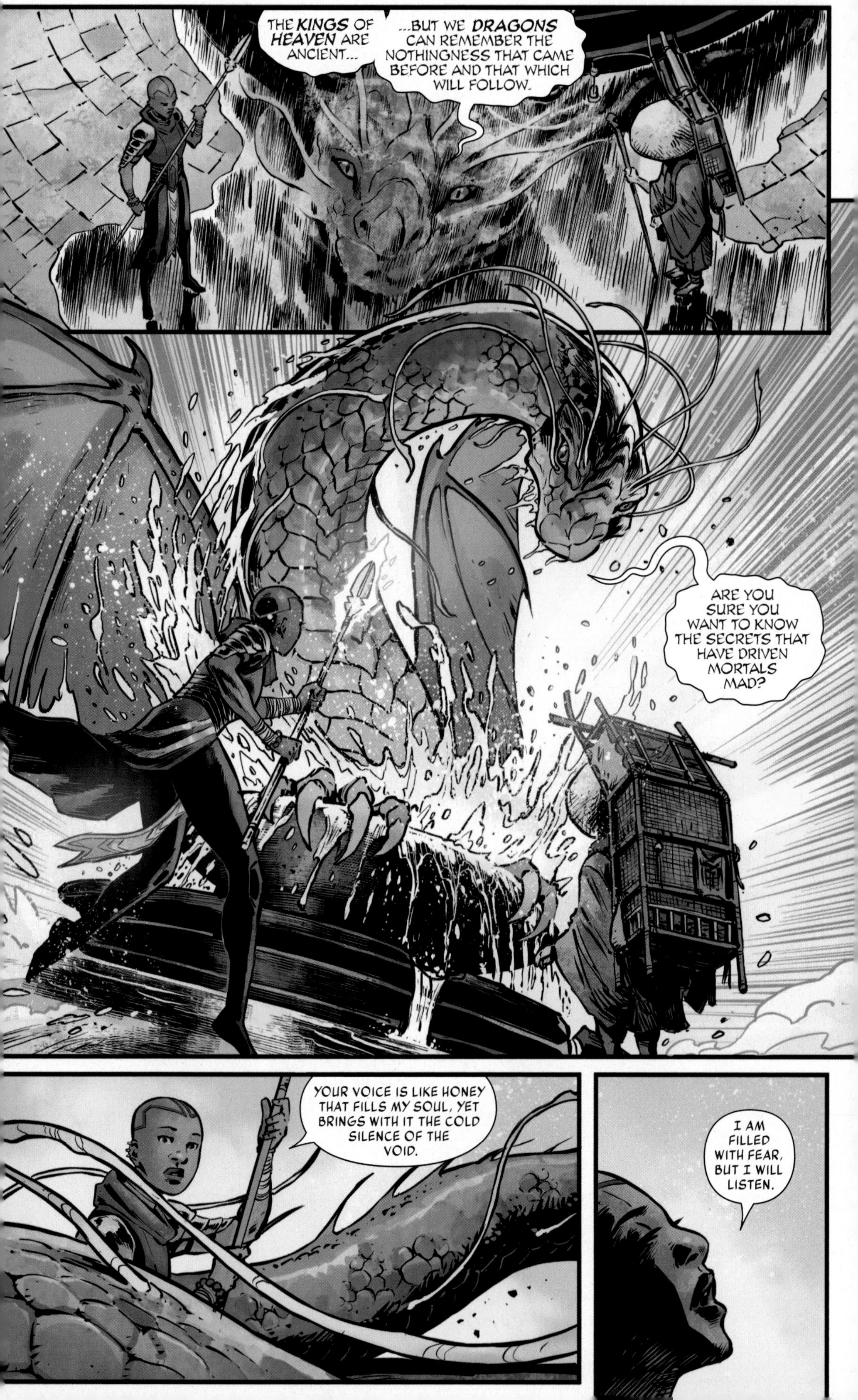

THE KINGS OF HEAVEN ARE ANCIENT...
...BUT WE DRAGONS CAN REMEMBER THE NOTHINGNESS THAT CAME BEFORE AND THAT WHICH WILL FOLLOW.
ARE YOU SURE YOU WANT TO KNOW THE SECRETS THAT HAVE DRIVEN MORTALS MAD?
YOUR VOICE IS LIKE HONEY THAT FILLS MY SOUL, YET BRINGS WITH IT THE COLD SILENCE OF THE VOID.
I AM FILLED WITH FEAR, BUT I WILL LISTEN.

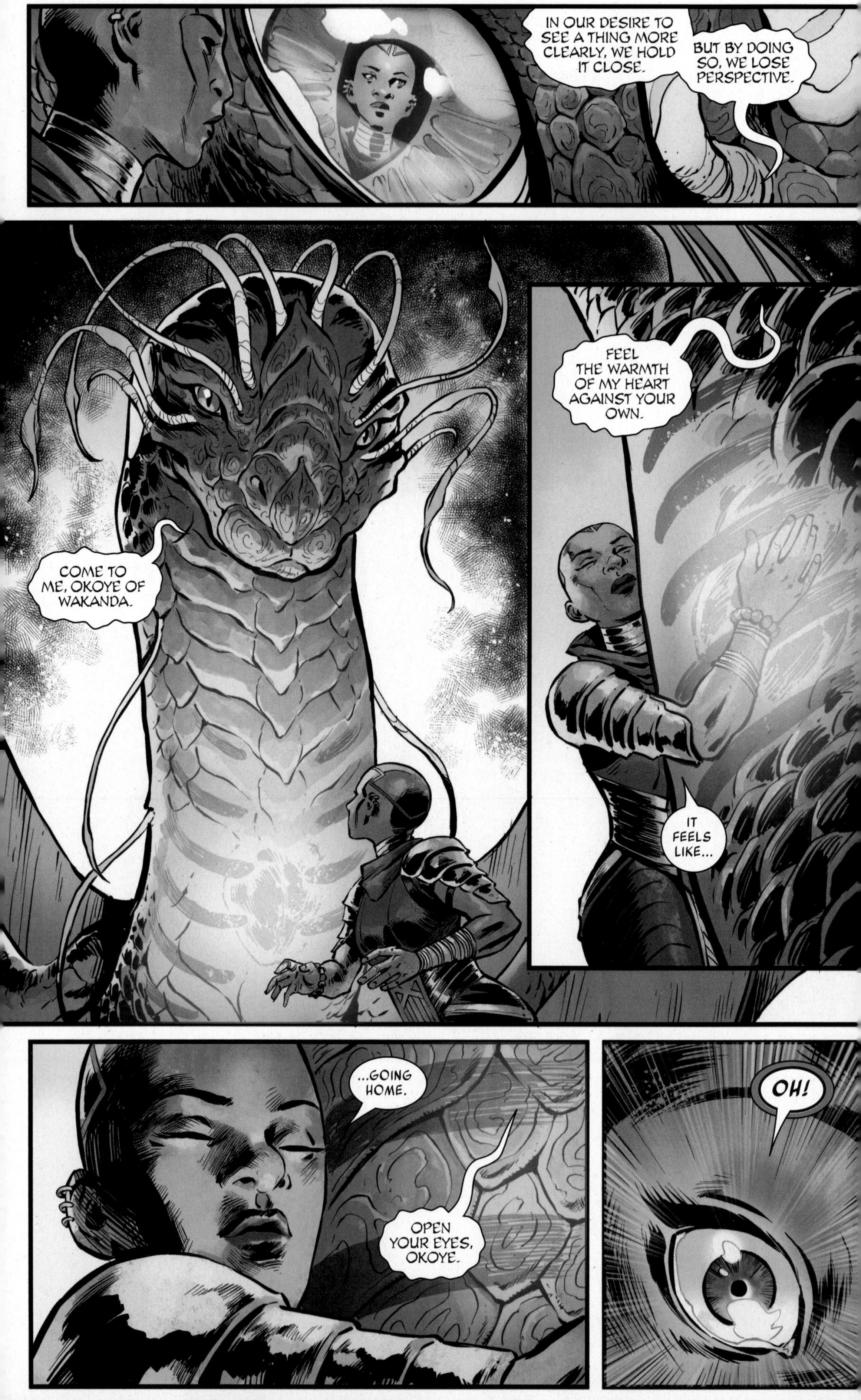
IN OUR DESIRE TO SEE A THING MORE CLEARLY, WE HOLD IT CLOSE.
BUT BY DOING SO, WE LOSE PERSPECTIVE.
COME TO ME, OKOYE OF WAKANDA.
FEEL THE WARMTH OF MY HEART AGAINST YOUR OWN.
IT FEELS LIKE...
...GOING HOME.
OPEN YOUR EYES, OKOYE.
OH!

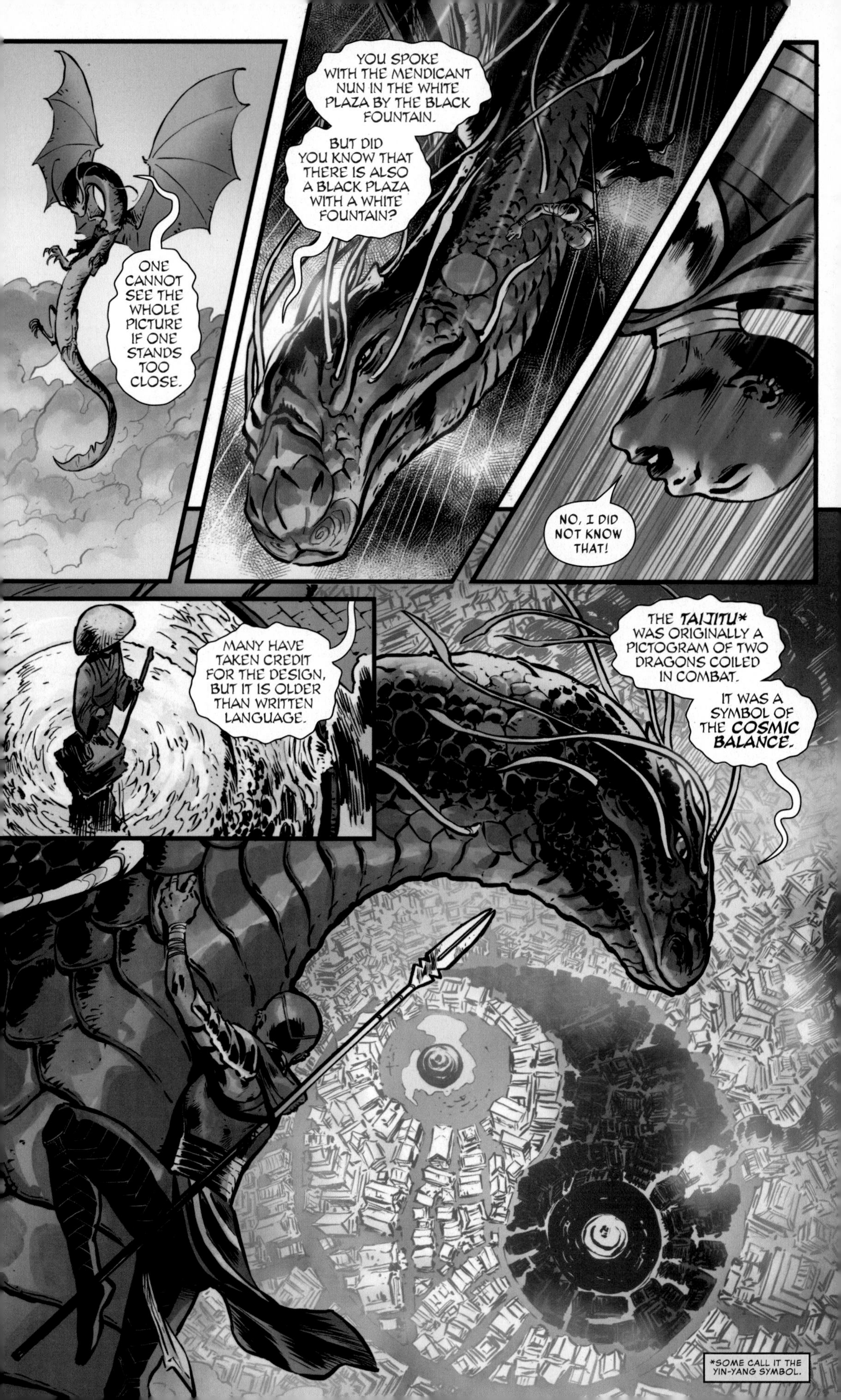
ONE CANNOT SEE THE WHOLE PICTURE IF ONE STANDS TOO CLOSE.
YOU SPOKE WITH THE MENDICANT NUN IN THE WHITE PLAZA BY THE BLACK FOUNTAIN.
BUT DID YOU KNOW THAT THERE IS ALSO A BLACK PLAZA WITH A WHITE FOUNTAIN?
NO, I DID NOT KNOW THAT!
MANY HAVE TAKEN CREDIT FOR THE DESIGN, BUT IT IS OLDER THAN WRITTEN LANGUAGE.
THE ***TAIJITU**** WAS ORIGINALLY A PICTOGRAM OF TWO DRAGONS COILED IN COMBAT.
IT WAS A SYMBOL OF THE **COSMIC BALANCE**.
*SOME CALL IT THE YIN-YANG SYMBOL.

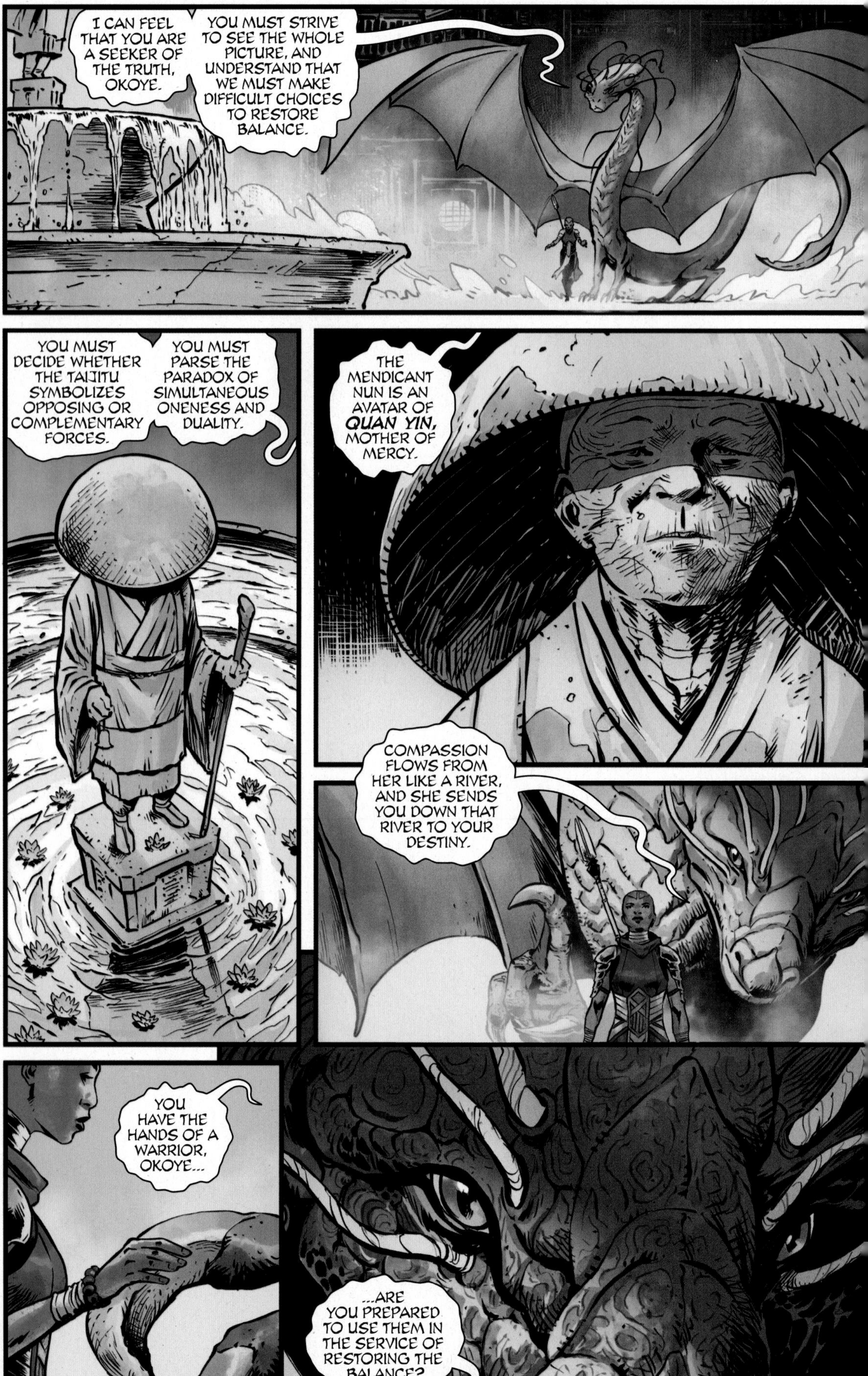
I CAN FEEL THAT YOU ARE A SEEKER OF THE TRUTH, OKOYE.
YOU MUST STRIVE TO SEE THE WHOLE PICTURE, AND UNDERSTAND THAT WE MUST MAKE DIFFICULT CHOICES TO RESTORE BALANCE.
YOU MUST DECIDE WHETHER THE TAIJITU SYMBOLIZES OPPOSING OR COMPLEMENTARY FORCES.
YOU MUST PARSE THE PARADOX OF SIMULTANEOUS ONENESS AND DUALITY.
THE MENDICANT NUN IS AN AVATAR OF QUAN YIN, MOTHER OF MERCY.
COMPASSION FLOWS FROM HER LIKE A RIVER, AND SHE SENDS YOU DOWN THAT RIVER TO YOUR DESTINY.
YOU HAVE THE HANDS OF A WARRIOR, OKOYE...
...ARE YOU PREPARED TO USE THEM IN THE SERVICE OF RESTORING THE BALANCE?

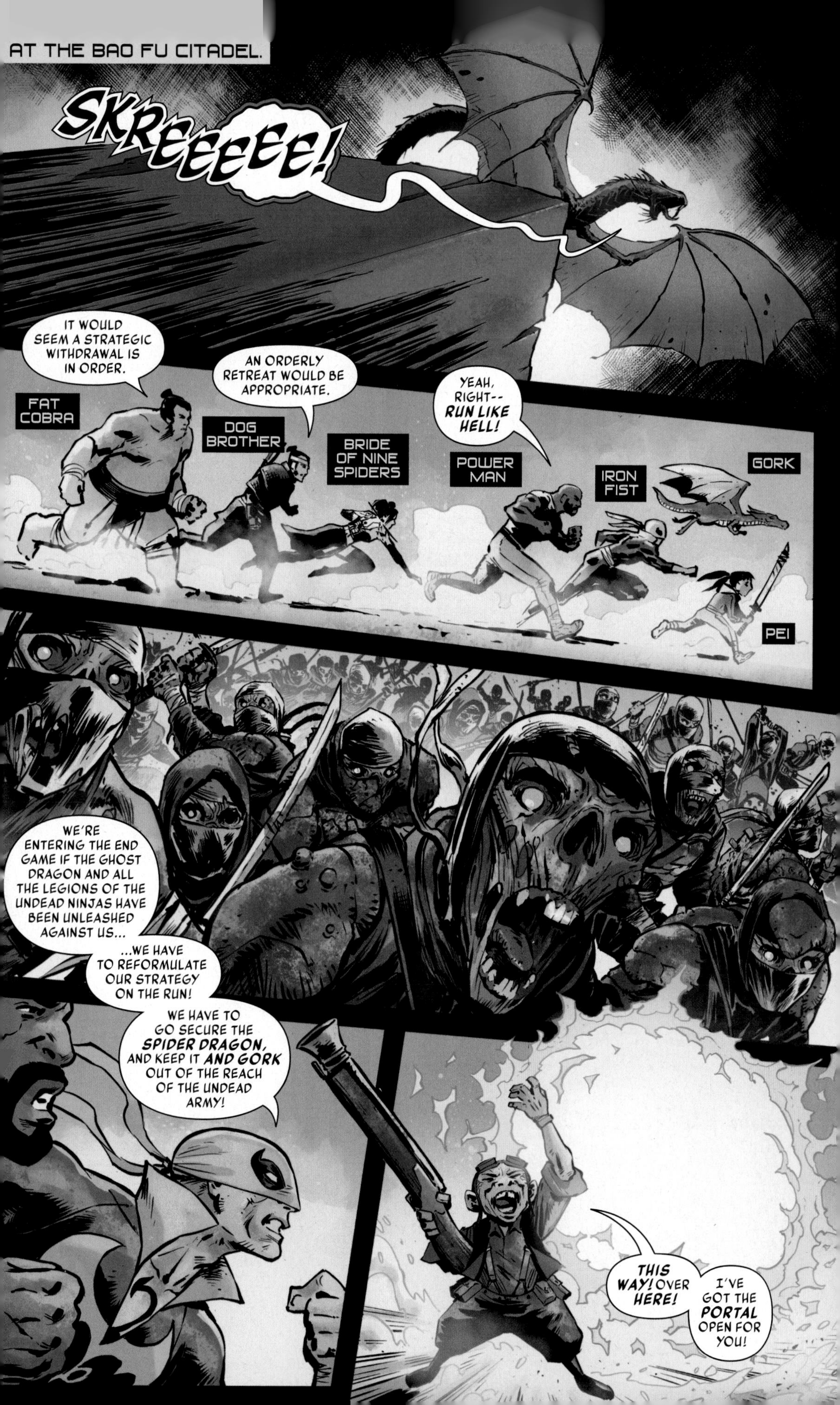

AT THE BAO FU CITADEL.
SKREEEEEE!
IT WOULD SEEM A STRATEGIC WITHDRAWAL IS IN ORDER.
FAT COBRA
AN ORDERLY RETREAT WOULD BE APPROPRIATE.
DOG BROTHER
BRIDE OF NINE SPIDERS
YEAH, RIGHT-- RUN LIKE HELL!
POWER MAN
IRON FIST
GORK
PEI
WE'RE ENTERING THE END GAME IF THE GHOST DRAGON AND ALL THE LEGIONS OF THE UNDEAD NINJAS HAVE BEEN UNLEASHED AGAINST US...
...WE HAVE TO REFORMULATE OUR STRATEGY ON THE RUN!
WE HAVE TO GO SECURE THE SPIDER DRAGON, AND KEEP IT AND GORK OUT OF THE REACH OF THE UNDEAD ARMY!
THIS WAY! OVER HERE!
I'VE GOT THE PORTAL OPEN FOR YOU!

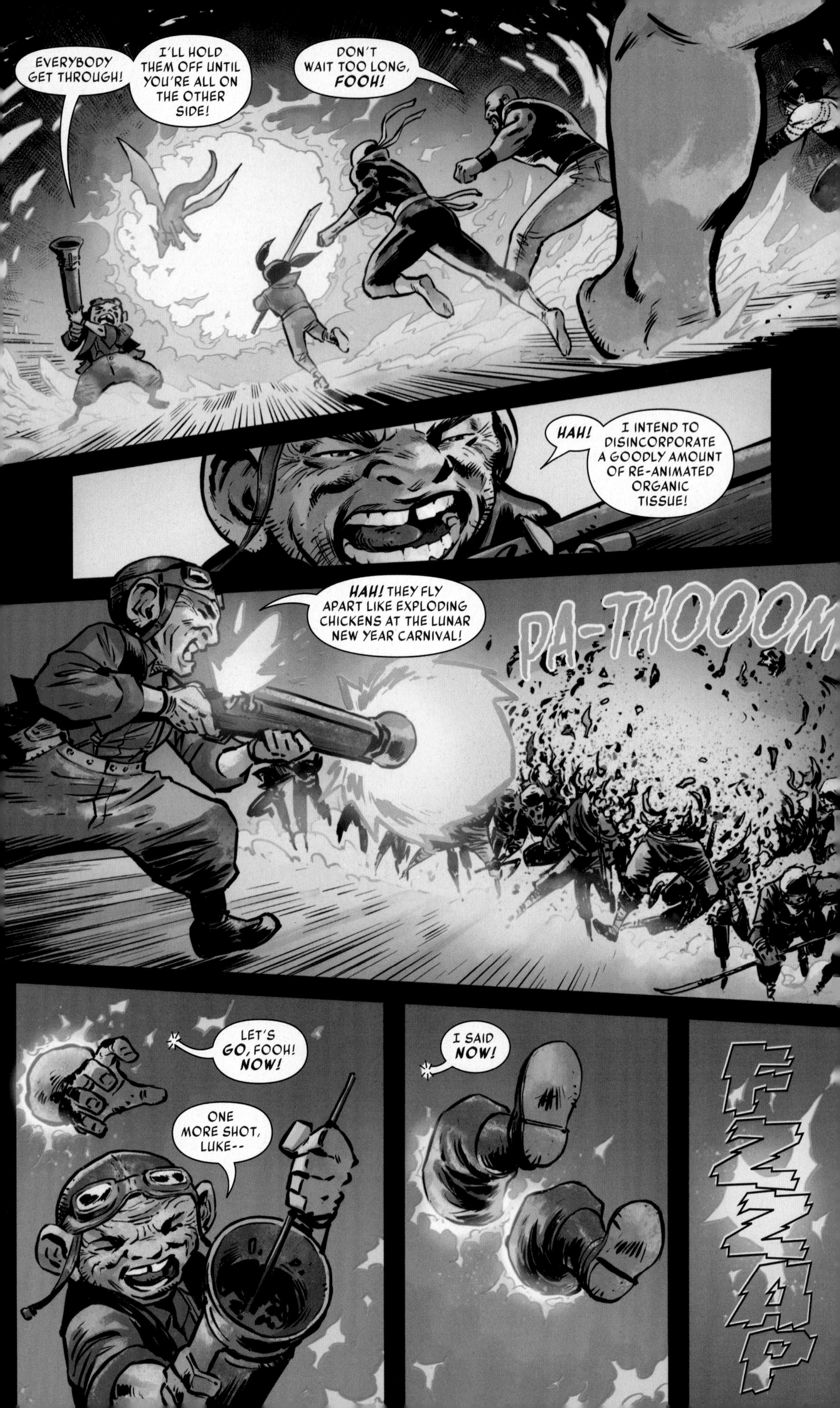
EVERYBODY GET THROUGH!
I'LL HOLD THEM OFF UNTIL YOU'RE ALL ON THE OTHER SIDE!
DON'T WAIT TOO LONG, FOOH!
HAH!
I INTEND TO DISINCORPORATE A GOODLY AMOUNT OF RE-ANIMATED ORGANIC TISSUE!
HAH! THEY FLY APART LIKE EXPLODING CHICKENS AT THE LUNAR NEW YEAR CARNIVAL!
PA-THOOOM
LET'S GO, FOOH! NOW!
ONE MORE SHOT, LUKE--
I SAID NOW!
FZZZAP

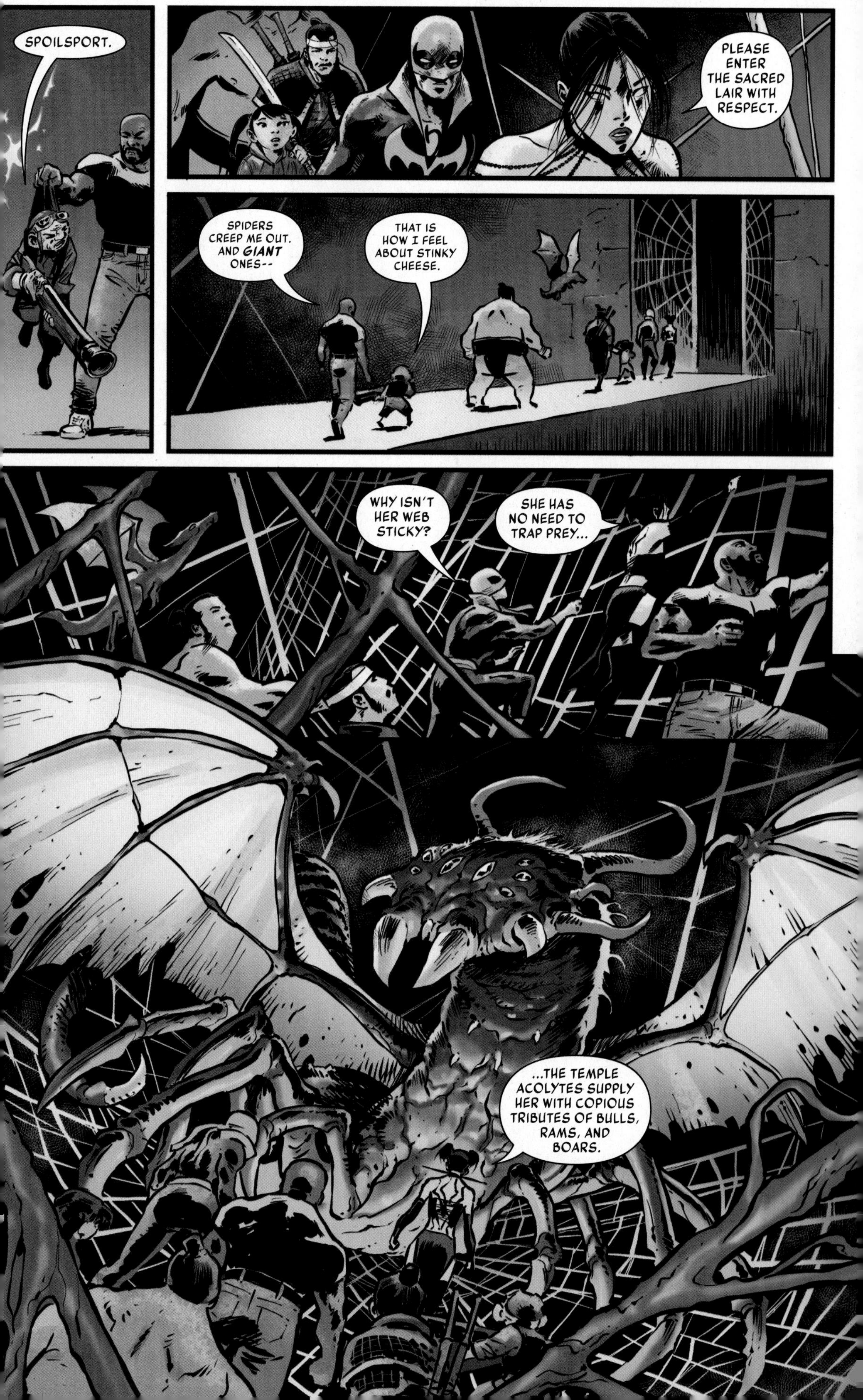
SPOILSPORT.
PLEASE ENTER THE SACRED LAIR WITH RESPECT.
SPIDERS CREEP ME OUT. AND GIANT ONES--
THAT IS HOW I FEEL ABOUT STINKY CHEESE.
WHY ISN'T HER WEB STICKY?
SHE HAS NO NEED TO TRAP PREY...
...THE TEMPLE ACOLYTES SUPPLY HER WITH COPIOUS TRIBUTES OF BULLS, RAMS, AND BOARS.

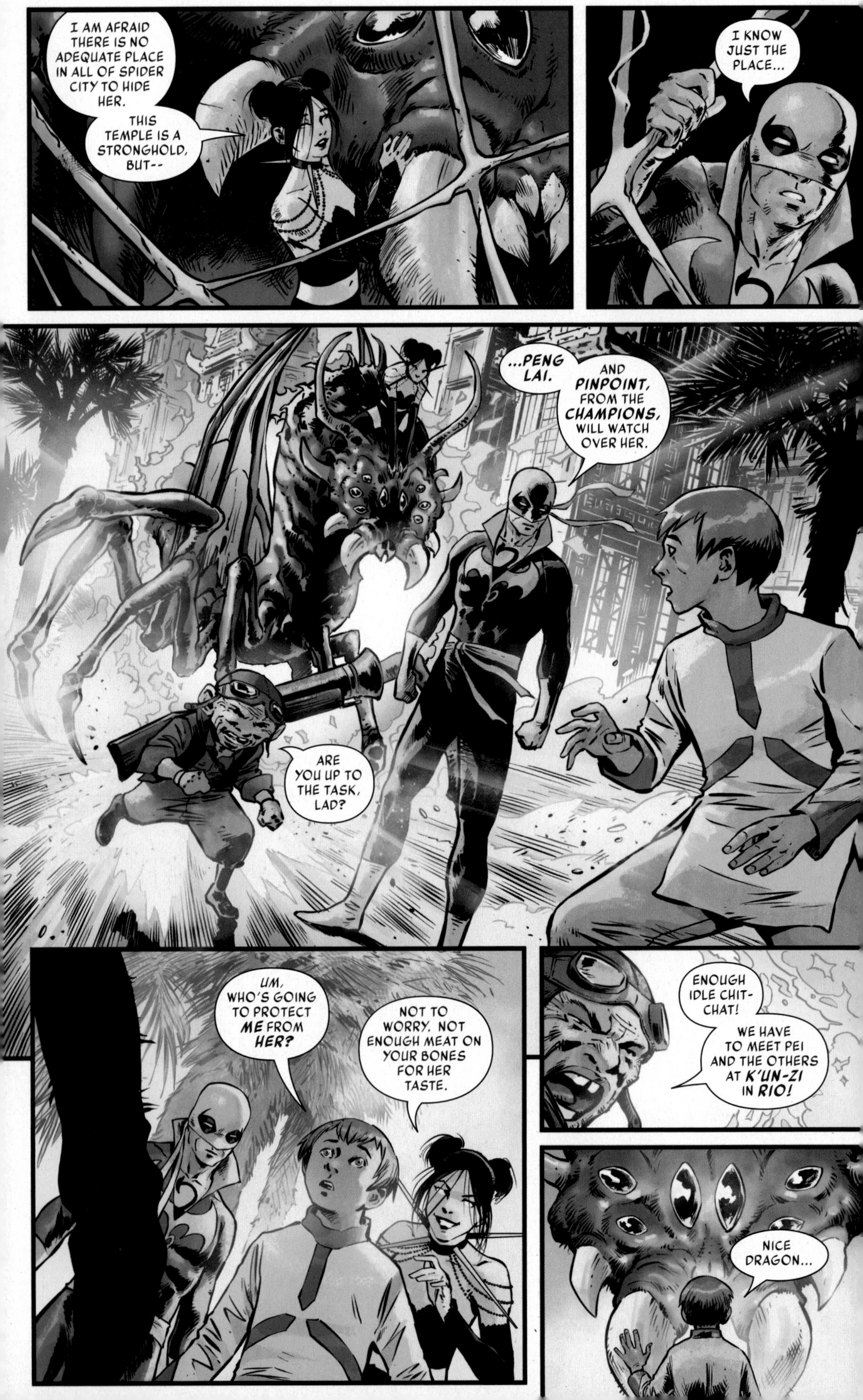
I AM AFRAID THERE IS NO ADEQUATE PLACE IN ALL OF SPIDER CITY TO HIDE HER.
THIS TEMPLE IS A STRONGHOLD, BUT--
I KNOW JUST THE PLACE...
...PENG LAI.
AND PINPOINT, FROM THE CHAMPIONS, WILL WATCH OVER HER.
ARE YOU UP TO THE TASK, LAD?
UM, WHO'S GOING TO PROTECT ME FROM HER?
NOT TO WORRY. NOT ENOUGH MEAT ON YOUR BONES FOR HER TASTE.
ENOUGH IDLE CHIT-CHAT!
WE HAVE TO MEET PEI AND THE OTHERS AT K'UN-ZI IN RIO!
NICE DRAGON...

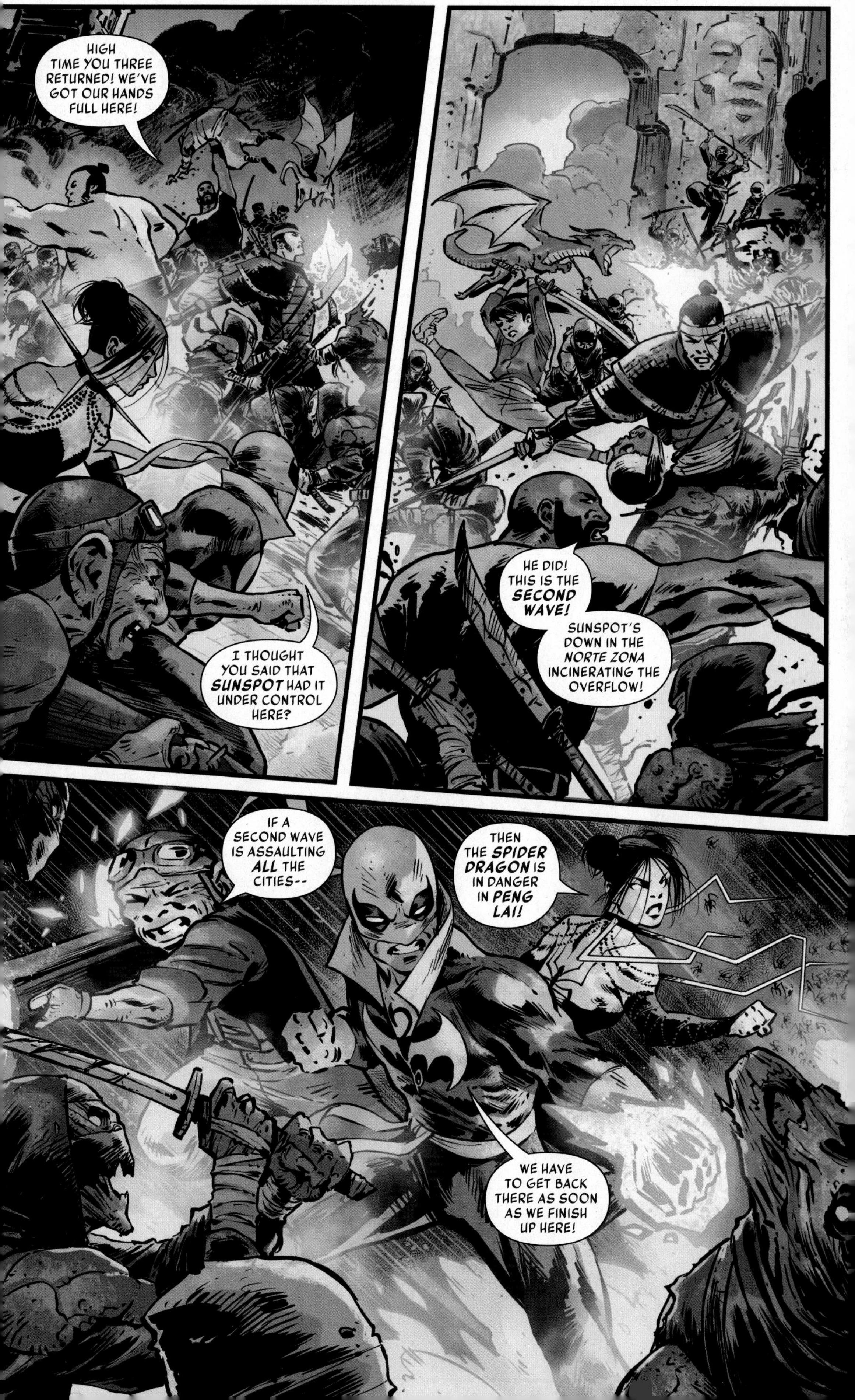
HIGH TIME YOU THREE RETURNED! WE'VE GOT OUR HANDS FULL HERE!
I THOUGHT YOU SAID THAT SUNSPOT HAD IT UNDER CONTROL HERE?
HE DID! THIS IS THE SECOND WAVE!
SUNSPOT'S DOWN IN THE NORTE ZONA INCINERATING THE OVERFLOW!
IF A SECOND WAVE IS ASSAULTING ALL THE CITIES--
THEN THE SPIDER DRAGON IS IN DANGER IN PENG LAI!
WE HAVE TO GET BACK THERE AS SOON AS WE FINISH UP HERE!

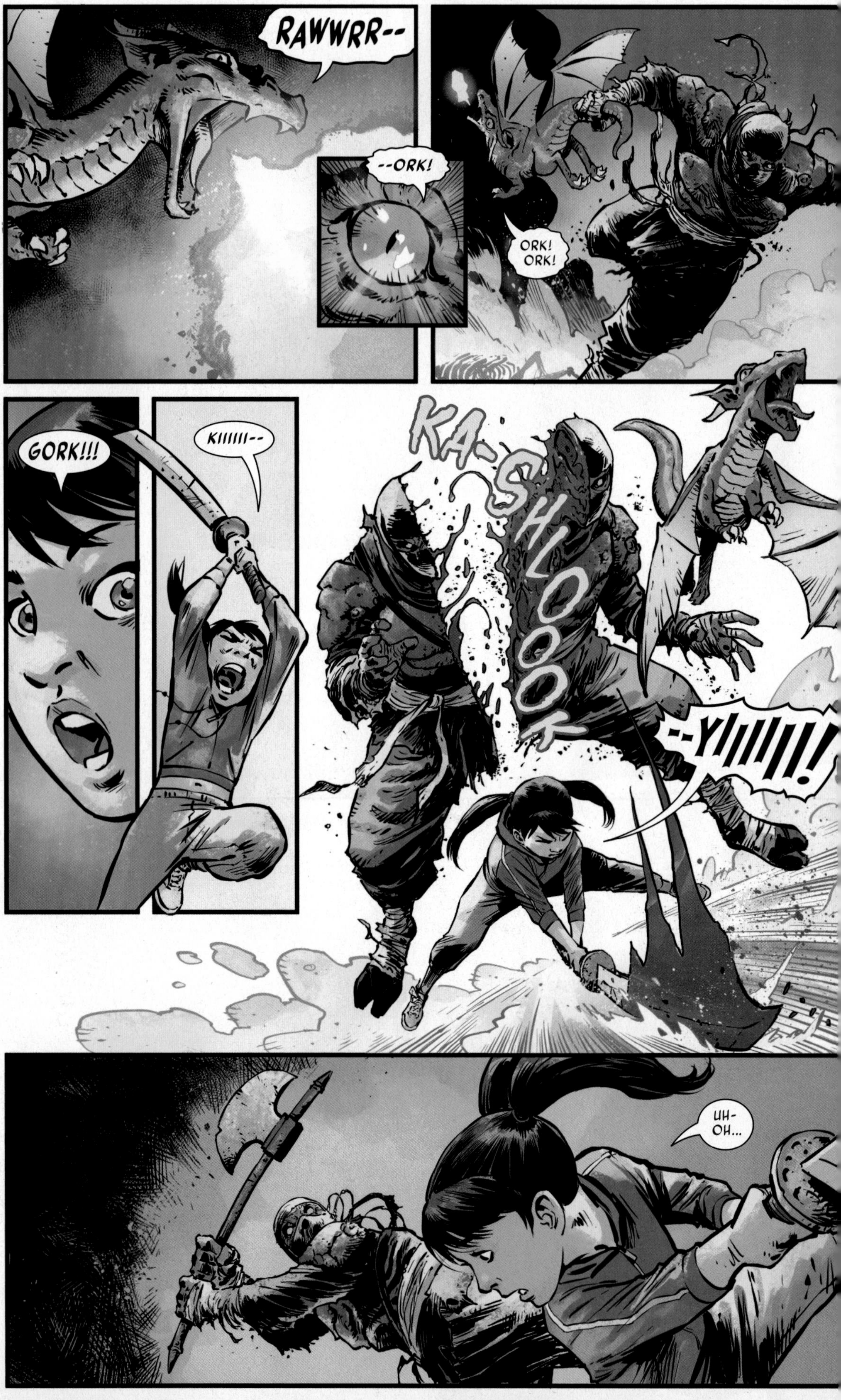
RAWWRR--
--ORK!
ORK! ORK!
GORK!!!
KIIIIII--
KA-SHLOOOOK
--YIIIIIII!
UH-OH...

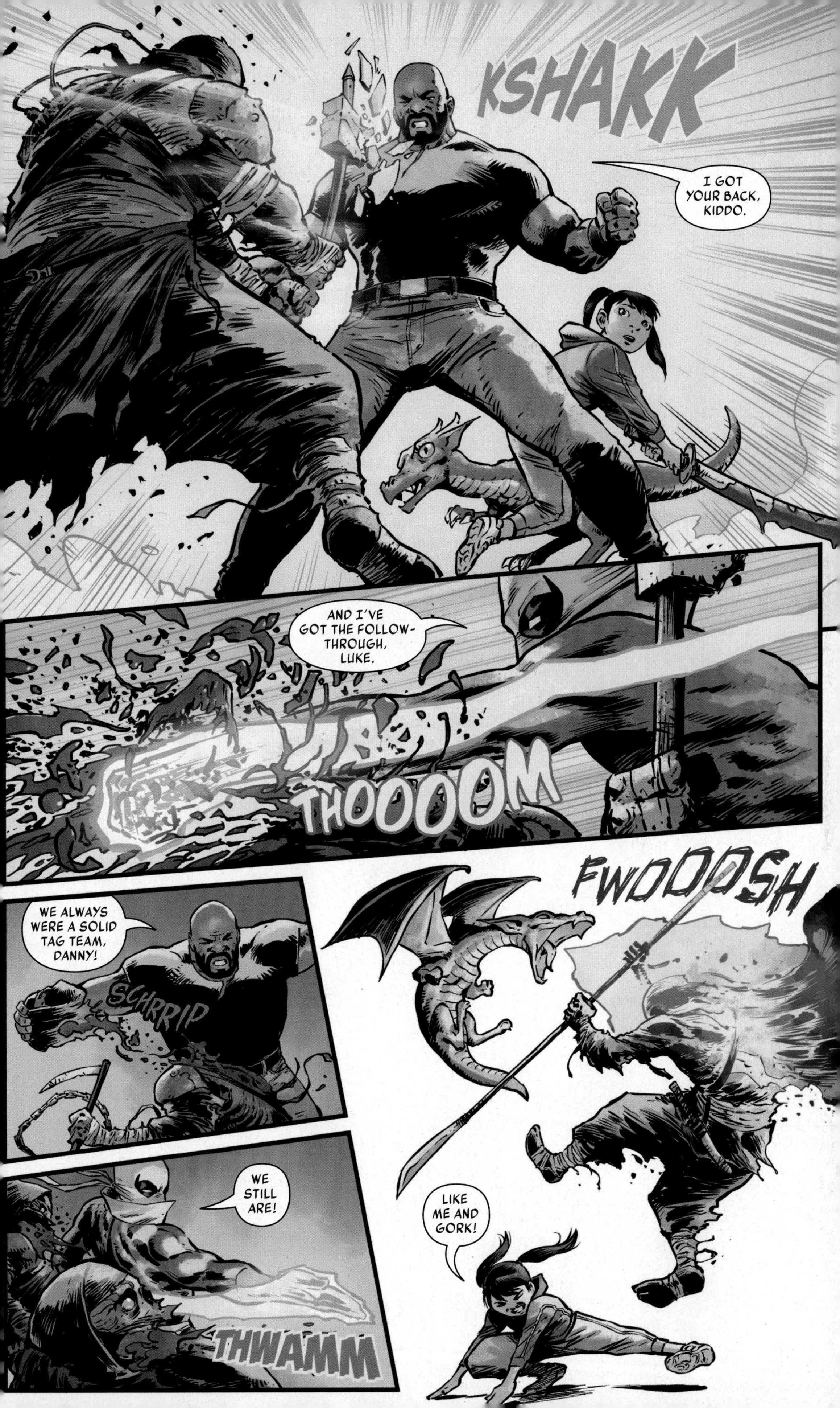
KSHAKK
I GOT YOUR BACK, KIDDO.
AND I'VE GOT THE FOLLOW-THROUGH, LUKE.
THOOOOM
FWOOOSH
WE ALWAYS WERE A SOLID TAG TEAM, DANNY!
SCHRRIP
WE STILL ARE!
THWAMM
LIKE ME AND GORK!

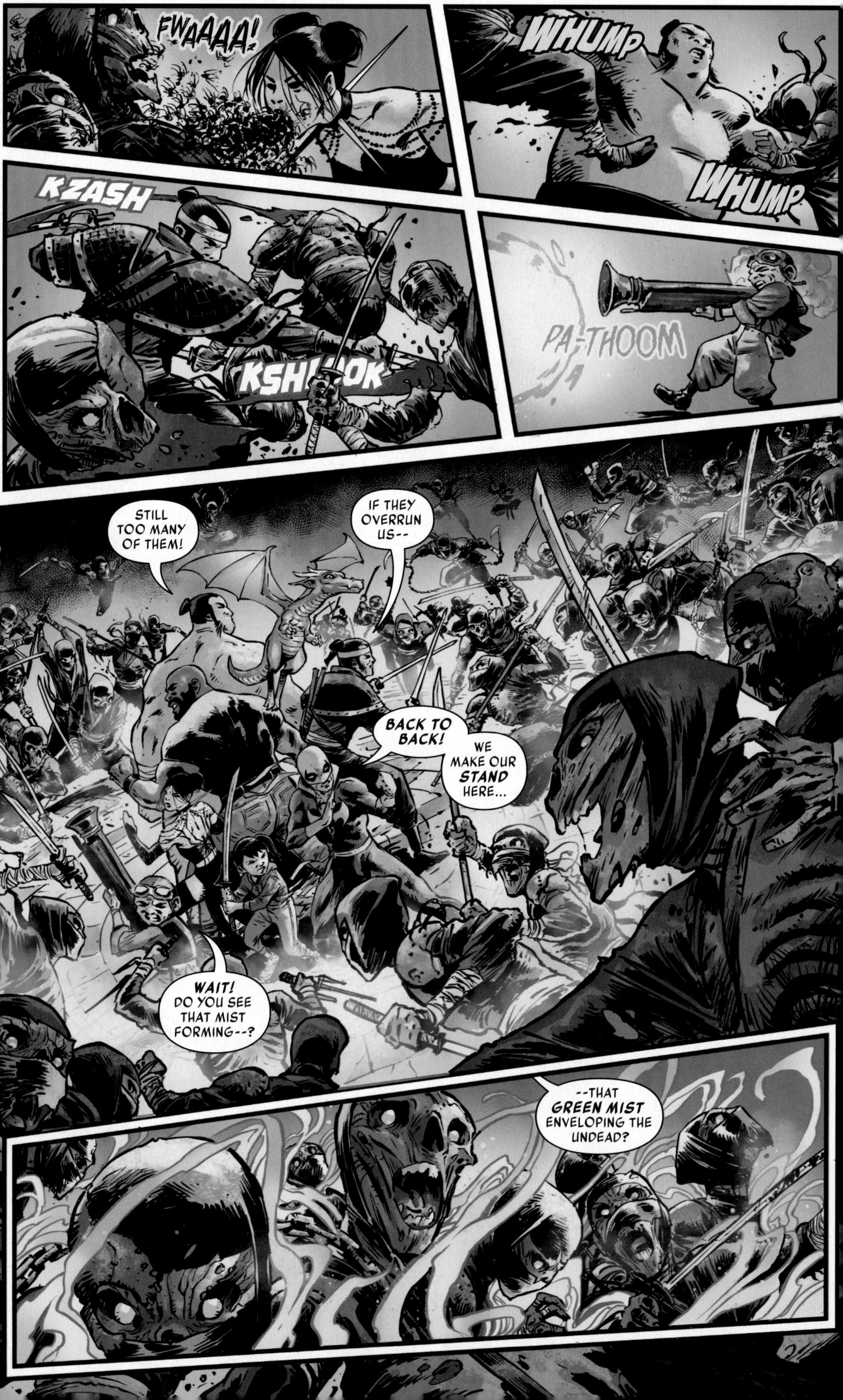
FWAAAA!
WHUMP
WHUMP
KZASH
KSHUNK
PA-THOOM
STILL TOO MANY OF THEM!
IF THEY OVERRUN US--
BACK TO BACK!
WE MAKE OUR STAND HERE...
WAIT! DO YOU SEE THAT MIST FORMING--?
--THAT GREEN MIST ENVELOPING THE UNDEAD?

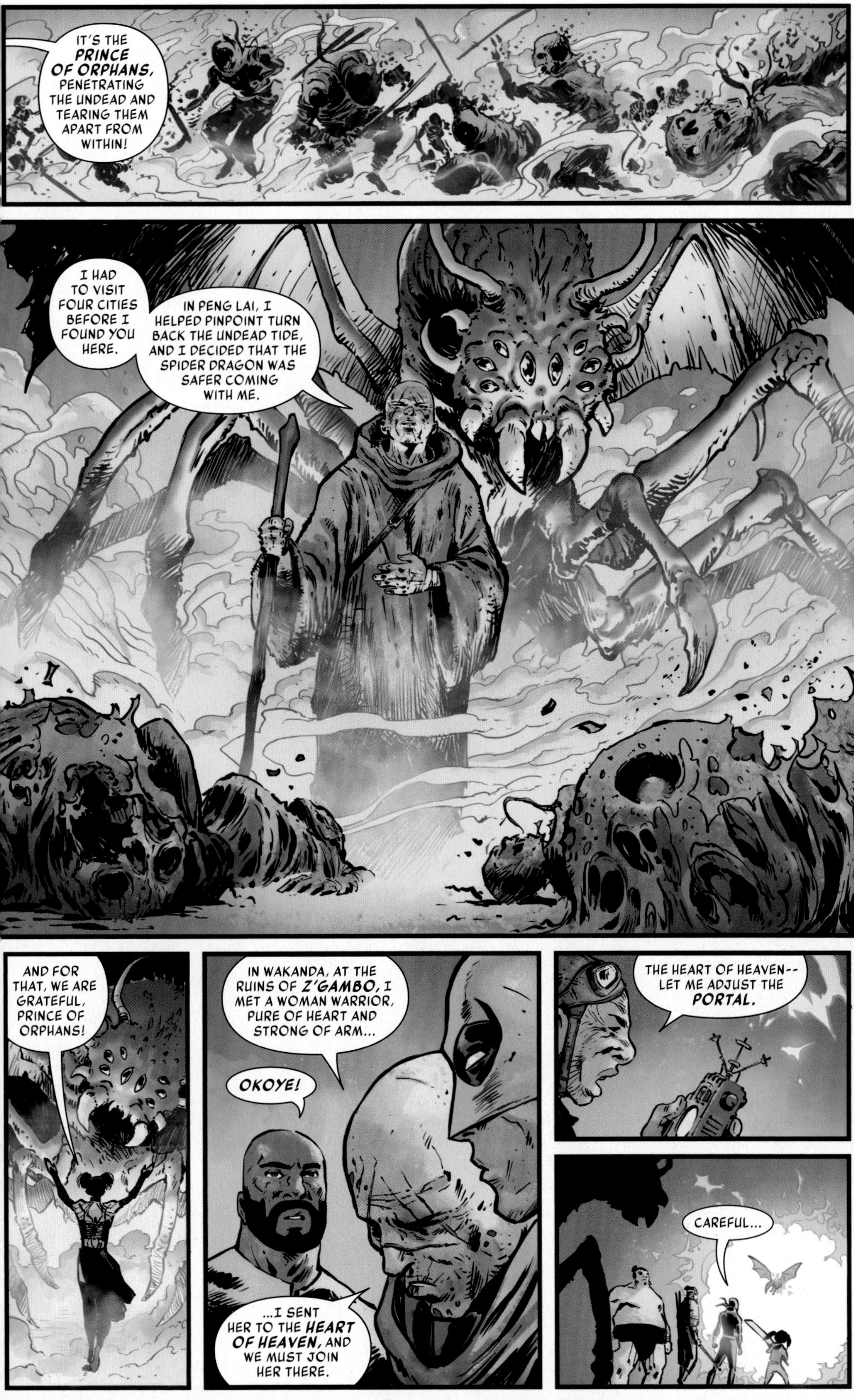
IT'S THE PRINCE OF ORPHANS, PENETRATING THE UNDEAD AND TEARING THEM APART FROM WITHIN!
I HAD TO VISIT FOUR CITIES BEFORE I FOUND YOU HERE.
IN PENG LAI, I HELPED PINPOINT TURN BACK THE UNDEAD TIDE, AND I DECIDED THAT THE SPIDER DRAGON WAS SAFER COMING WITH ME.
AND FOR THAT, WE ARE GRATEFUL, PRINCE OF ORPHANS!
IN WAKANDA, AT THE RUINS OF Z'GAMBO, I MET A WOMAN WARRIOR, PURE OF HEART AND STRONG OF ARM...
OKOYE!
...I SENT HER TO THE HEART OF HEAVEN, AND WE MUST JOIN HER THERE.
THE HEART OF HEAVEN-- LET ME ADJUST THE PORTAL.
CAREFUL...

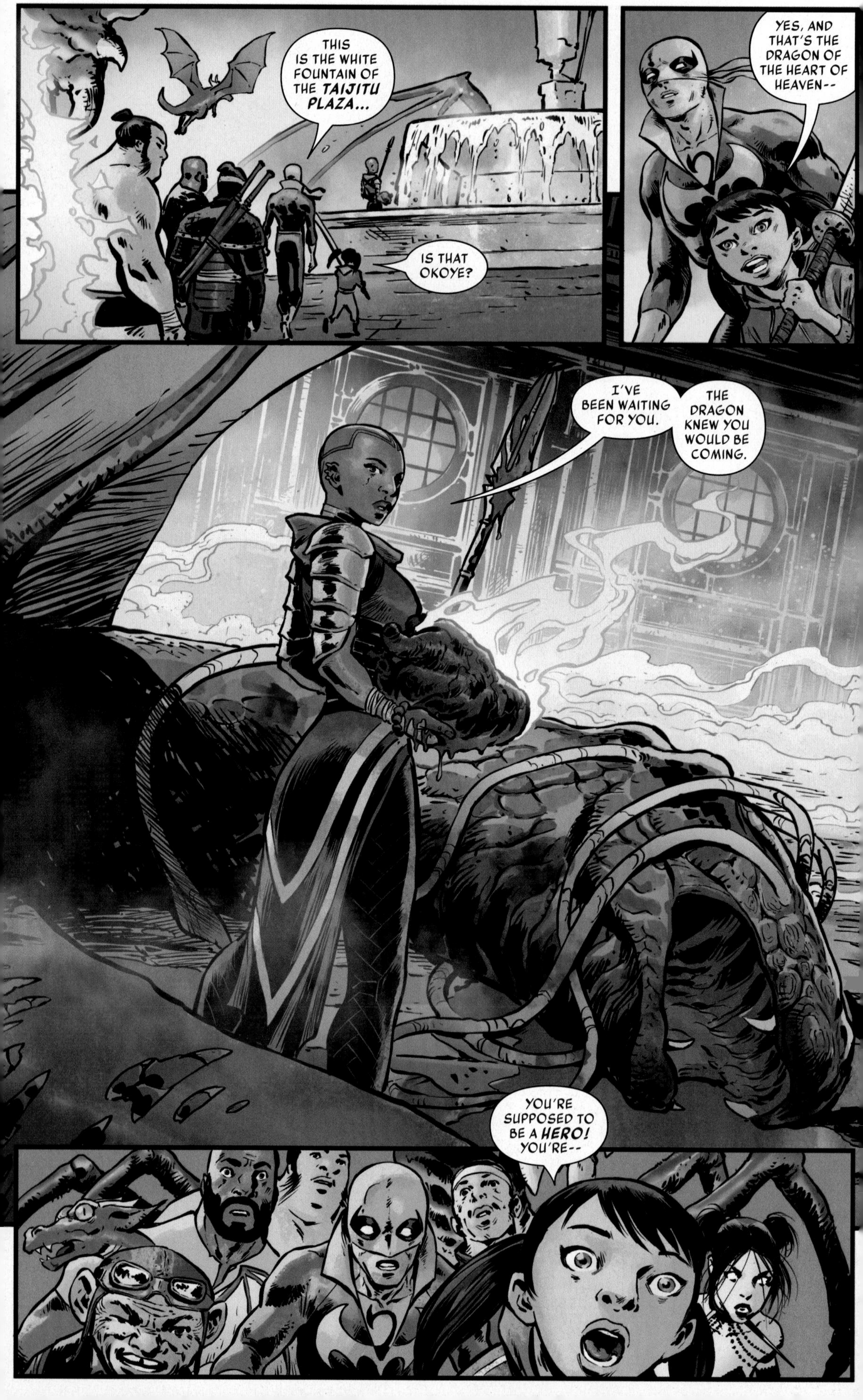
THIS IS THE WHITE FOUNTAIN OF THE *TAIJITU PLAZA*...
IS THAT OKOYE?
YES, AND THAT'S THE DRAGON OF THE HEART OF HEAVEN--
I'VE BEEN WAITING FOR YOU.
THE DRAGON KNEW YOU WOULD BE COMING.
YOU'RE SUPPOSED TO BE A *HERO!* YOU'RE--

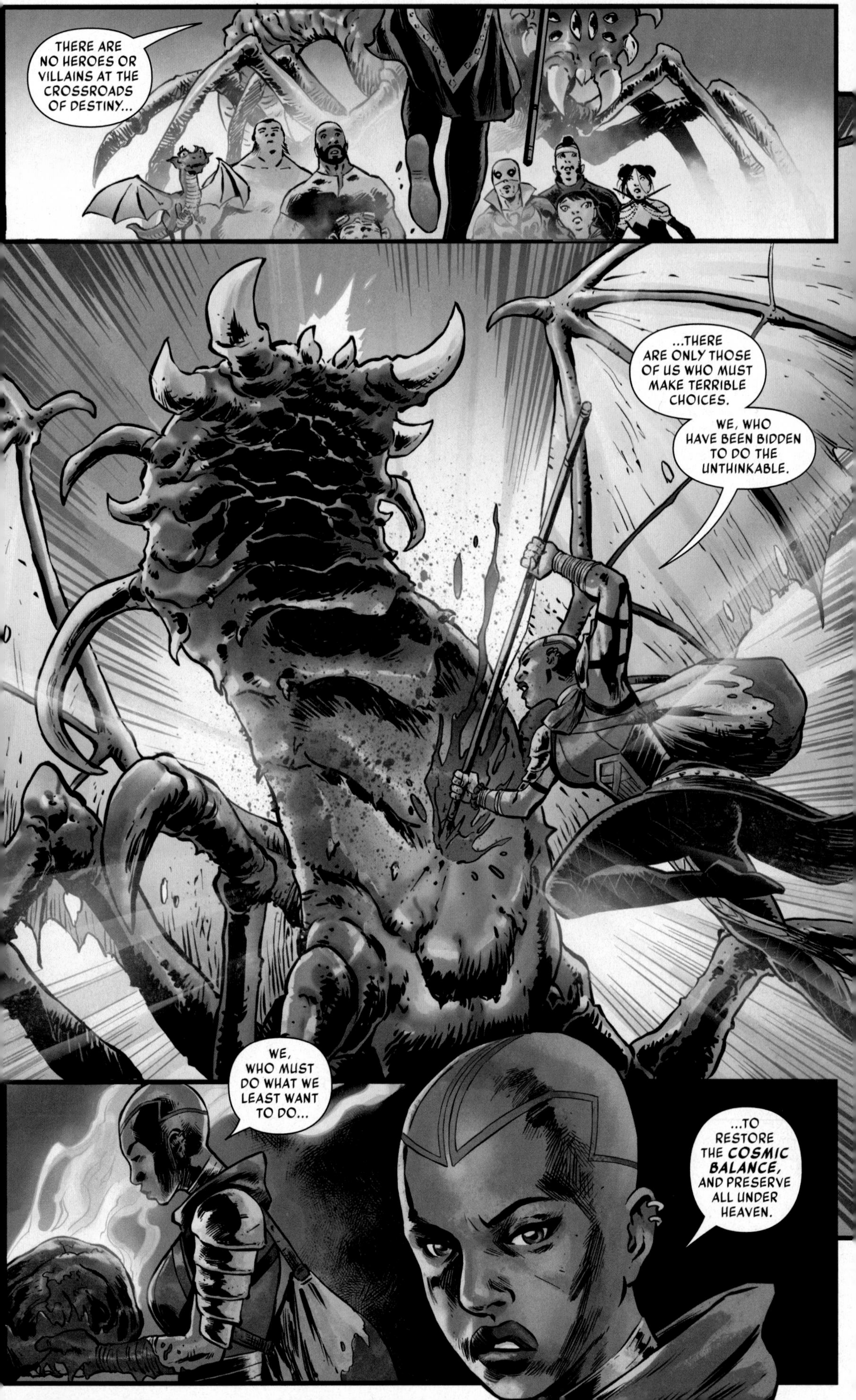
THERE ARE NO HEROES OR VILLAINS AT THE CROSSROADS OF DESTINY...
...THERE ARE ONLY THOSE OF US WHO MUST MAKE TERRIBLE CHOICES.
WE, WHO HAVE BEEN BIDDEN TO DO THE UNTHINKABLE.
WE, WHO MUST DO WHAT WE LEAST WANT TO DO...
...TO RESTORE THE COSMIC BALANCE, AND PRESERVE ALL UNDER HEAVEN.

# FIVE

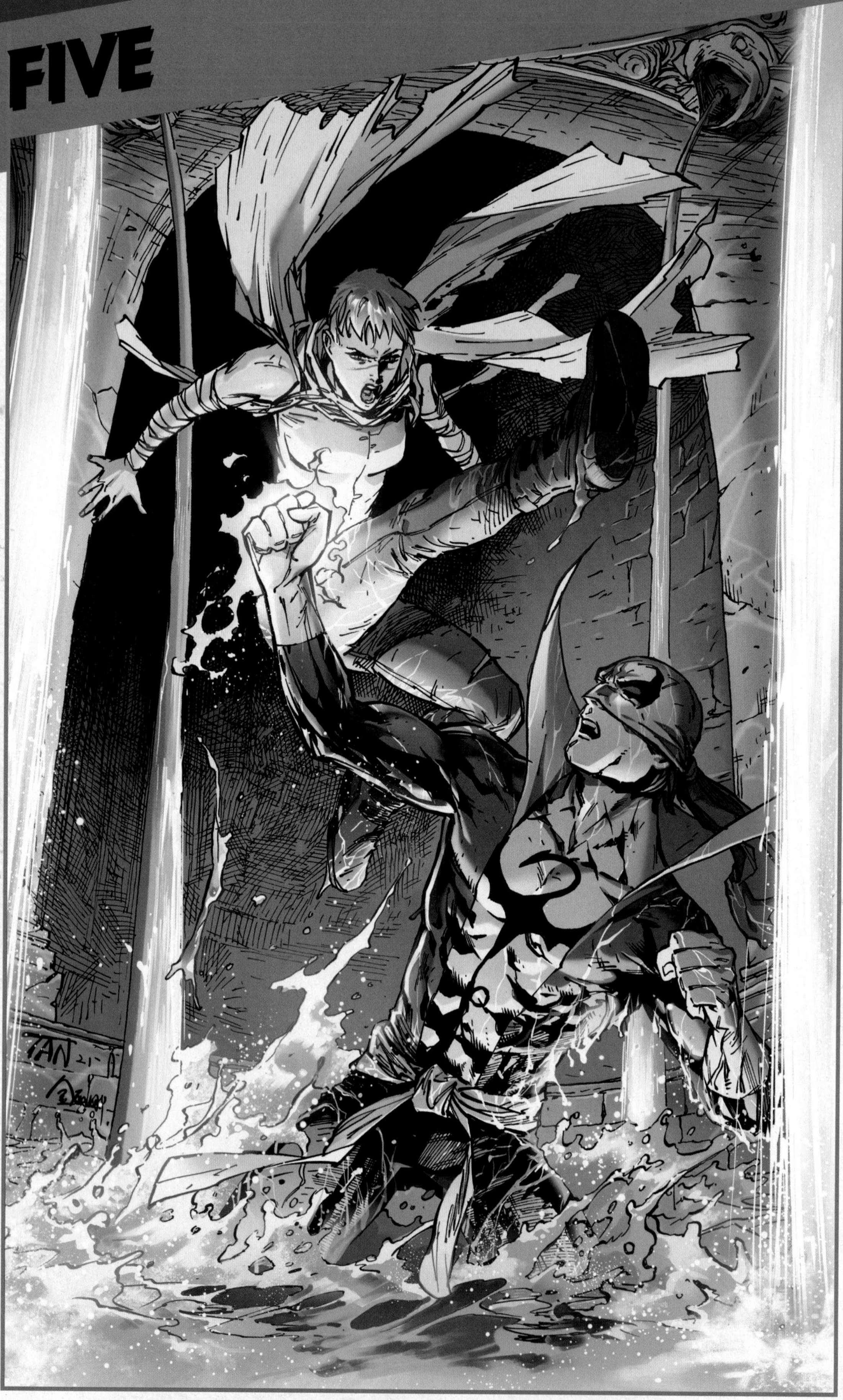

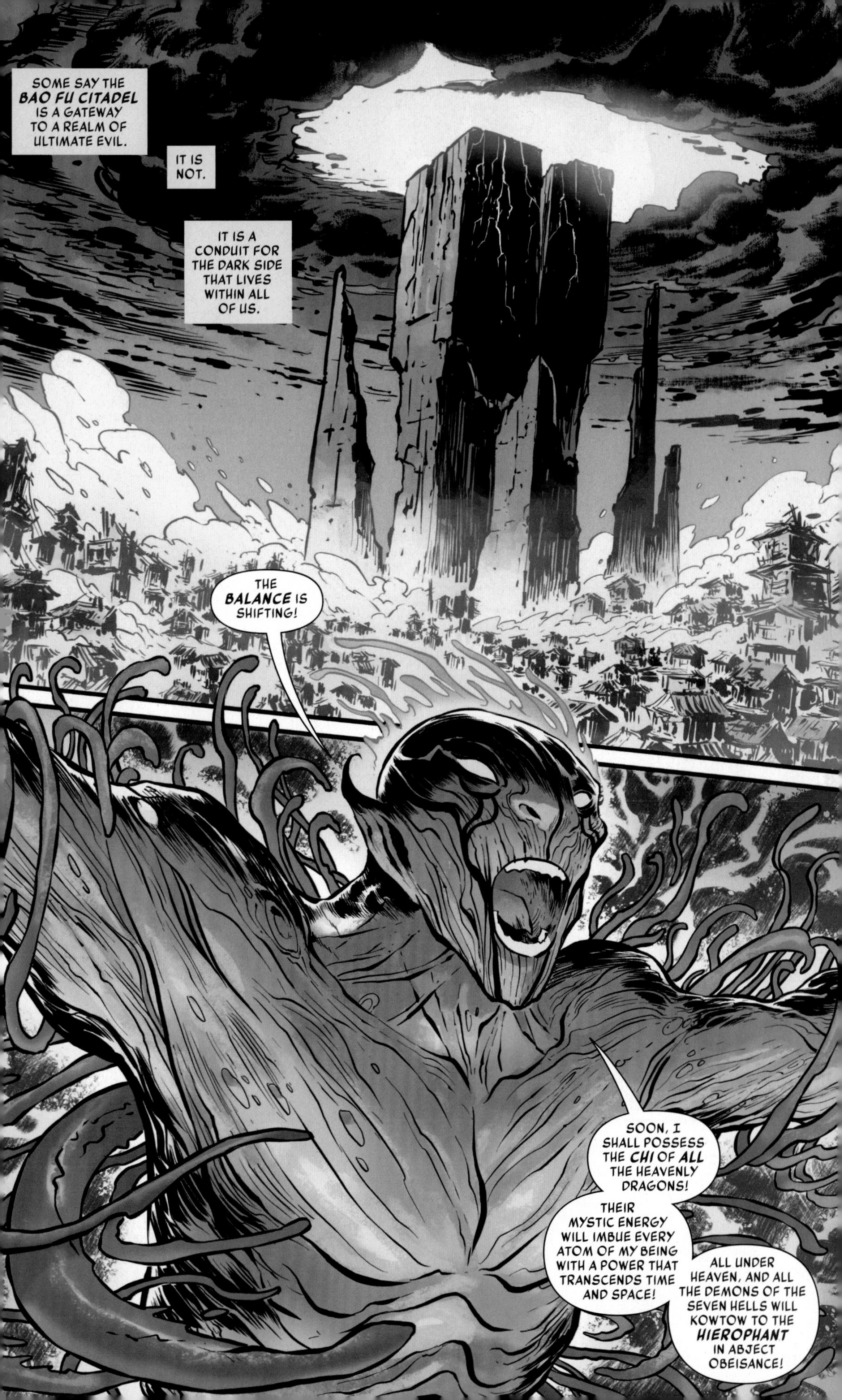

SOME SAY THE BAO FU CITADEL IS A GATEWAY TO A REALM OF ULTIMATE EVIL.
IT IS NOT.
IT IS A CONDUIT FOR THE DARK SIDE THAT LIVES WITHIN ALL OF US.
THE BALANCE IS SHIFTING!
SOON, I SHALL POSSESS THE CHI OF ALL THE HEAVENLY DRAGONS!
THEIR MYSTIC ENERGY WILL IMBUE EVERY ATOM OF MY BEING WITH A POWER THAT TRANSCENDS TIME AND SPACE!
ALL UNDER HEAVEN, AND ALL THE DEMONS OF THE SEVEN HELLS WILL KOWTOW TO THE HIEROPHANT IN ABJECT OBEISANCE!

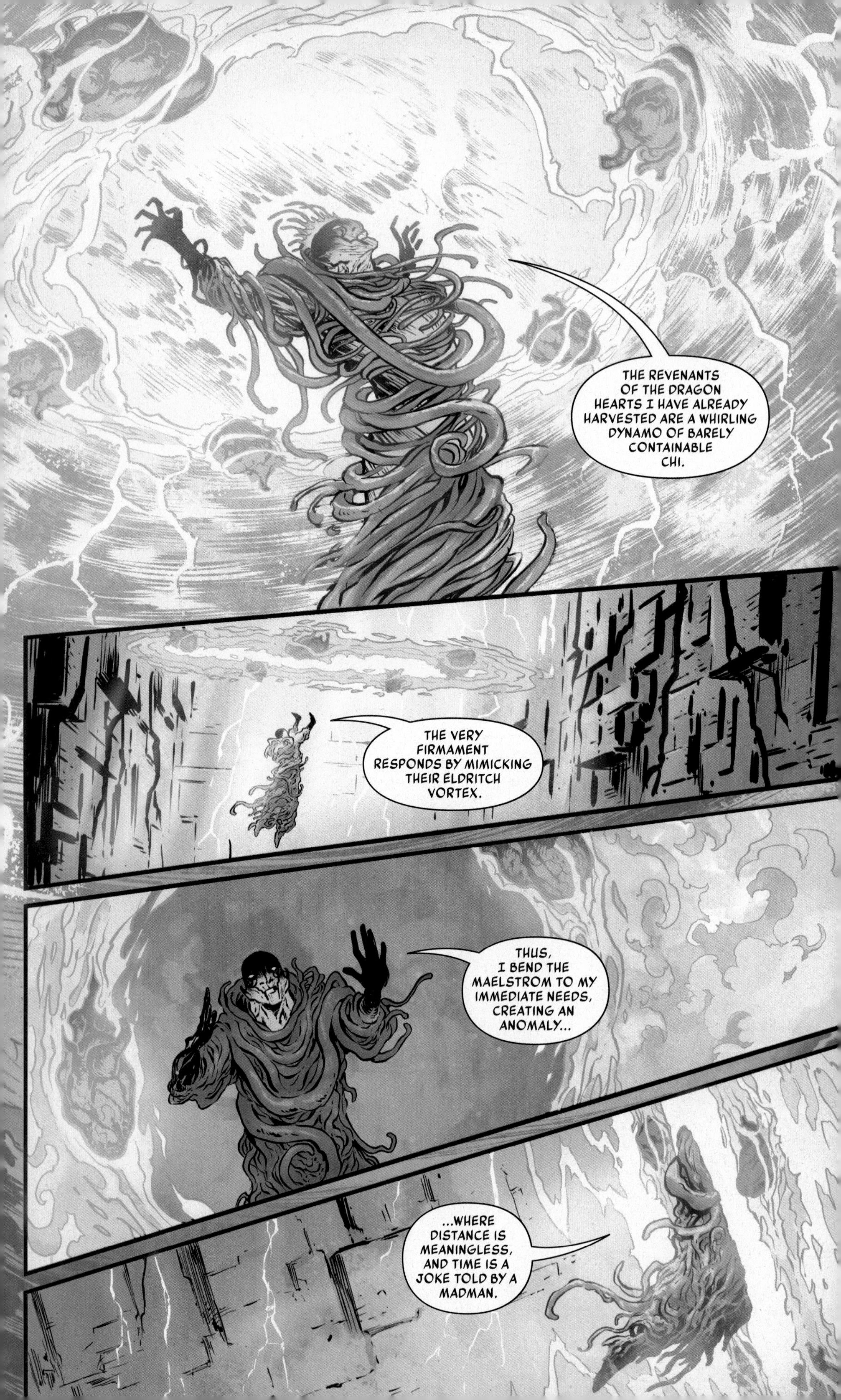
THE REVENANTS OF THE DRAGON HEARTS I HAVE ALREADY HARVESTED ARE A WHIRLING DYNAMO OF BARELY CONTAINABLE CHI.
THE VERY FIRMAMENT RESPONDS BY MIMICKING THEIR ELDRITCH VORTEX.
THUS, I BEND THE MAELSTROM TO MY IMMEDIATE NEEDS, CREATING AN ANOMALY...
...WHERE DISTANCE IS MEANINGLESS, AND TIME IS A JOKE TOLD BY A MADMAN.

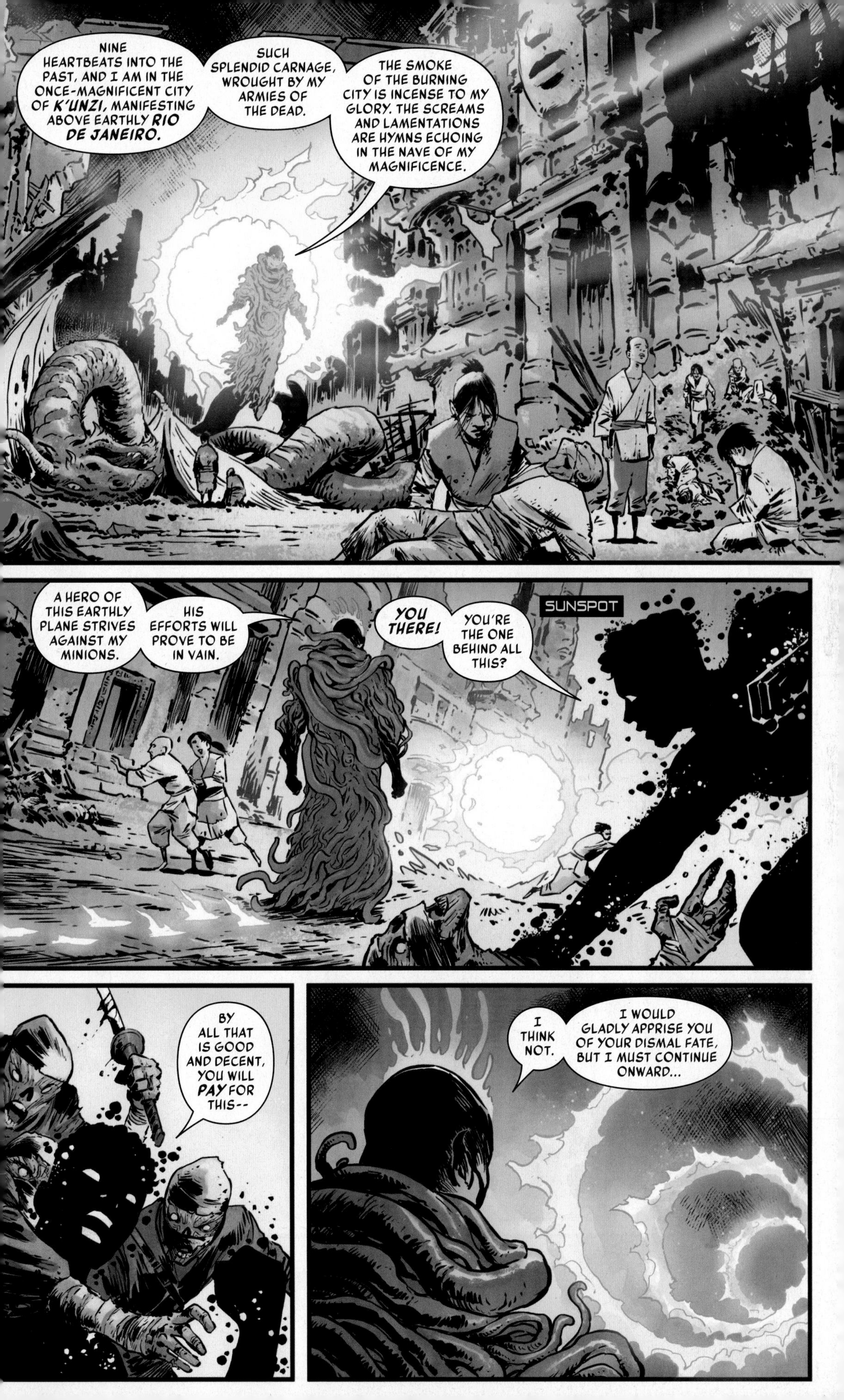
NINE HEARTBEATS INTO THE PAST, AND I AM IN THE ONCE-MAGNIFICENT CITY OF *K'UNZI,* MANIFESTING ABOVE EARTHLY *RIO DE JANEIRO.*
SUCH SPLENDID CARNAGE, WROUGHT BY MY ARMIES OF THE DEAD.
THE SMOKE OF THE BURNING CITY IS INCENSE TO MY GLORY. THE SCREAMS AND LAMENTATIONS ARE HYMNS ECHOING IN THE NAVE OF MY MAGNIFICENCE.
A HERO OF THIS EARTHLY PLANE STRIVES AGAINST MY MINIONS.
HIS EFFORTS WILL PROVE TO BE IN VAIN.
SUNSPOT
*YOU THERE!*
YOU'RE THE ONE BEHIND ALL THIS?
BY ALL THAT IS GOOD AND DECENT, YOU WILL *PAY* FOR THIS--
I THINK NOT.
I WOULD GLADLY APPRISE YOU OF YOUR DISMAL FATE, BUT I MUST CONTINUE ONWARD...

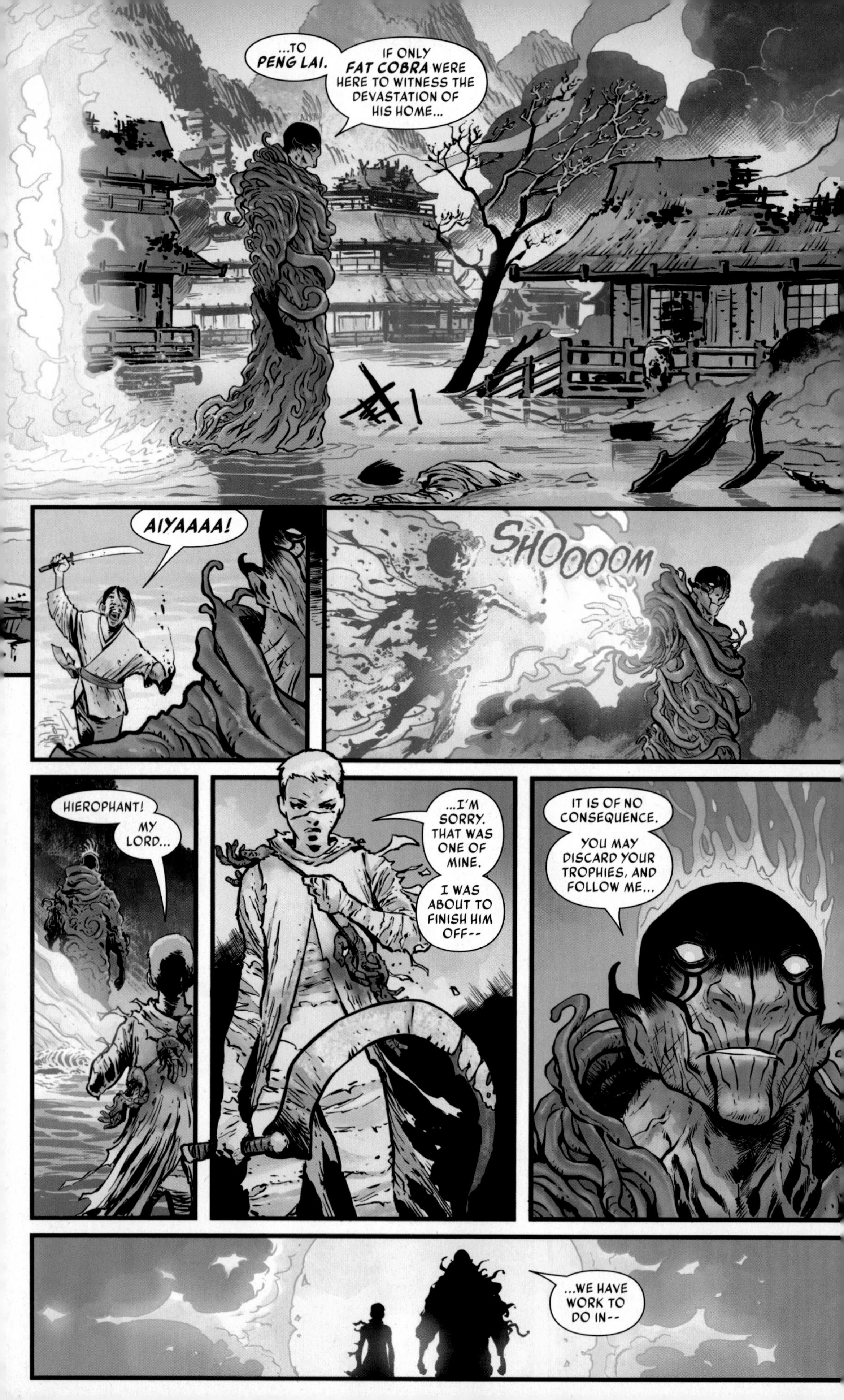
...TO PENG LAI.
IF ONLY FAT COBRA WERE HERE TO WITNESS THE DEVASTATION OF HIS HOME...
AIYAAAA!
SHOOOOM
HIEROPHANT! MY LORD...
...I'M SORRY. THAT WAS ONE OF MINE.
I WAS ABOUT TO FINISH HIM OFF--
IT IS OF NO CONSEQUENCE.
YOU MAY DISCARD YOUR TROPHIES, AND FOLLOW ME...
...WE HAVE WORK TO DO IN--

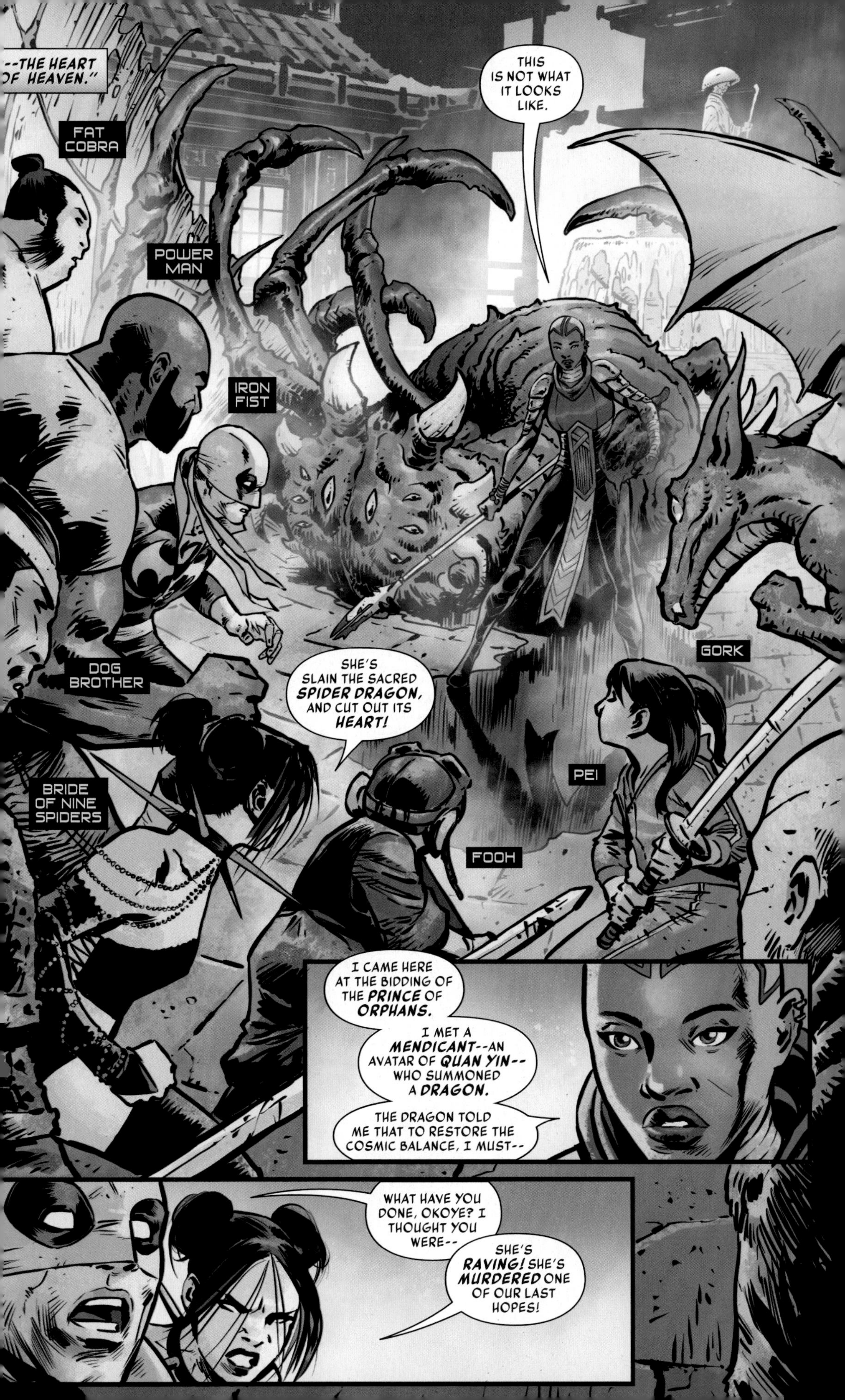
--THE HEART OF HEAVEN."
FAT COBRA
POWER MAN
IRON FIST
THIS IS NOT WHAT IT LOOKS LIKE.
DOG BROTHER
GORK
SHE'S SLAIN THE SACRED SPIDER DRAGON, AND CUT OUT ITS HEART!
BRIDE OF NINE SPIDERS
PEI
FOOH
I CAME HERE AT THE BIDDING OF THE PRINCE OF ORPHANS.
I MET A MENDICANT--AN AVATAR OF QUAN YIN--WHO SUMMONED A DRAGON.
THE DRAGON TOLD ME THAT TO RESTORE THE COSMIC BALANCE, I MUST--
WHAT HAVE YOU DONE, OKOYE? I THOUGHT YOU WERE--
SHE'S RAVING! SHE'S MURDERED ONE OF OUR LAST HOPES!

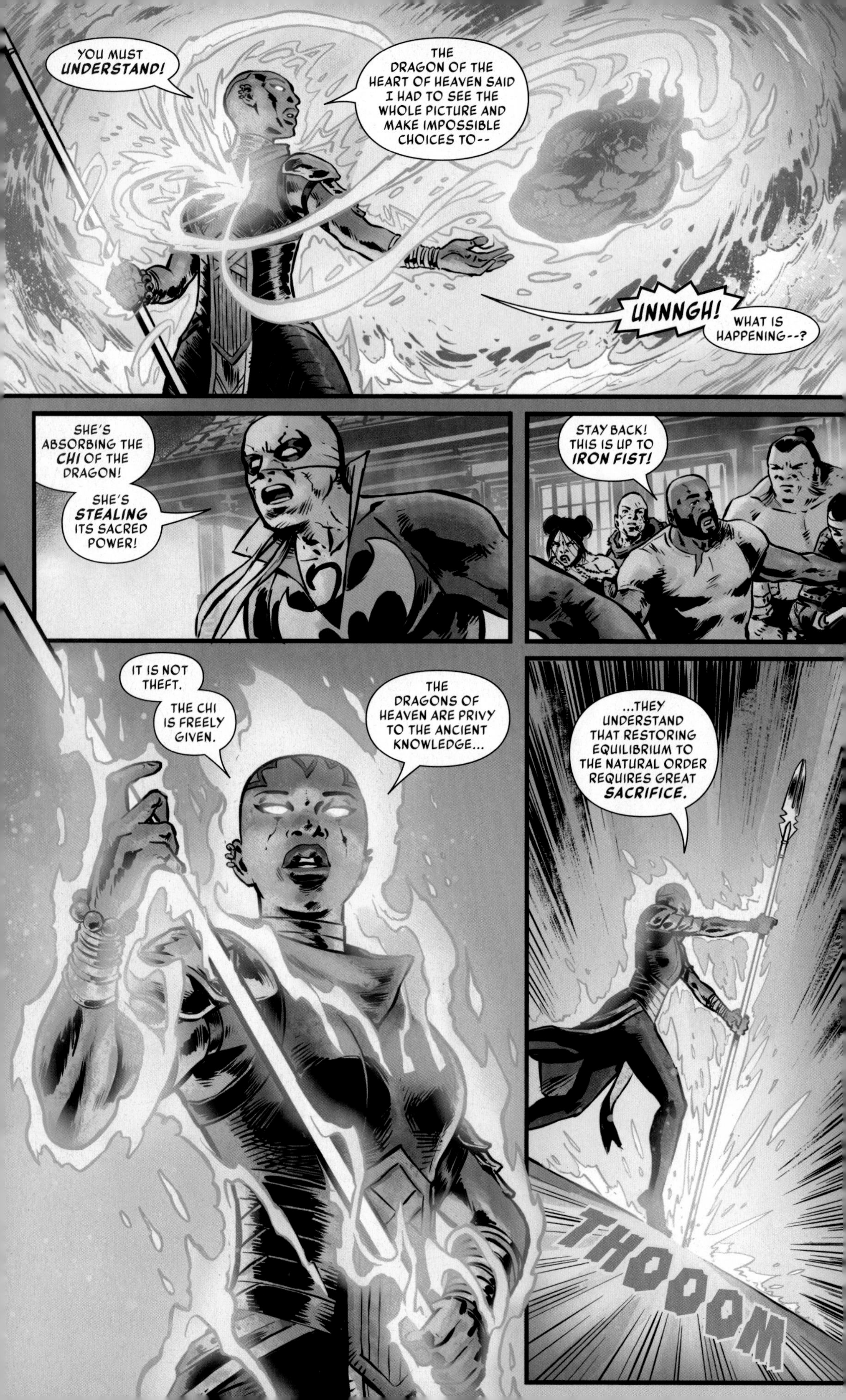
YOU MUST UNDERSTAND!
THE DRAGON OF THE HEART OF HEAVEN SAID I HAD TO SEE THE WHOLE PICTURE AND MAKE IMPOSSIBLE CHOICES TO--
UNNNGH! WHAT IS HAPPENING--?
SHE'S ABSORBING THE CHI OF THE DRAGON!
SHE'S STEALING ITS SACRED POWER!
STAY BACK! THIS IS UP TO IRON FIST!
IT IS NOT THEFT.
THE CHI IS FREELY GIVEN.
THE DRAGONS OF HEAVEN ARE PRIVY TO THE ANCIENT KNOWLEDGE...
...THEY UNDERSTAND THAT RESTORING EQUILIBRIUM TO THE NATURAL ORDER REQUIRES GREAT SACRIFICE.
THOOOM

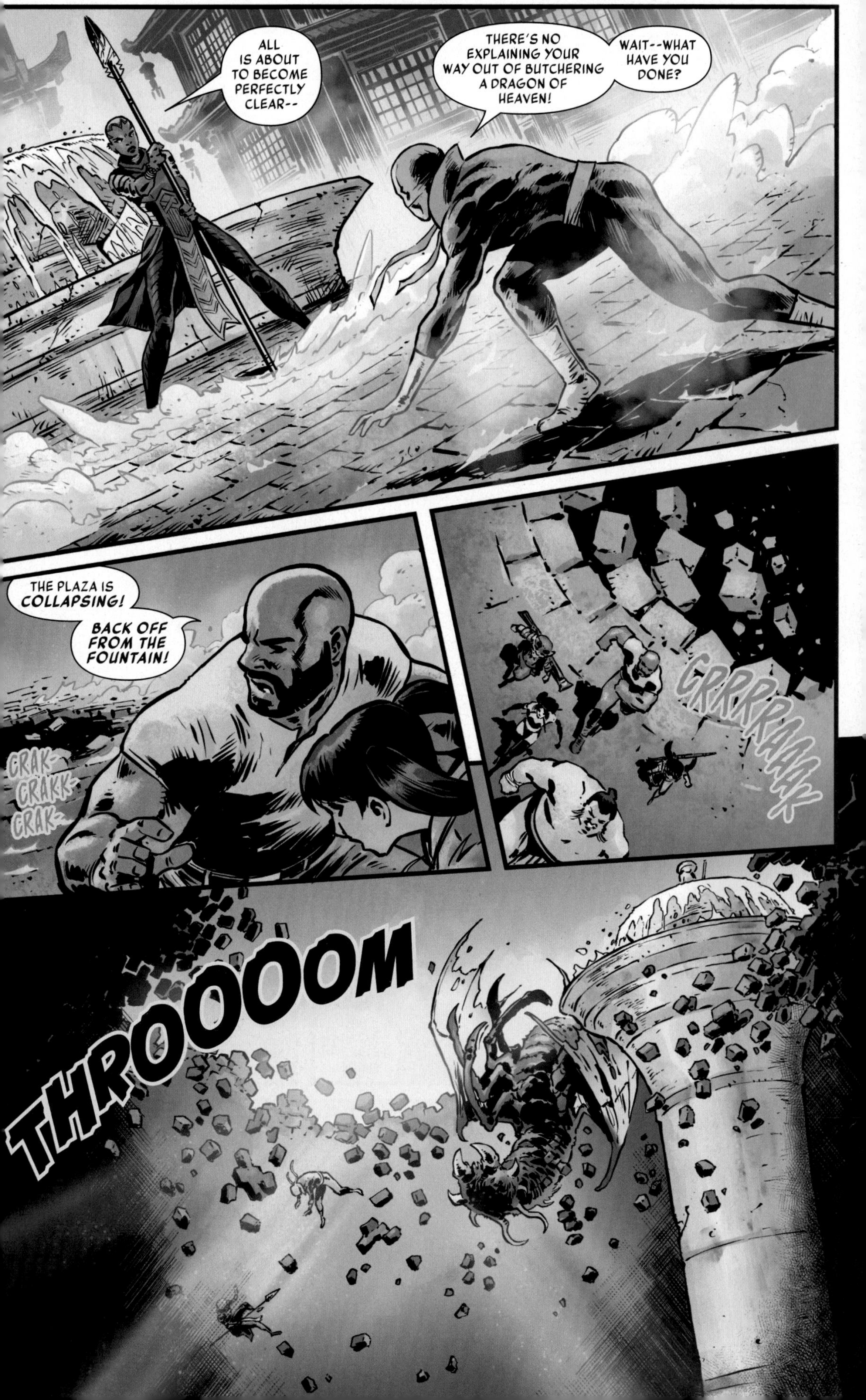
ALL IS ABOUT TO BECOME PERFECTLY CLEAR--
THERE'S NO EXPLAINING YOUR WAY OUT OF BUTCHERING A DRAGON OF HEAVEN!
WAIT--WHAT HAVE YOU DONE?
THE PLAZA IS COLLAPSING!
BACK OFF FROM THE FOUNTAIN!
CRAK-CRAKK-CRAK
CRRRRAAAAK
THROOOOOM

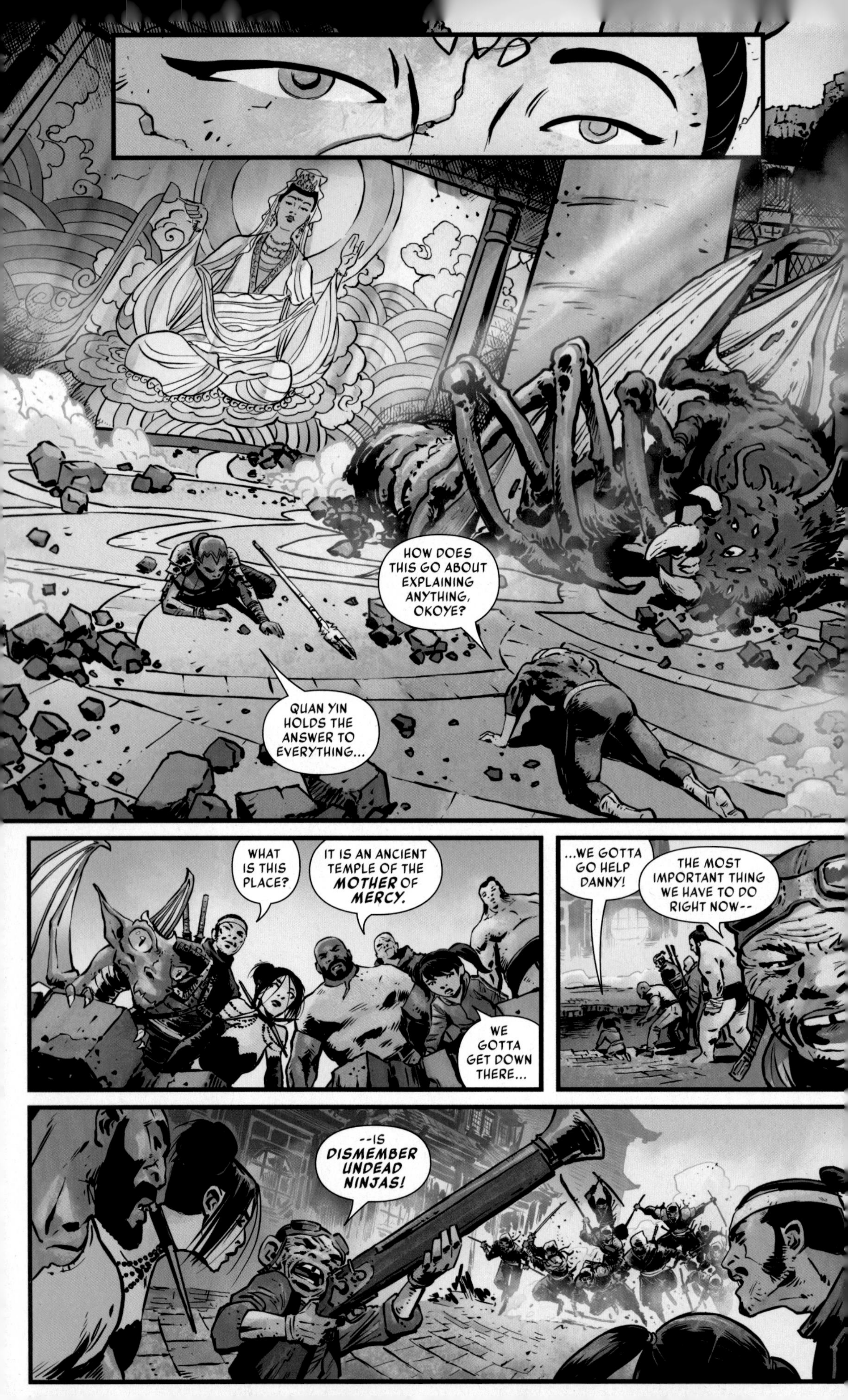
HOW DOES THIS GO ABOUT EXPLAINING ANYTHING, OKOYE?
QUAN YIN HOLDS THE ANSWER TO EVERYTHING...
WHAT IS THIS PLACE?
IT IS AN ANCIENT TEMPLE OF THE *MOTHER* OF *MERCY.*
WE GOTTA GET DOWN THERE...
...WE GOTTA GO HELP DANNY!
THE MOST IMPORTANT THING WE HAVE TO DO RIGHT NOW--
--IS *DISMEMBER UNDEAD NINJAS!*

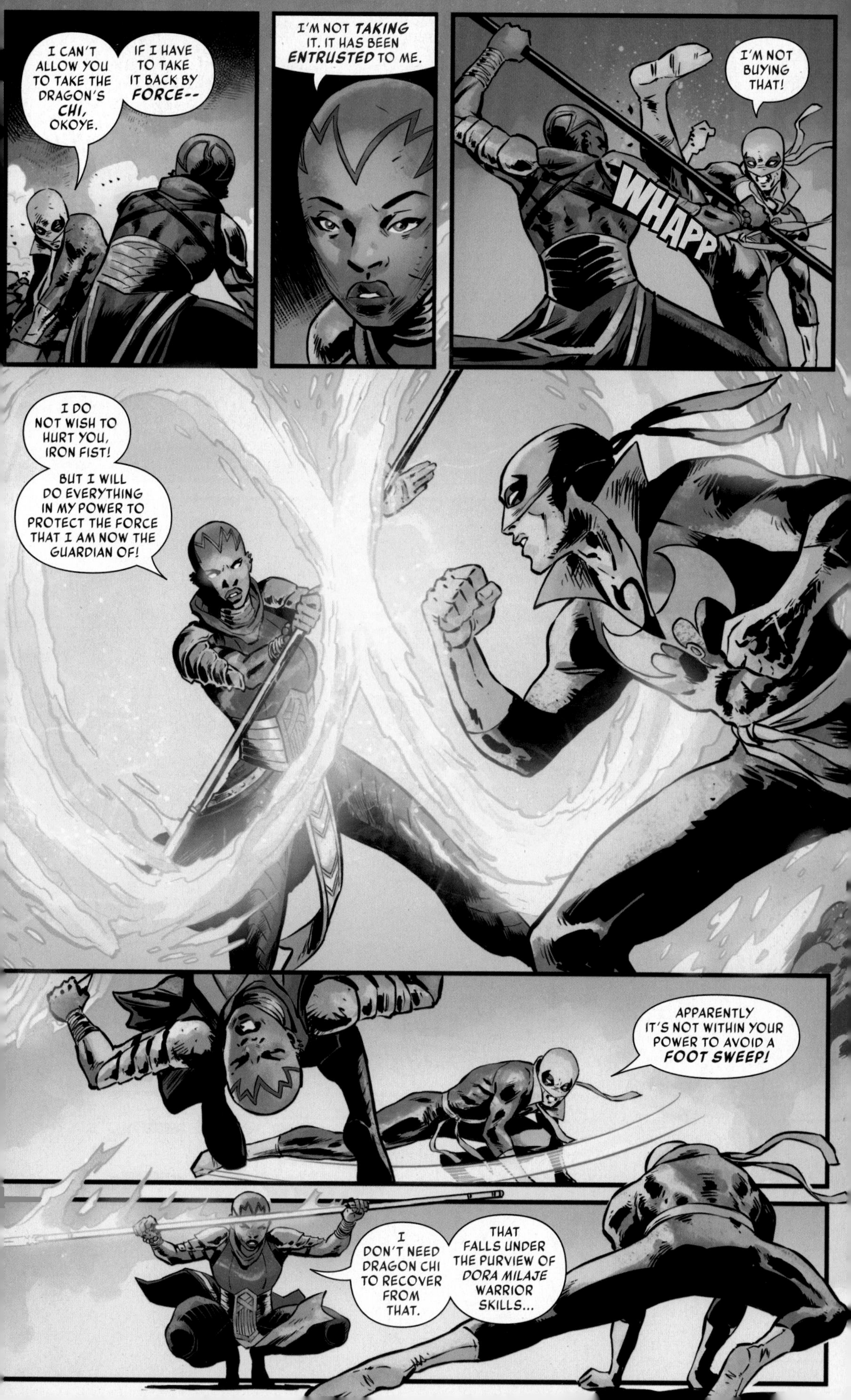

I CAN'T ALLOW YOU TO TAKE THE DRAGON'S CHI, OKOYE.
IF I HAVE TO TAKE IT BACK BY FORCE--
I'M NOT TAKING IT. IT HAS BEEN ENTRUSTED TO ME.
I'M NOT BUYING THAT!
WHAPP
I DO NOT WISH TO HURT YOU, IRON FIST!
BUT I WILL DO EVERYTHING IN MY POWER TO PROTECT THE FORCE THAT I AM NOW THE GUARDIAN OF!
APPARENTLY IT'S NOT WITHIN YOUR POWER TO AVOID A FOOT SWEEP!
I DON'T NEED DRAGON CHI TO RECOVER FROM THAT.
THAT FALLS UNDER THE PURVIEW OF DORA MILAJE WARRIOR SKILLS...

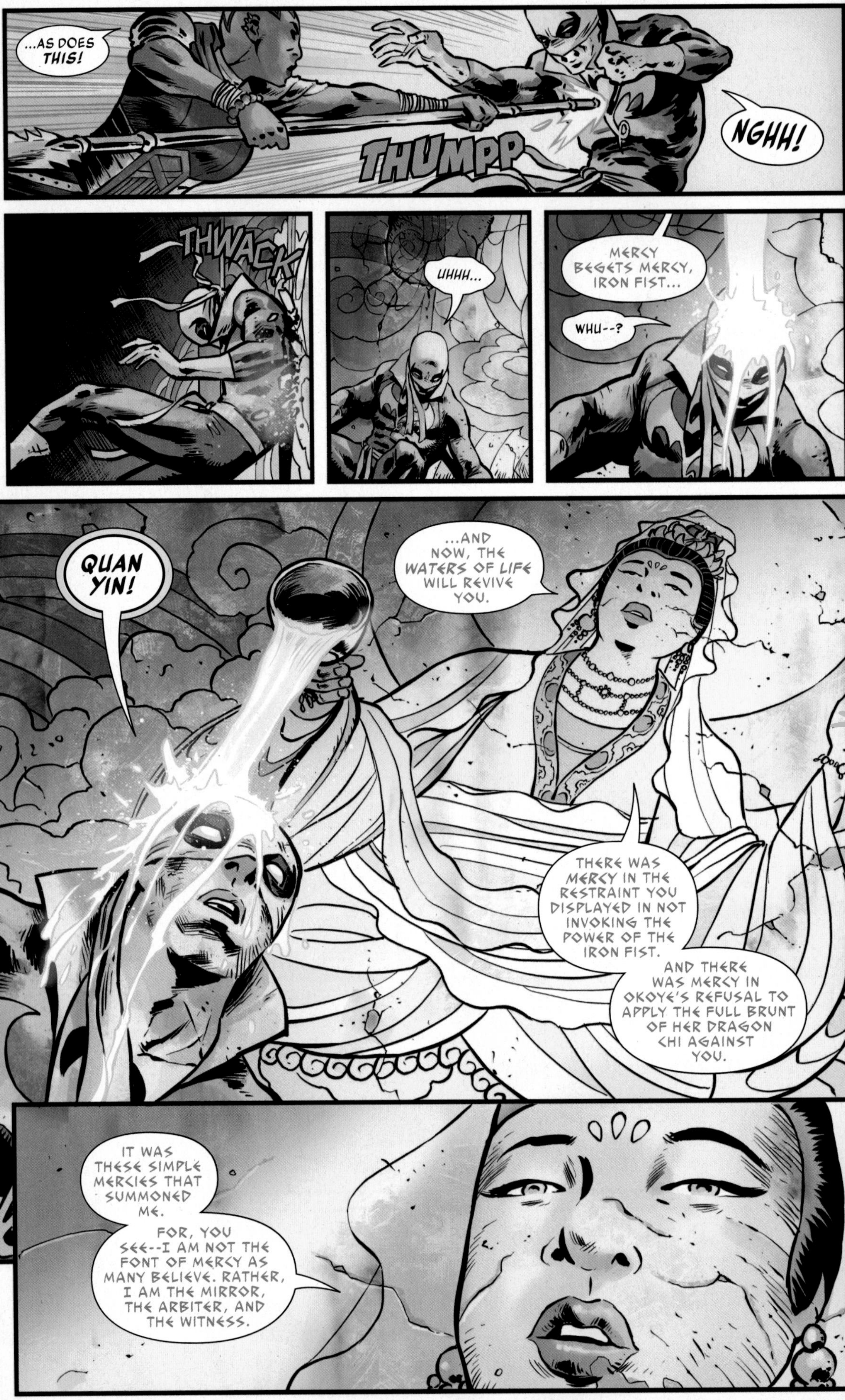
...AS DOES THIS!
THUMPP
NGHH!
THWACK
UHHH...
MERCY BEGETS MERCY, IRON FIST...
WHU--?
QUAN YIN!
...AND NOW, THE WATERS OF LIFE WILL REVIVE YOU.
THERE WAS MERCY IN THE RESTRAINT YOU DISPLAYED IN NOT INVOKING THE POWER OF THE IRON FIST.
AND THERE WAS MERCY IN OKOYE'S REFUSAL TO APPLY THE FULL BRUNT OF HER DRAGON CHI AGAINST YOU.
IT WAS THESE SIMPLE MERCIES THAT SUMMONED ME.
FOR, YOU SEE--I AM NOT THE FONT OF MERCY AS MANY BELIEVE. RATHER, I AM THE MIRROR, THE ARBITER, AND THE WITNESS.

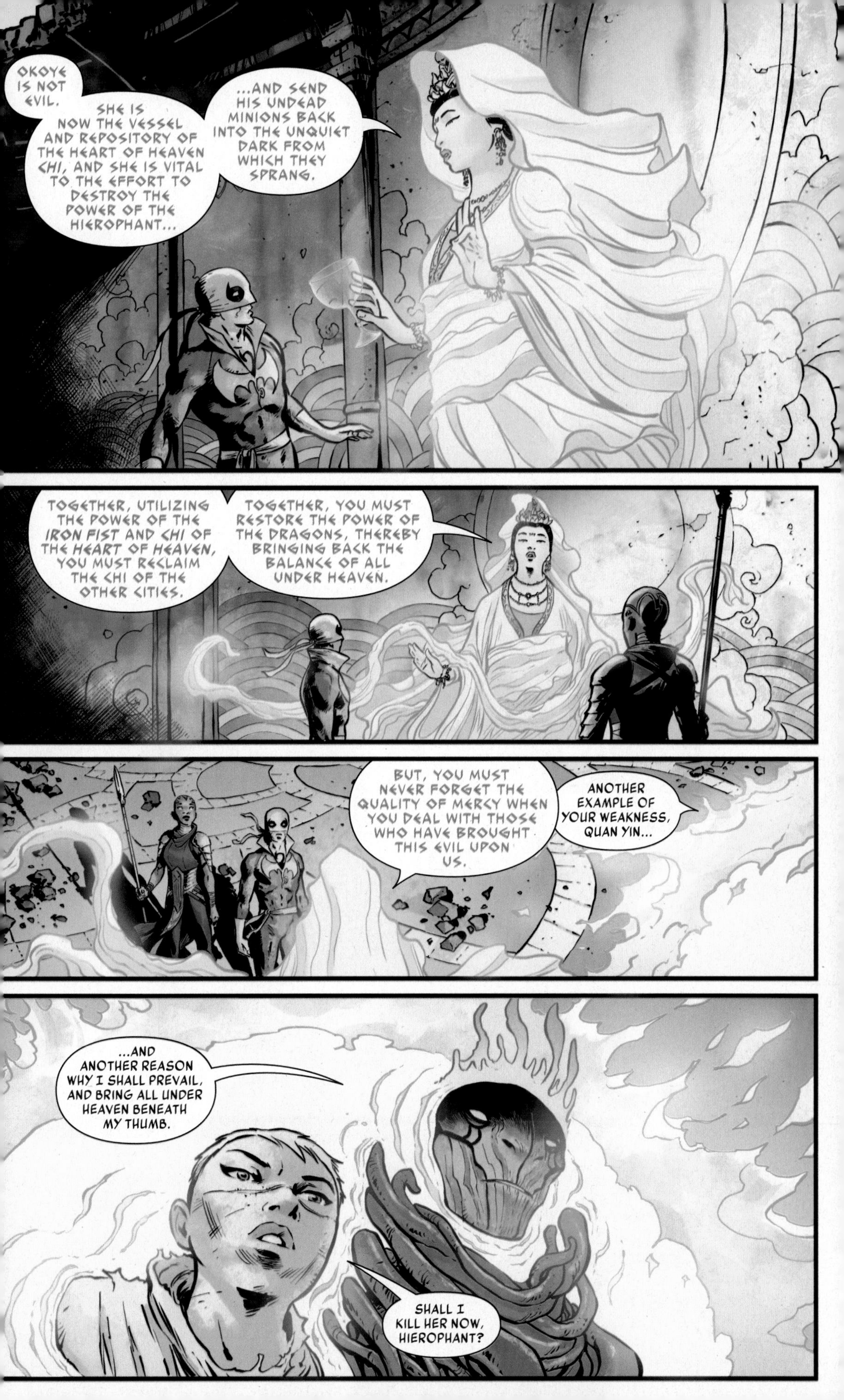
OKOYE IS NOT EVIL.
SHE IS NOW THE VESSEL AND REPOSITORY OF THE HEART OF HEAVEN *CHI*, AND SHE IS VITAL TO THE EFFORT TO DESTROY THE POWER OF THE HIEROPHANT...
...AND SEND HIS UNDEAD MINIONS BACK INTO THE UNQUIET DARK FROM WHICH THEY SPRANG.
TOGETHER, UTILIZING THE POWER OF THE *IRON FIST* AND *CHI* OF THE *HEART OF HEAVEN*, YOU MUST RECLAIM THE CHI OF THE OTHER CITIES.
TOGETHER, YOU MUST RESTORE THE POWER OF THE DRAGONS, THEREBY BRINGING BACK THE BALANCE OF ALL UNDER HEAVEN.
BUT, YOU MUST NEVER FORGET THE QUALITY OF MERCY WHEN YOU DEAL WITH THOSE WHO HAVE BROUGHT THIS EVIL UPON US.
ANOTHER EXAMPLE OF YOUR WEAKNESS, QUAN YIN...
...AND ANOTHER REASON WHY I SHALL PREVAIL, AND BRING ALL UNDER HEAVEN BENEATH MY THUMB.
SHALL I KILL HER NOW, HIEROPHANT?

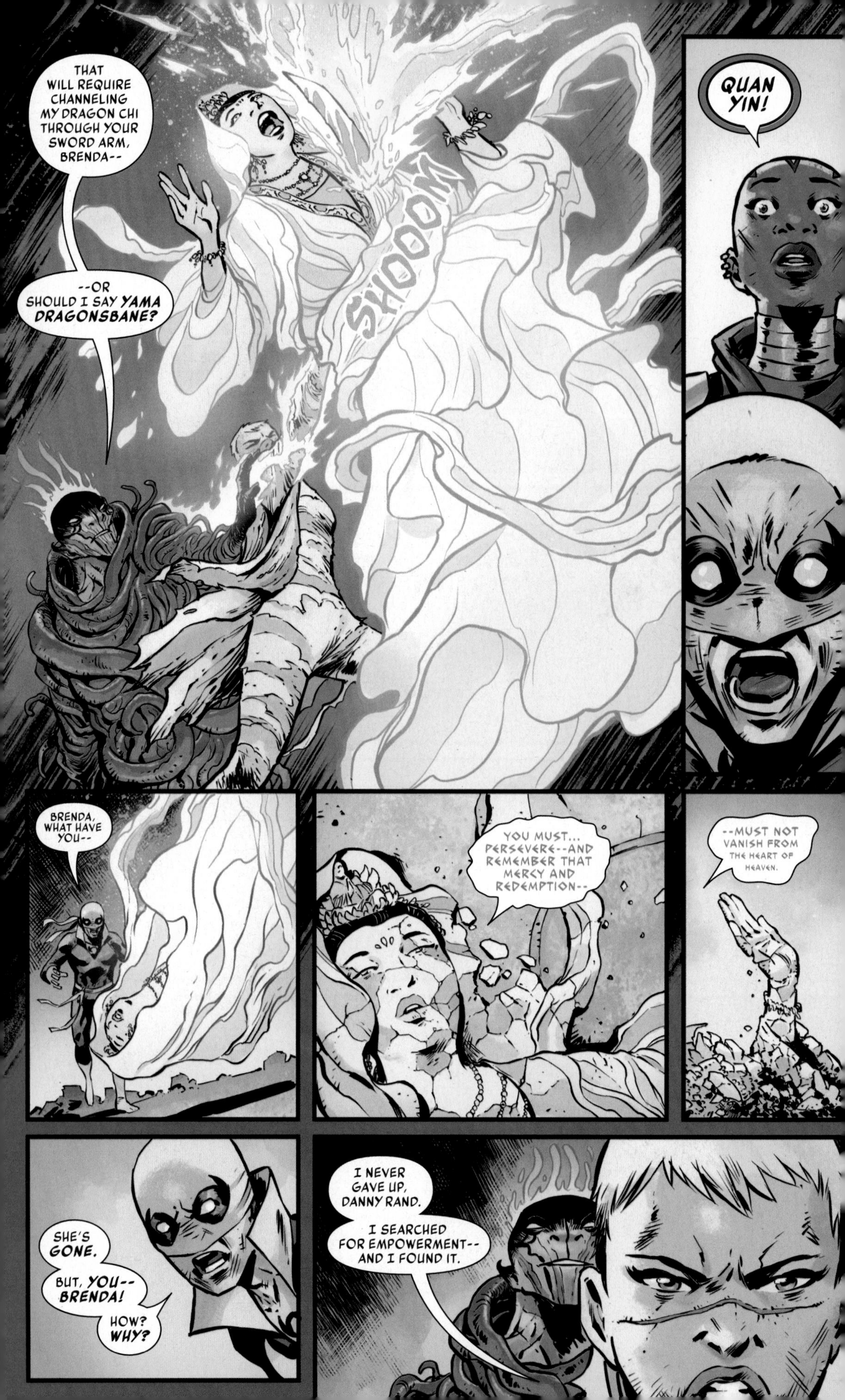

THAT WILL REQUIRE CHANNELING MY DRAGON CHI THROUGH YOUR SWORD ARM, BRENDA--
--OR SHOULD I SAY YAMA DRAGONSBANE?
SHOOOM
QUAN YIN!
BRENDA, WHAT HAVE YOU--
YOU MUST... PERSEVERE--AND REMEMBER THAT MERCY AND REDEMPTION--
--MUST NOT VANISH FROM THE HEART OF HEAVEN.
SHE'S GONE.
BUT, YOU-- BRENDA!
HOW? WHY?
I NEVER GAVE UP, DANNY RAND.
I SEARCHED FOR EMPOWERMENT-- AND I FOUND IT.

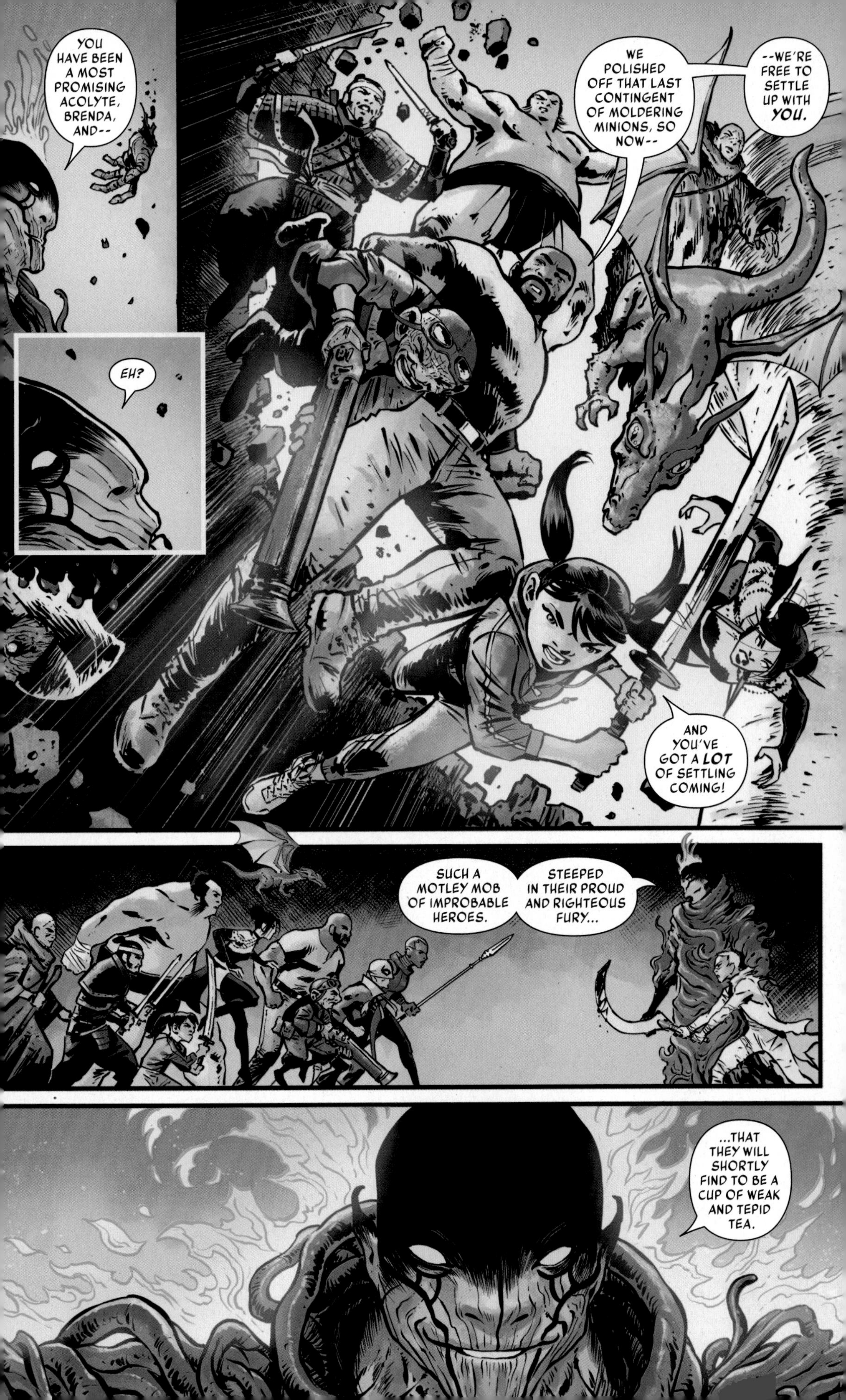
YOU HAVE BEEN A MOST PROMISING ACOLYTE, BRENDA, AND--
WE POLISHED OFF THAT LAST CONTINGENT OF MOLDERING MINIONS, SO NOW--
--WE'RE FREE TO SETTLE UP WITH YOU.
EH?
AND YOU'VE GOT A LOT OF SETTLING COMING!
SUCH A MOTLEY MOB OF IMPROBABLE HEROES.
STEEPED IN THEIR PROUD AND RIGHTEOUS FURY...
...THAT THEY WILL SHORTLY FIND TO BE A CUP OF WEAK AND TEPID TEA.

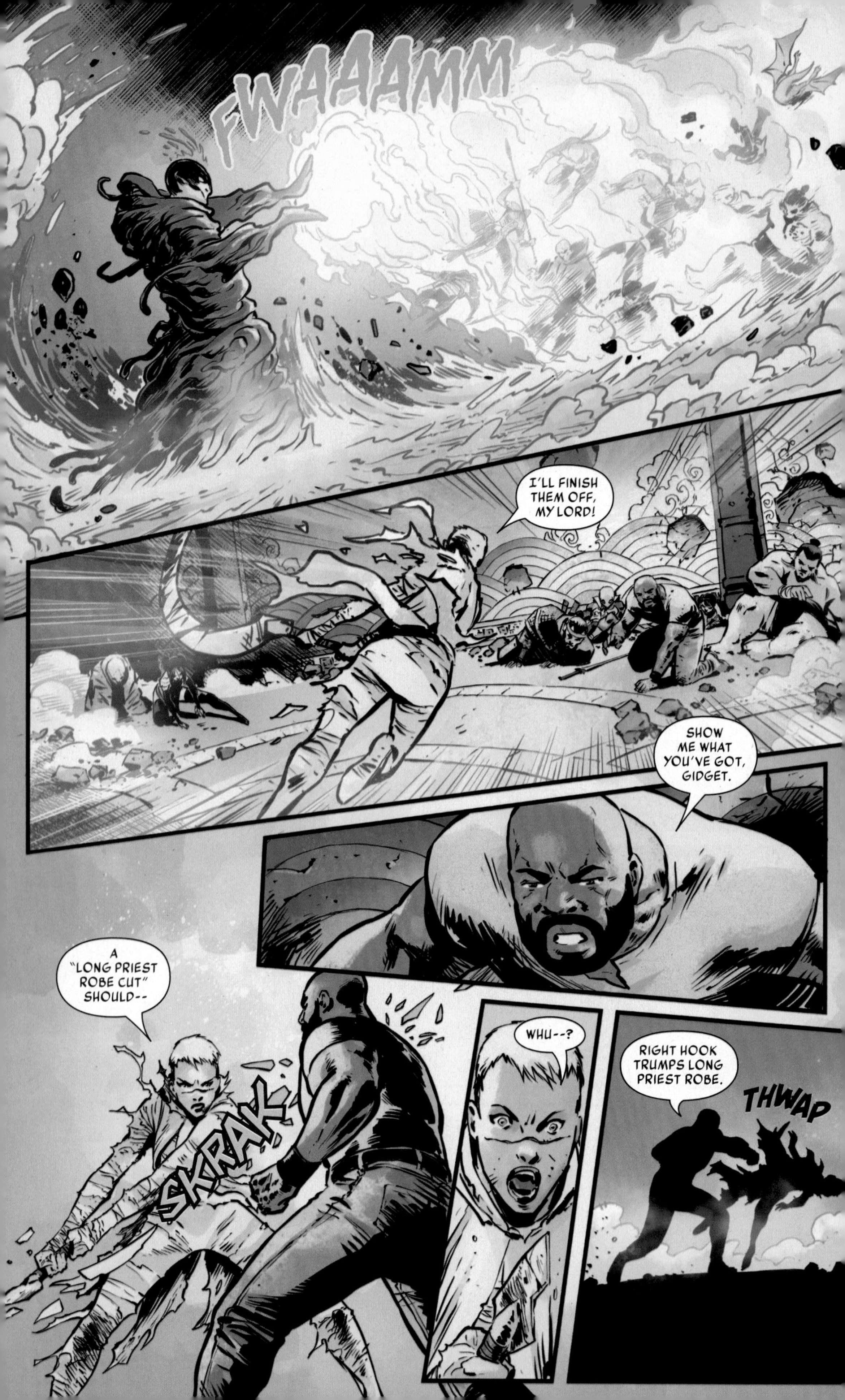
FWAAAAMM
I'LL FINISH THEM OFF, MY LORD!
SHOW ME WHAT YOU'VE GOT, GIDGET.
A "LONG PRIEST ROBE CUT" SHOULD--
SKRAK
WHU--?
RIGHT HOOK TRUMPS LONG PRIEST ROBE.
THWAP

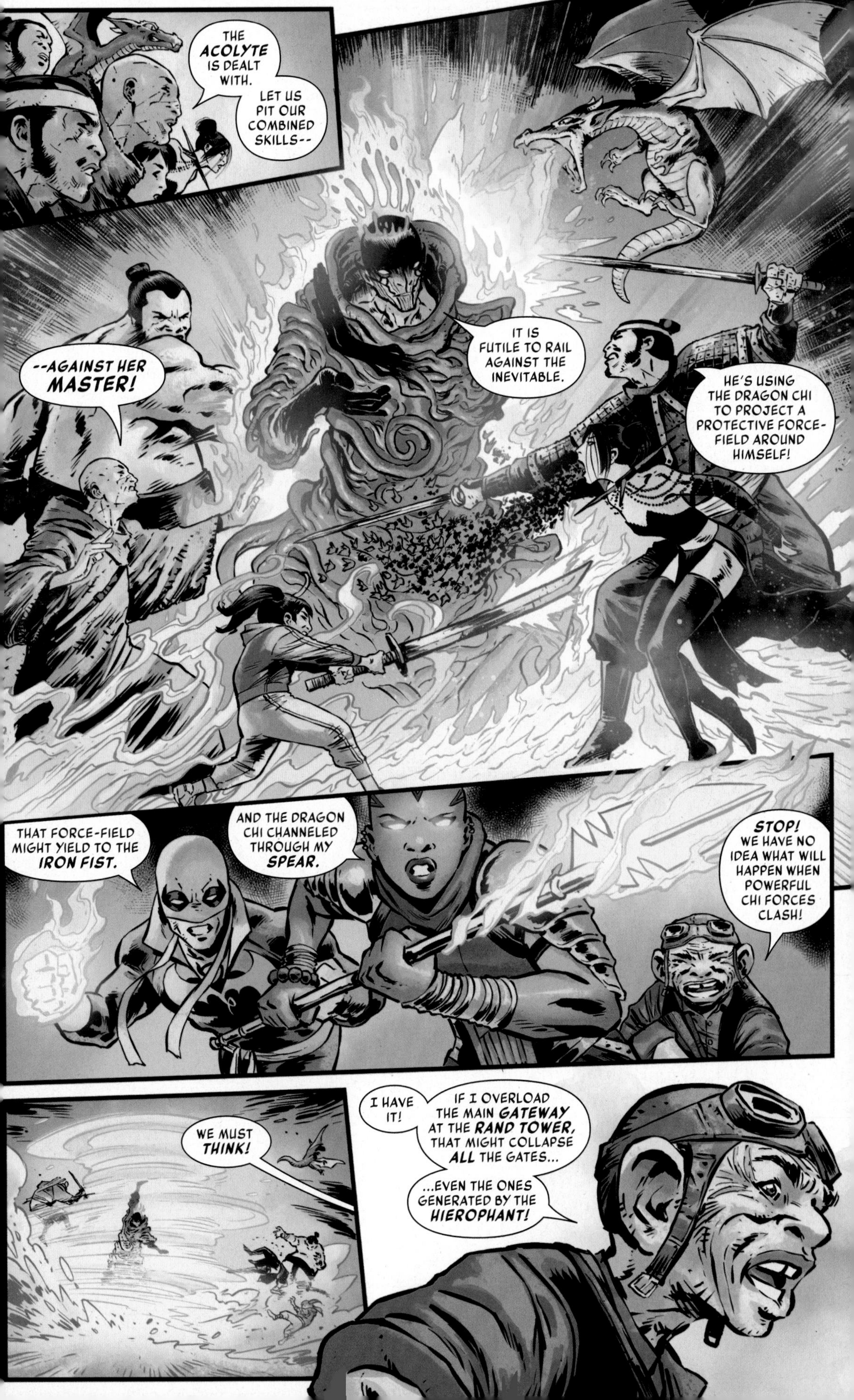

THE ACOLYTE IS DEALT WITH.
LET US PIT OUR COMBINED SKILLS--
--AGAINST HER MASTER!
IT IS FUTILE TO RAIL AGAINST THE INEVITABLE.
HE'S USING THE DRAGON CHI TO PROJECT A PROTECTIVE FORCE-FIELD AROUND HIMSELF!
THAT FORCE-FIELD MIGHT YIELD TO THE IRON FIST.
AND THE DRAGON CHI CHANNELED THROUGH MY SPEAR.
STOP! WE HAVE NO IDEA WHAT WILL HAPPEN WHEN POWERFUL CHI FORCES CLASH!
WE MUST THINK!
I HAVE IT!
IF I OVERLOAD THE MAIN GATEWAY AT THE RAND TOWER, THAT MIGHT COLLAPSE ALL THE GATES...
...EVEN THE ONES GENERATED BY THE HIEROPHANT!

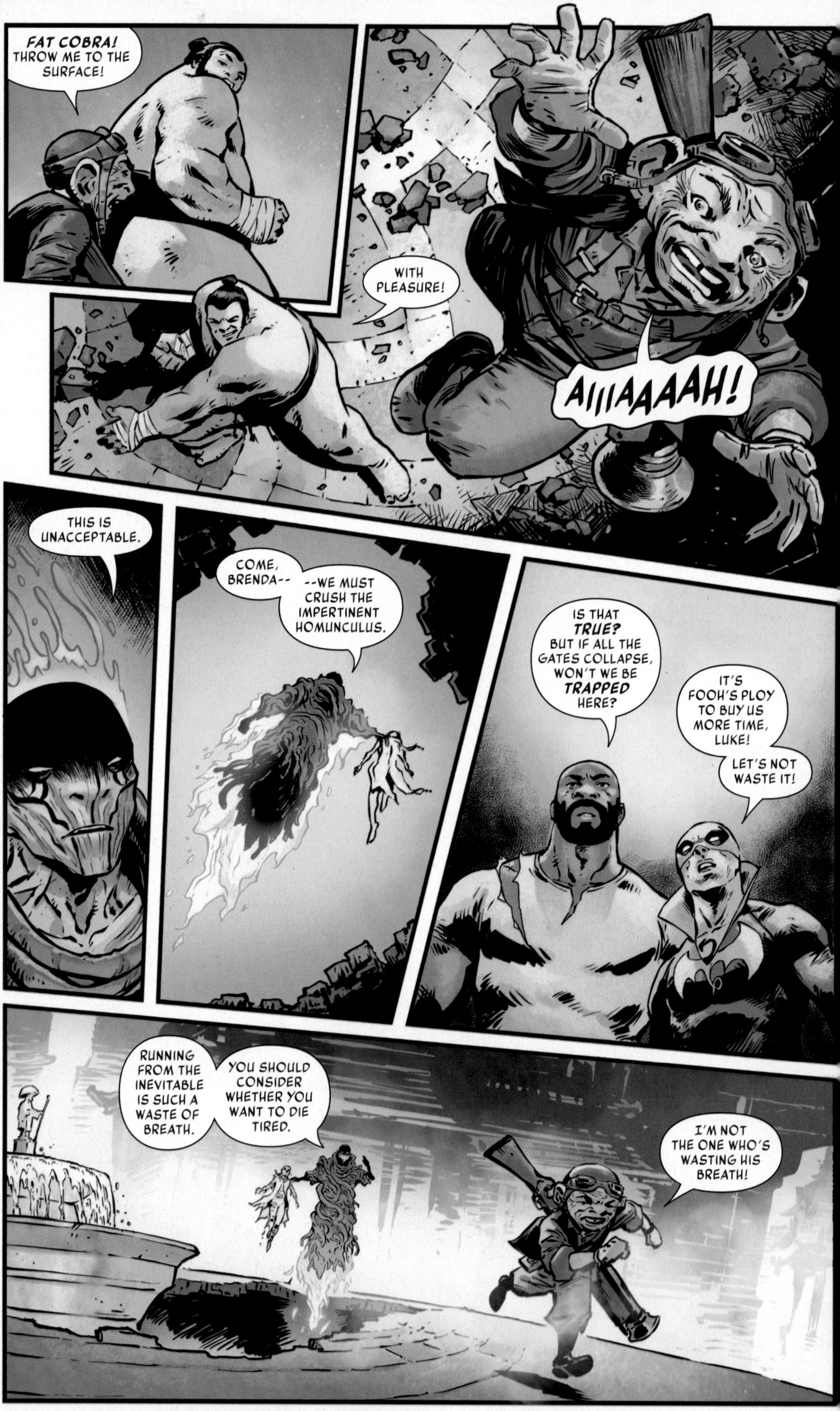
FAT COBRA! THROW ME TO THE SURFACE!
WITH PLEASURE!
AIIIAAAAH!
THIS IS UNACCEPTABLE.
COME, BRENDA--
--WE MUST CRUSH THE IMPERTINENT HOMUNCULUS.
IS THAT TRUE? BUT IF ALL THE GATES COLLAPSE, WON'T WE BE TRAPPED HERE?
IT'S FOOH'S PLOY TO BUY US MORE TIME, LUKE!
LET'S NOT WASTE IT!
RUNNING FROM THE INEVITABLE IS SUCH A WASTE OF BREATH.
YOU SHOULD CONSIDER WHETHER YOU WANT TO DIE TIRED.
I'M NOT THE ONE WHO'S WASTING HIS BREATH!

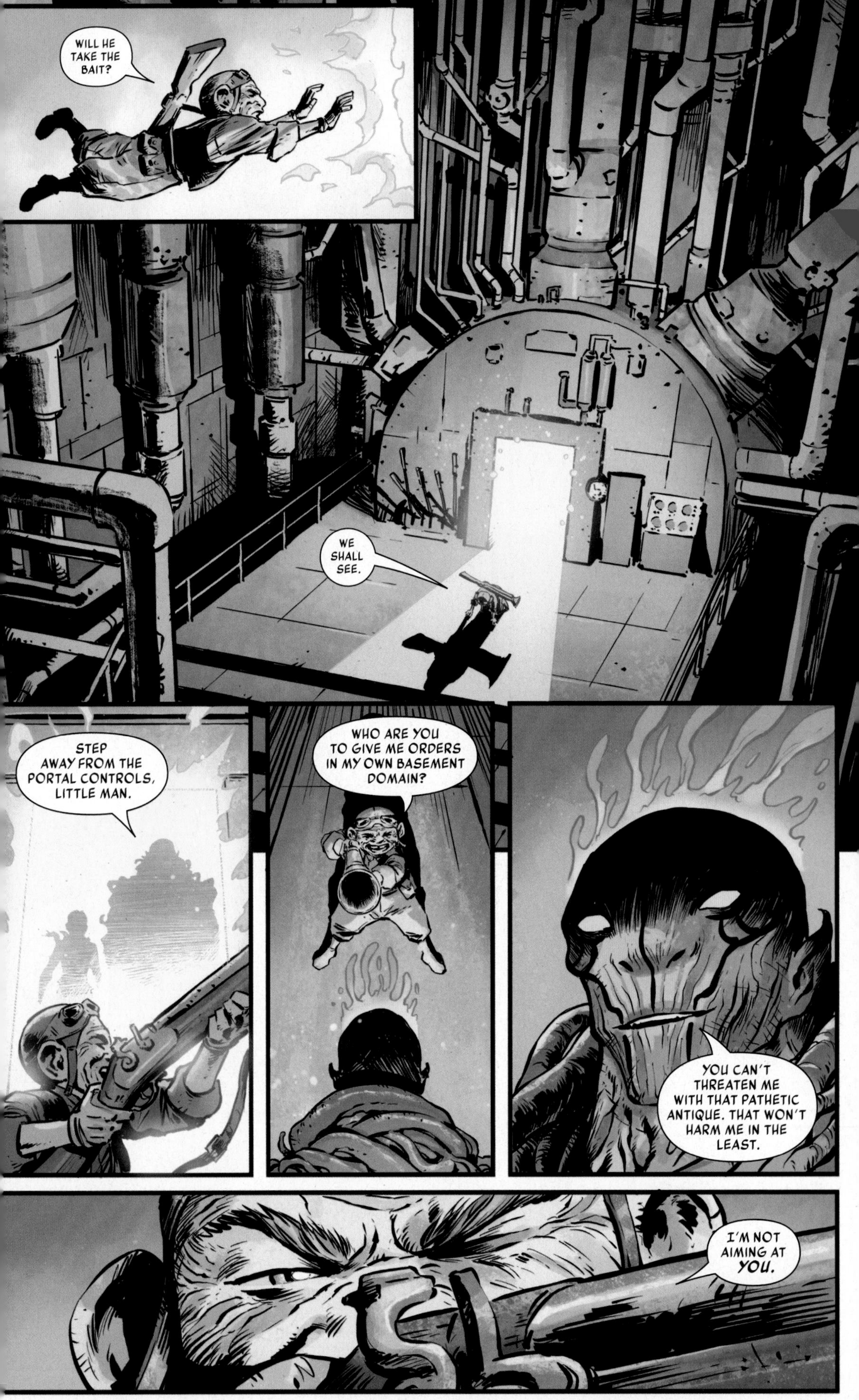
WILL HE TAKE THE BAIT?
WE SHALL SEE.
STEP AWAY FROM THE PORTAL CONTROLS, LITTLE MAN.
WHO ARE YOU TO GIVE ME ORDERS IN MY OWN BASEMENT DOMAIN?
YOU CAN'T THREATEN ME WITH THAT PATHETIC ANTIQUE. THAT WON'T HARM ME IN THE LEAST.
I'M NOT AIMING AT *YOU.*

PA-**THOOOM**

RAND

EXCUSE ME...

...I HAVE AN APPOINTMENT WITH JENI MUNN AT THOMAS & BALLESTEROS ON 26.

SIGN IN, PLEASE. I NEED TO SEE A PHOTO I.D.

SHHHHHHHHHSHHHHSHHHSHH

DID YOU FEEL THAT TREMOR? ARE WE HAVING AN EARTHQUAKE?

NOTHING TO WORRY ABOUT.

WHEN THEY REBUILT THE TOWER, THEY MADE IT BLAST-PROOF.

K-POK

THEY TELL ME THE BASEMENT RIVALS CHEYENNE MOUNTAIN.

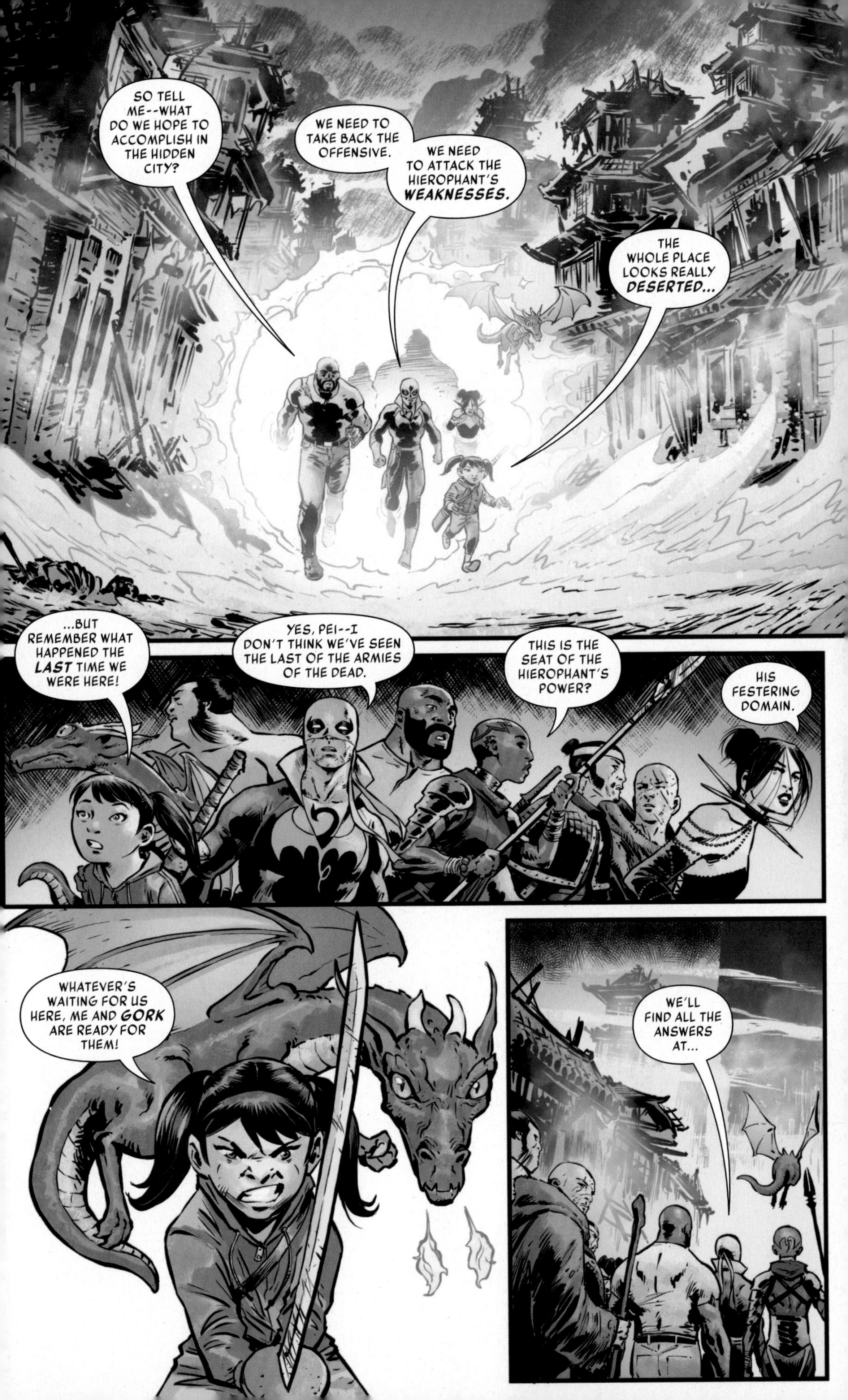
SO TELL ME--WHAT DO WE HOPE TO ACCOMPLISH IN THE HIDDEN CITY?
WE NEED TO TAKE BACK THE OFFENSIVE.
WE NEED TO ATTACK THE HIEROPHANT'S WEAKNESSES.
THE WHOLE PLACE LOOKS REALLY DESERTED...
...BUT REMEMBER WHAT HAPPENED THE LAST TIME WE WERE HERE!
YES, PEI--I DON'T THINK WE'VE SEEN THE LAST OF THE ARMIES OF THE DEAD.
THIS IS THE SEAT OF THE HIEROPHANT'S POWER?
HIS FESTERING DOMAIN.
WHATEVER'S WAITING FOR US HERE, ME AND GORK ARE READY FOR THEM!
WE'LL FIND ALL THE ANSWERS AT...

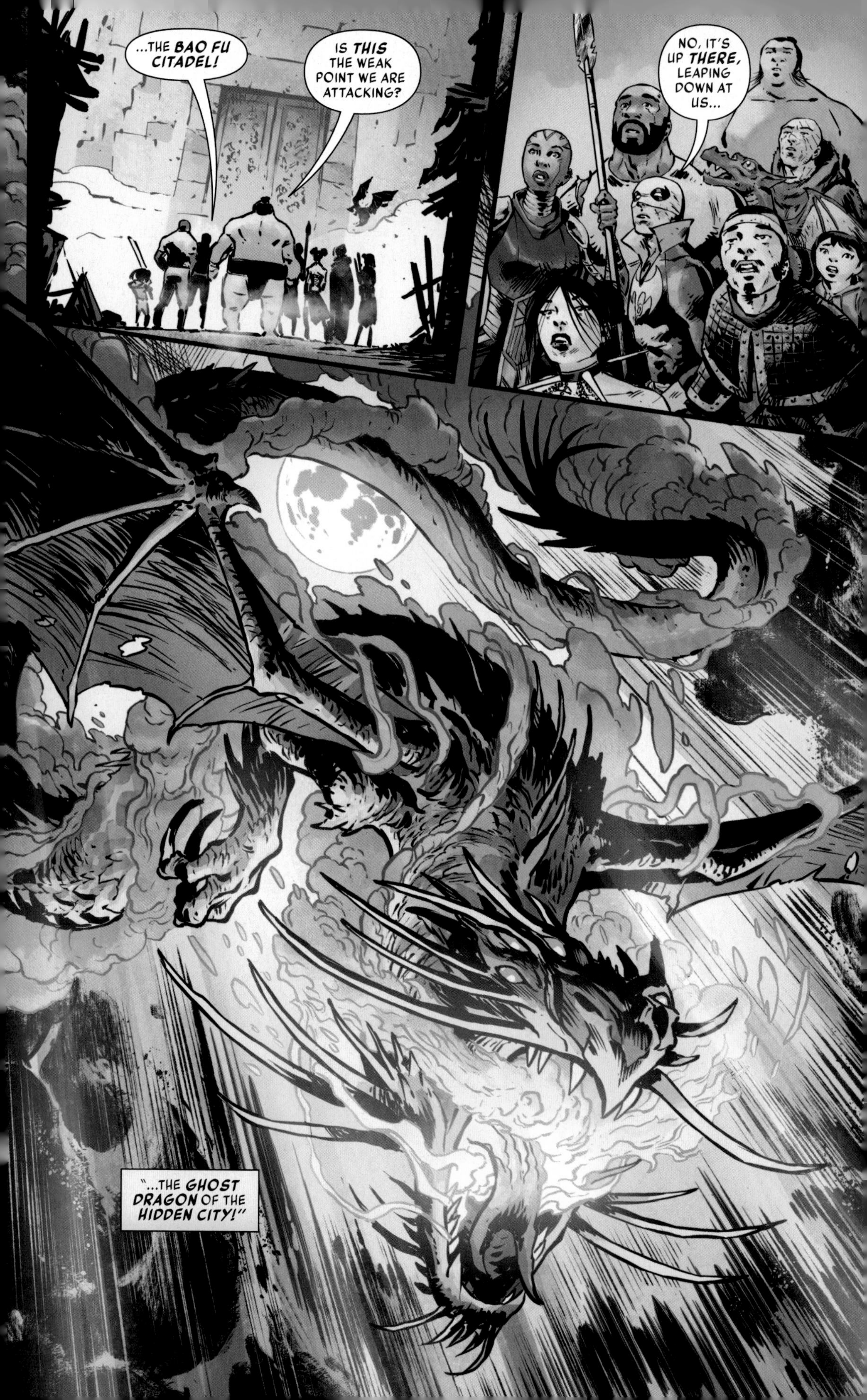
...THE BAO FU CITADEL!
IS THIS THE WEAK POINT WE ARE ATTACKING?
NO, IT'S UP THERE, LEAPING DOWN AT US...
"...THE GHOST DRAGON OF THE HIDDEN CITY!"

# SIX

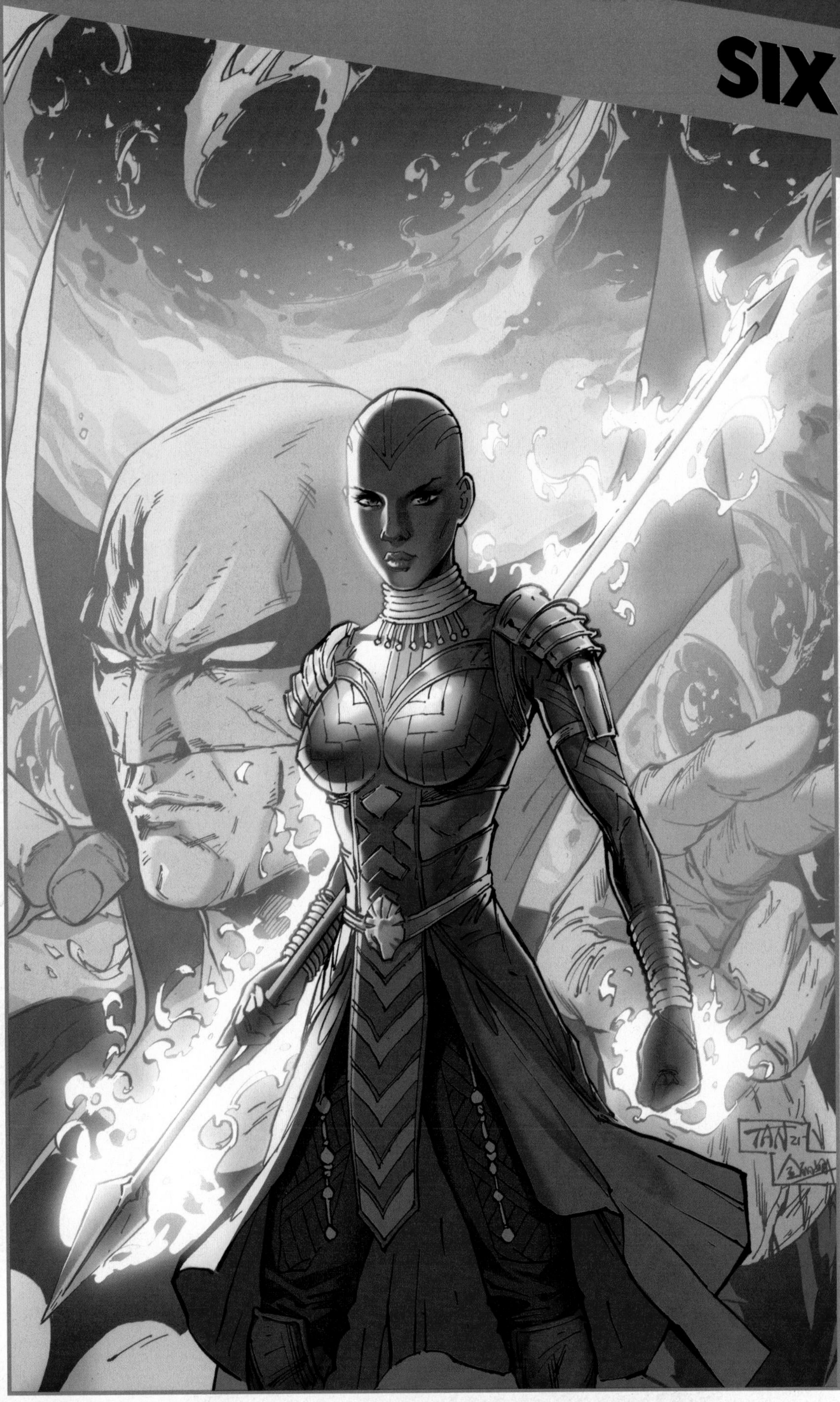

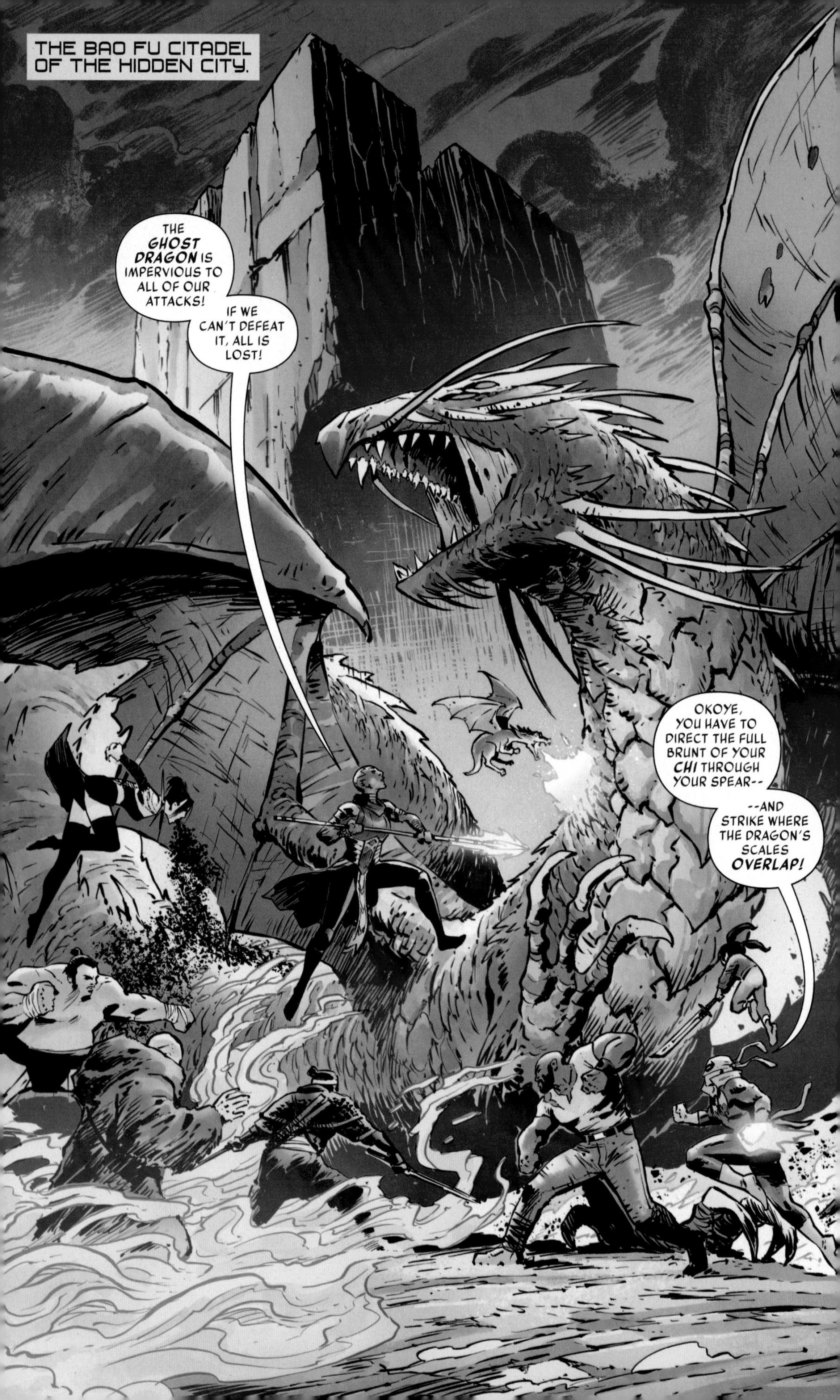
THE BAO FU CITADEL OF THE HIDDEN CITY.
THE GHOST DRAGON IS IMPERVIOUS TO ALL OF OUR ATTACKS!
IF WE CAN'T DEFEAT IT, ALL IS LOST!
OKOYE, YOU HAVE TO DIRECT THE FULL BRUNT OF YOUR CHI THROUGH YOUR SPEAR--
--AND STRIKE WHERE THE DRAGON'S SCALES OVERLAP!

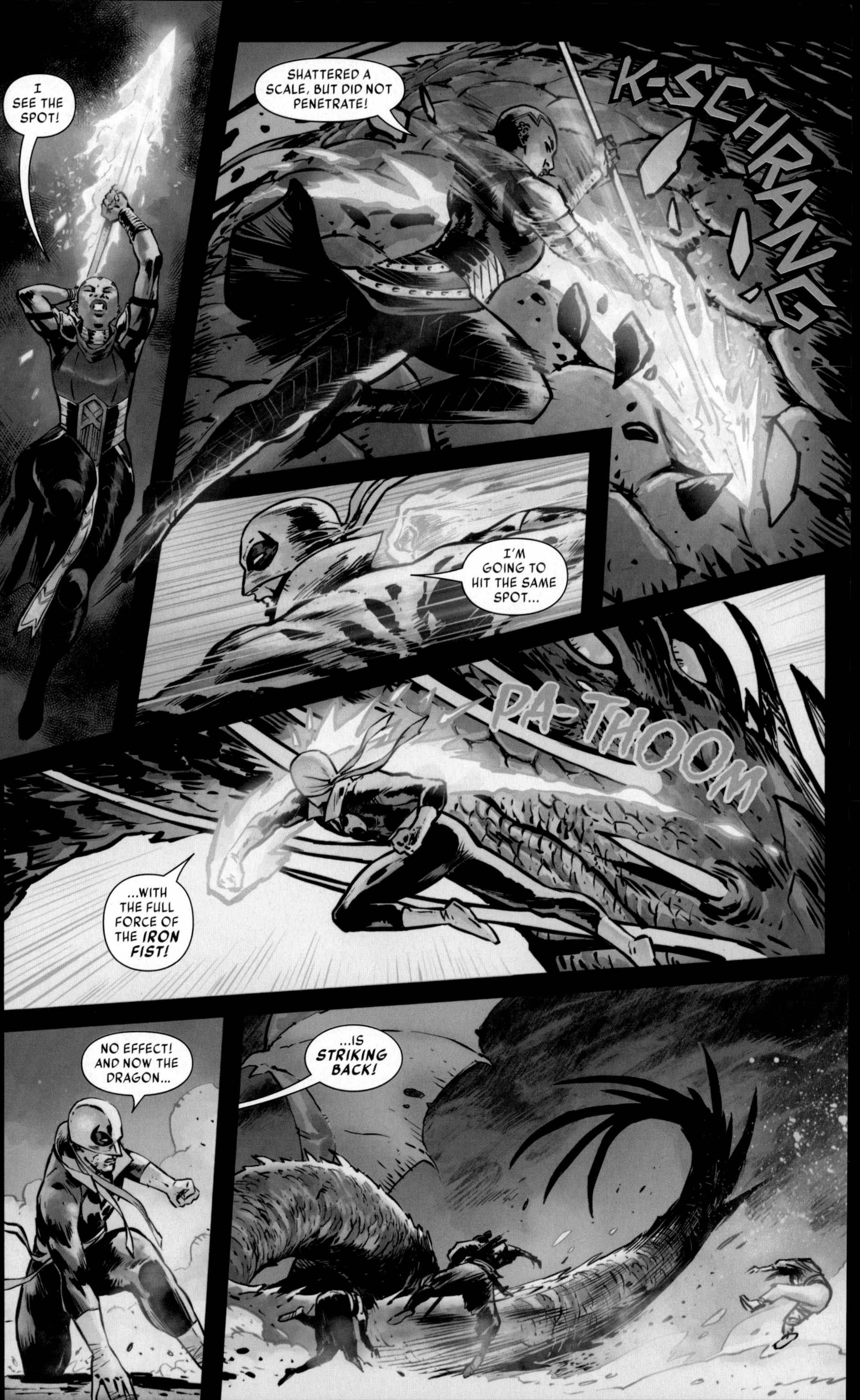
I SEE THE SPOT!
SHATTERED A SCALE, BUT DID NOT PENETRATE!
K-SCHRANG
I'M GOING TO HIT THE SAME SPOT...
PA-THOOM
...WITH THE FULL FORCE OF THE IRON FIST!
NO EFFECT! AND NOW THE DRAGON...
...IS STRIKING BACK!

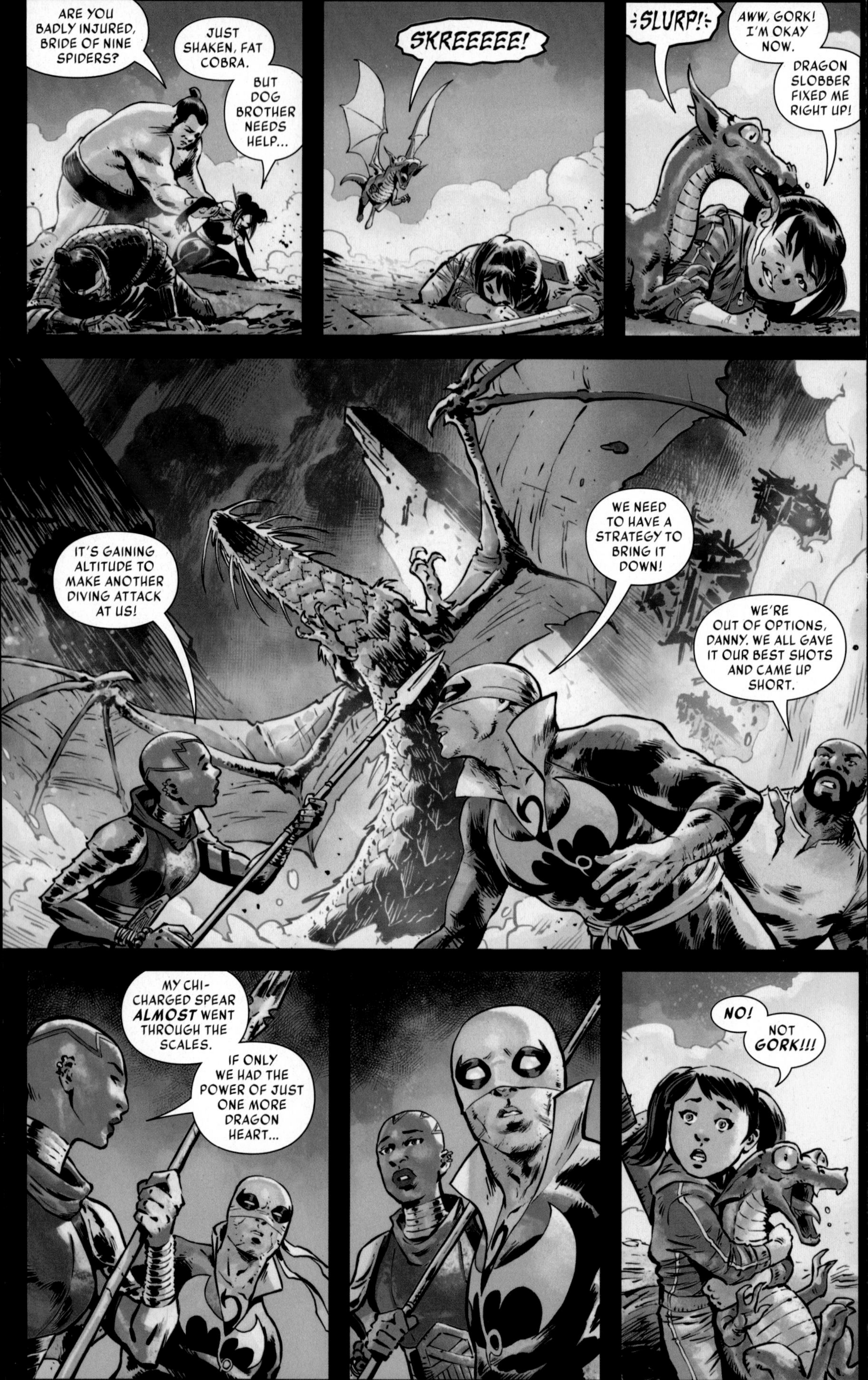

ARE YOU BADLY INJURED, BRIDE OF NINE SPIDERS?
JUST SHAKEN, FAT COBRA.
BUT DOG BROTHER NEEDS HELP...
SKREEEEEE!
SLURP!
AWW, GORK! I'M OKAY NOW.
DRAGON SLOBBER FIXED ME RIGHT UP!
IT'S GAINING ALTITUDE TO MAKE ANOTHER DIVING ATTACK AT US!
WE NEED TO HAVE A STRATEGY TO BRING IT DOWN!
WE'RE OUT OF OPTIONS, DANNY. WE ALL GAVE IT OUR BEST SHOTS AND CAME UP SHORT.
MY CHI-CHARGED SPEAR **ALMOST** WENT THROUGH THE SCALES.
IF ONLY WE HAD THE POWER OF JUST ONE MORE DRAGON HEART...
**NO!**
NOT **GORK!!!**

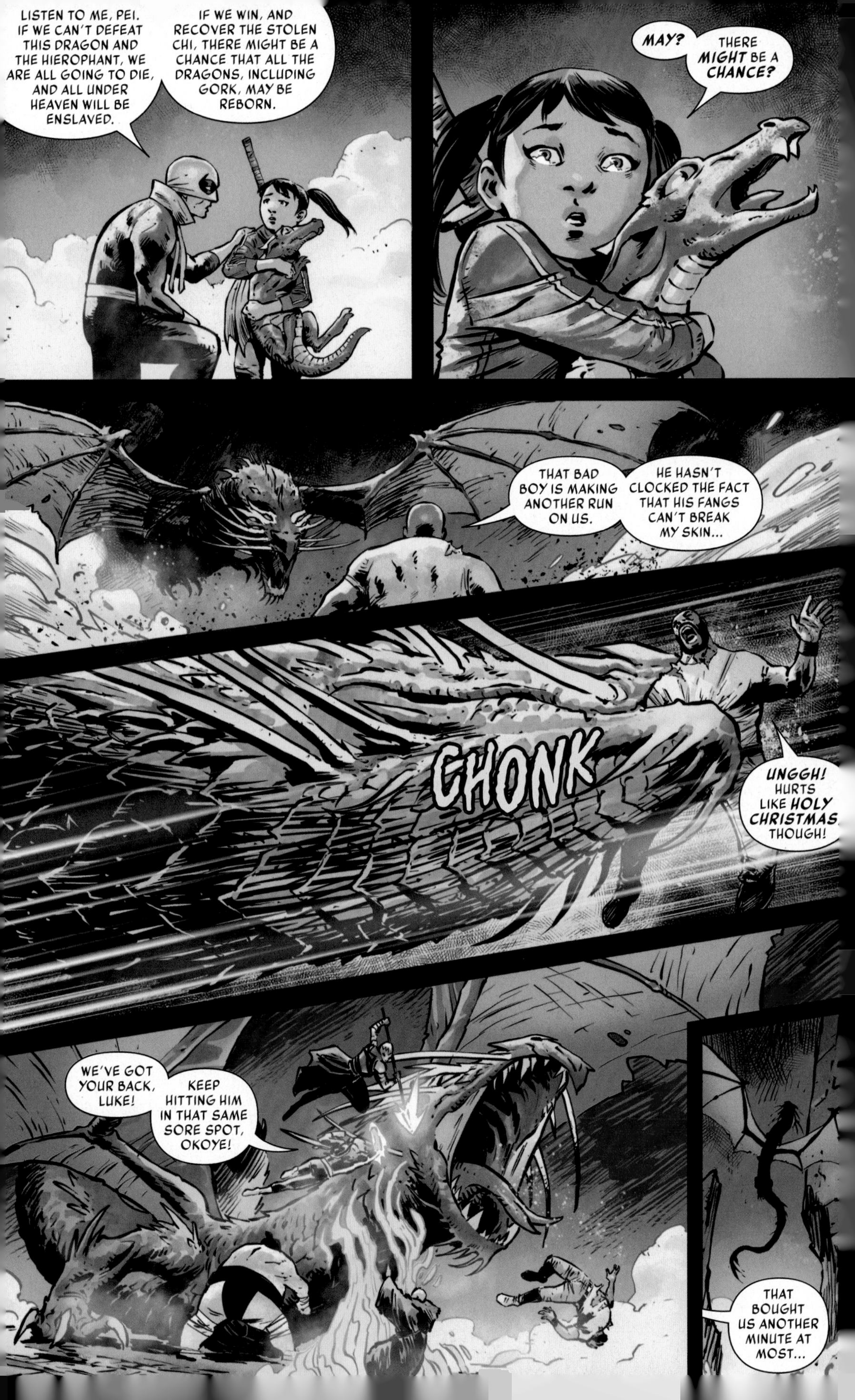
LISTEN TO ME, PEI. IF WE CAN'T DEFEAT THIS DRAGON AND THE HIEROPHANT, WE ARE ALL GOING TO DIE, AND ALL UNDER HEAVEN WILL BE ENSLAVED.
IF WE WIN, AND RECOVER THE STOLEN CHI, THERE MIGHT BE A CHANCE THAT ALL THE DRAGONS, INCLUDING GORK, MAY BE REBORN.
MAY?
THERE MIGHT BE A CHANCE?
THAT BAD BOY IS MAKING ANOTHER RUN ON US.
HE HASN'T CLOCKED THE FACT THAT HIS FANGS CAN'T BREAK MY SKIN...
CHONK
UNGGH! HURTS LIKE HOLY CHRISTMAS THOUGH!
WE'VE GOT YOUR BACK, LUKE!
KEEP HITTING HIM IN THAT SAME SORE SPOT, OKOYE!
THAT BOUGHT US ANOTHER MINUTE AT MOST...

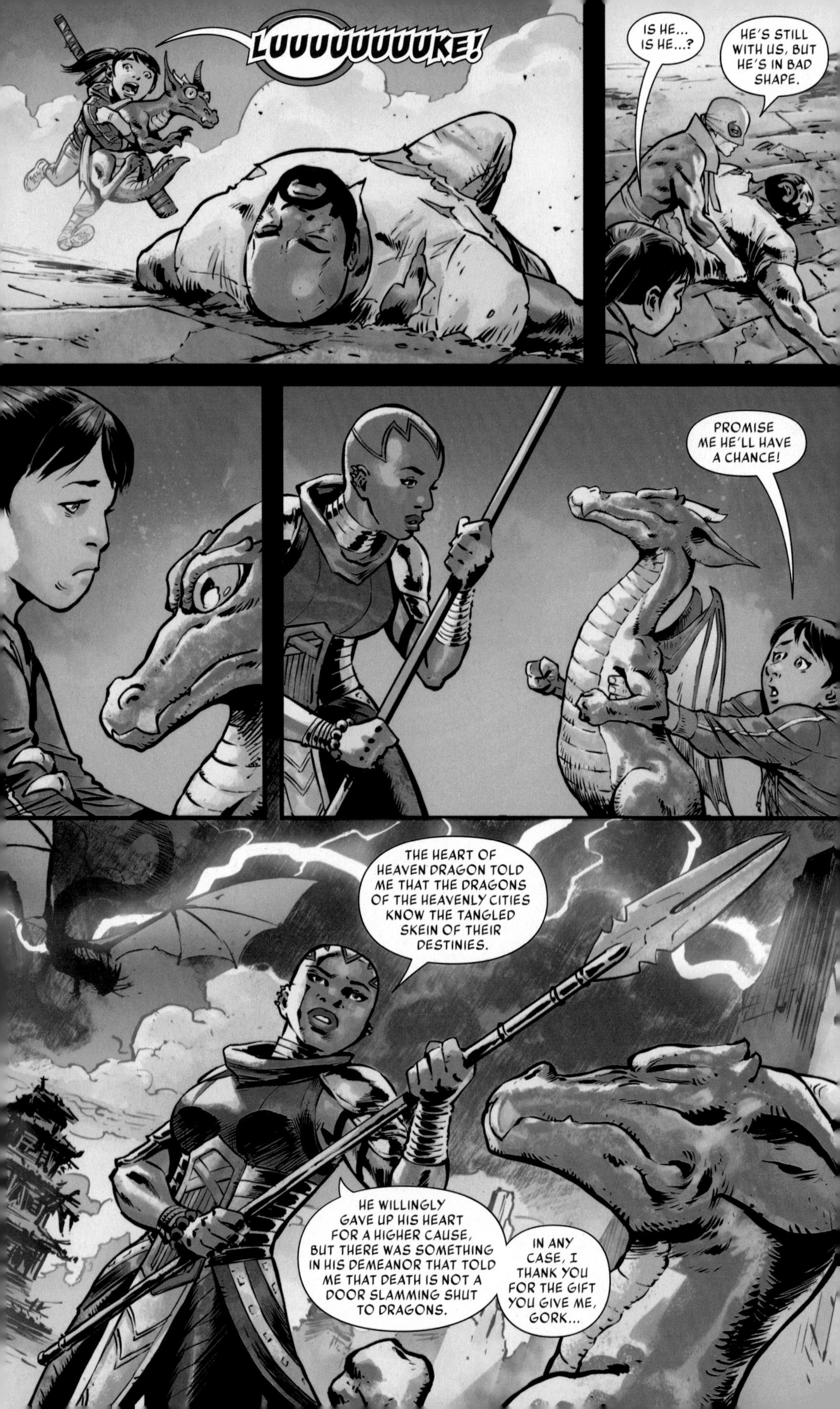
LUUUUUUUUKE!
IS HE... IS HE...?
HE'S STILL WITH US, BUT HE'S IN BAD SHAPE.
PROMISE ME HE'LL HAVE A CHANCE!
THE HEART OF HEAVEN DRAGON TOLD ME THAT THE DRAGONS OF THE HEAVENLY CITIES KNOW THE TANGLED SKEIN OF THEIR DESTINIES.
HE WILLINGLY GAVE UP HIS HEART FOR A HIGHER CAUSE, BUT THERE WAS SOMETHING IN HIS DEMEANOR THAT TOLD ME THAT DEATH IS NOT A DOOR SLAMMING SHUT TO DRAGONS.
IN ANY CASE, I THANK YOU FOR THE GIFT YOU GIVE ME, GORK...

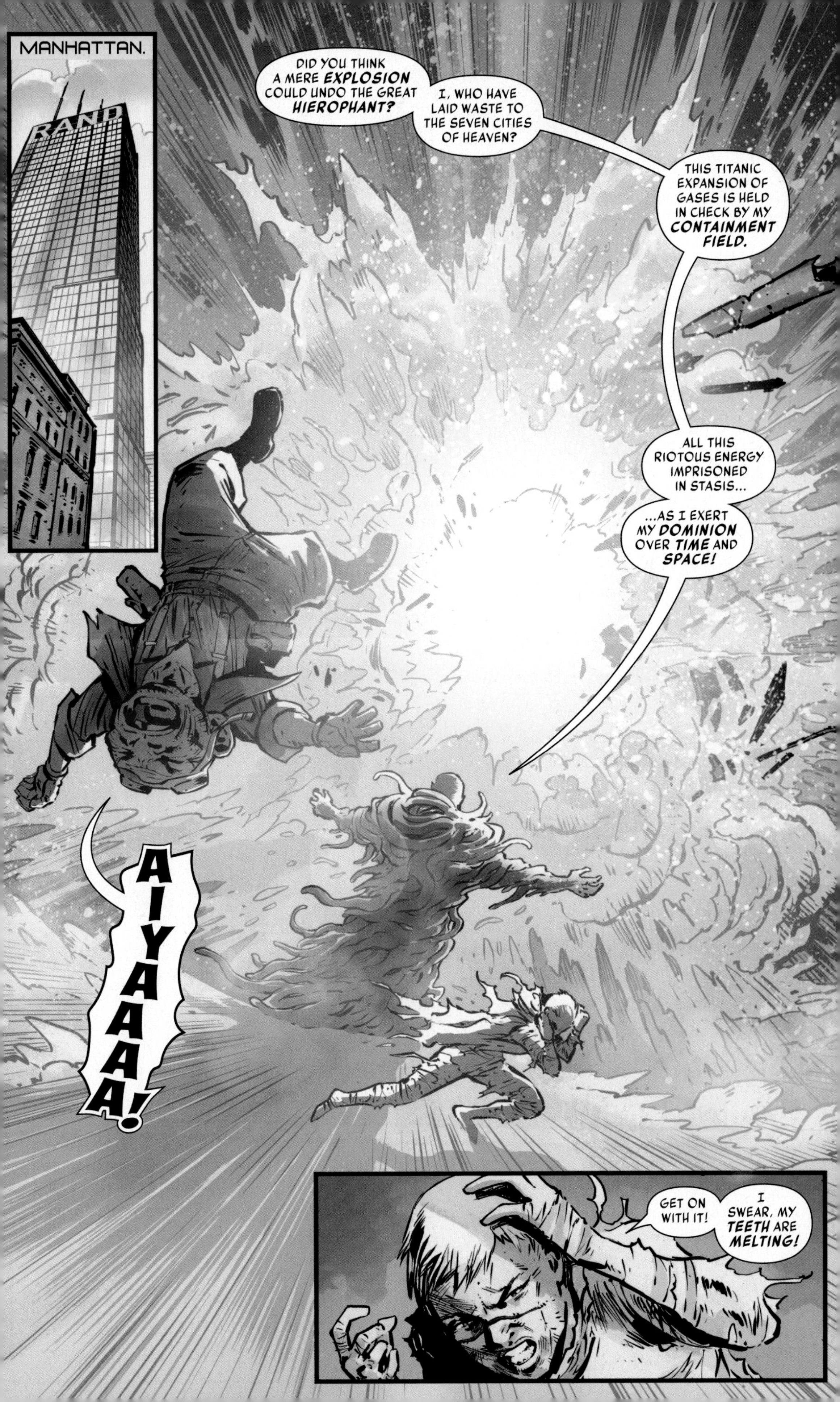

MANHATTAN.
RAND
DID YOU THINK A MERE EXPLOSION COULD UNDO THE GREAT HIEROPHANT?
I, WHO HAVE LAID WASTE TO THE SEVEN CITIES OF HEAVEN?
THIS TITANIC EXPANSION OF GASES IS HELD IN CHECK BY MY CONTAINMENT FIELD.
ALL THIS RIOTOUS ENERGY IMPRISONED IN STASIS...
...AS I EXERT MY DOMINION OVER TIME AND SPACE!
AIYAAAAA!
GET ON WITH IT!
I SWEAR, MY TEETH ARE MELTING!

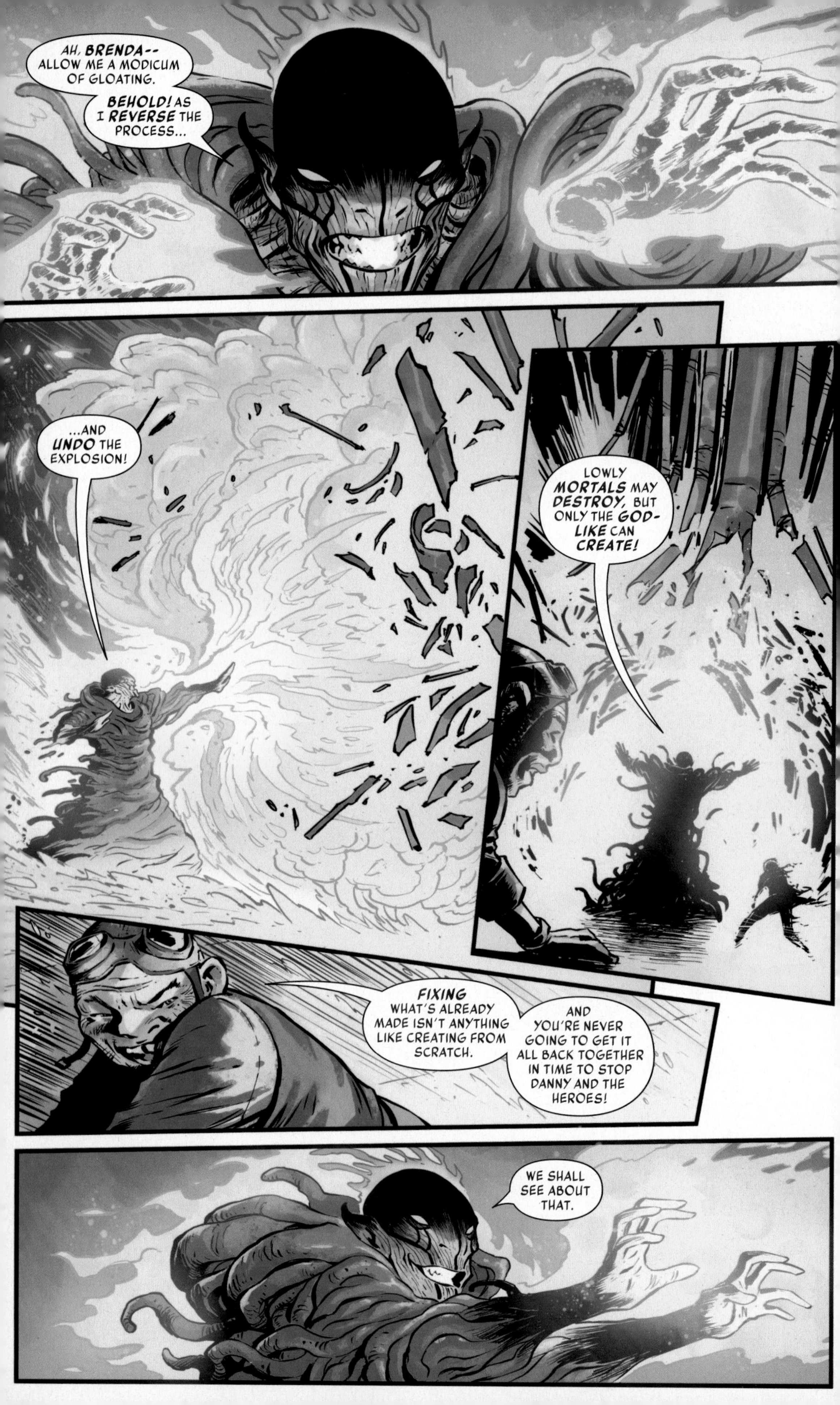

AH, BRENDA-- ALLOW ME A MODICUM OF GLOATING.
BEHOLD! AS I REVERSE THE PROCESS...
...AND UNDO THE EXPLOSION!
LOWLY MORTALS MAY DESTROY, BUT ONLY THE GOD-LIKE CAN CREATE!
FIXING WHAT'S ALREADY MADE ISN'T ANYTHING LIKE CREATING FROM SCRATCH.
AND YOU'RE NEVER GOING TO GET IT ALL BACK TOGETHER IN TIME TO STOP DANNY AND THE HEROES!
WE SHALL SEE ABOUT THAT.

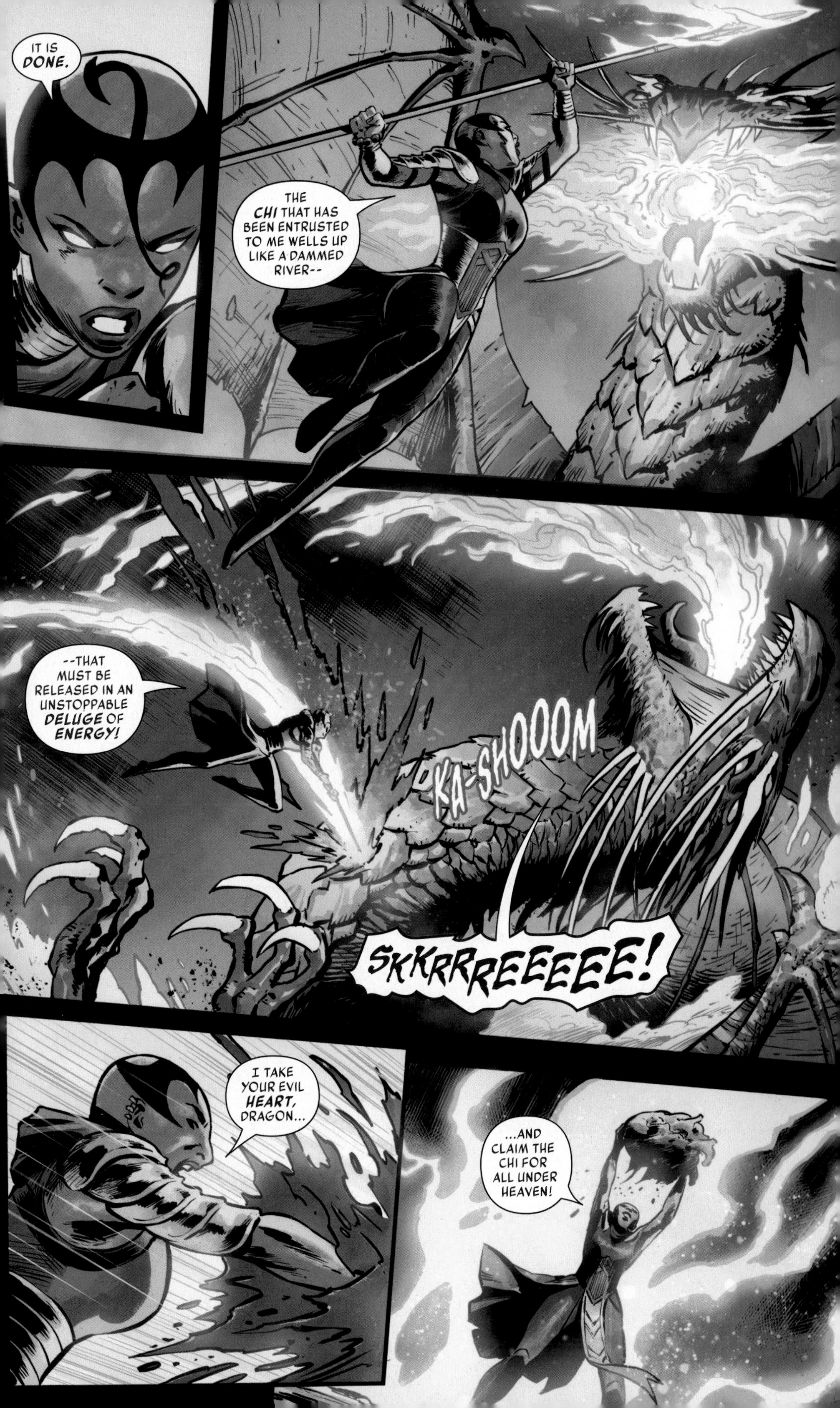
IT IS DONE.
THE CHI THAT HAS BEEN ENTRUSTED TO ME WELLS UP LIKE A DAMMED RIVER--
--THAT MUST BE RELEASED IN AN UNSTOPPABLE DELUGE OF ENERGY!
KA-SHOOOM
SKKRRREEEEEE!
I TAKE YOUR EVIL HEART, DRAGON...
...AND CLAIM THE CHI FOR ALL UNDER HEAVEN!

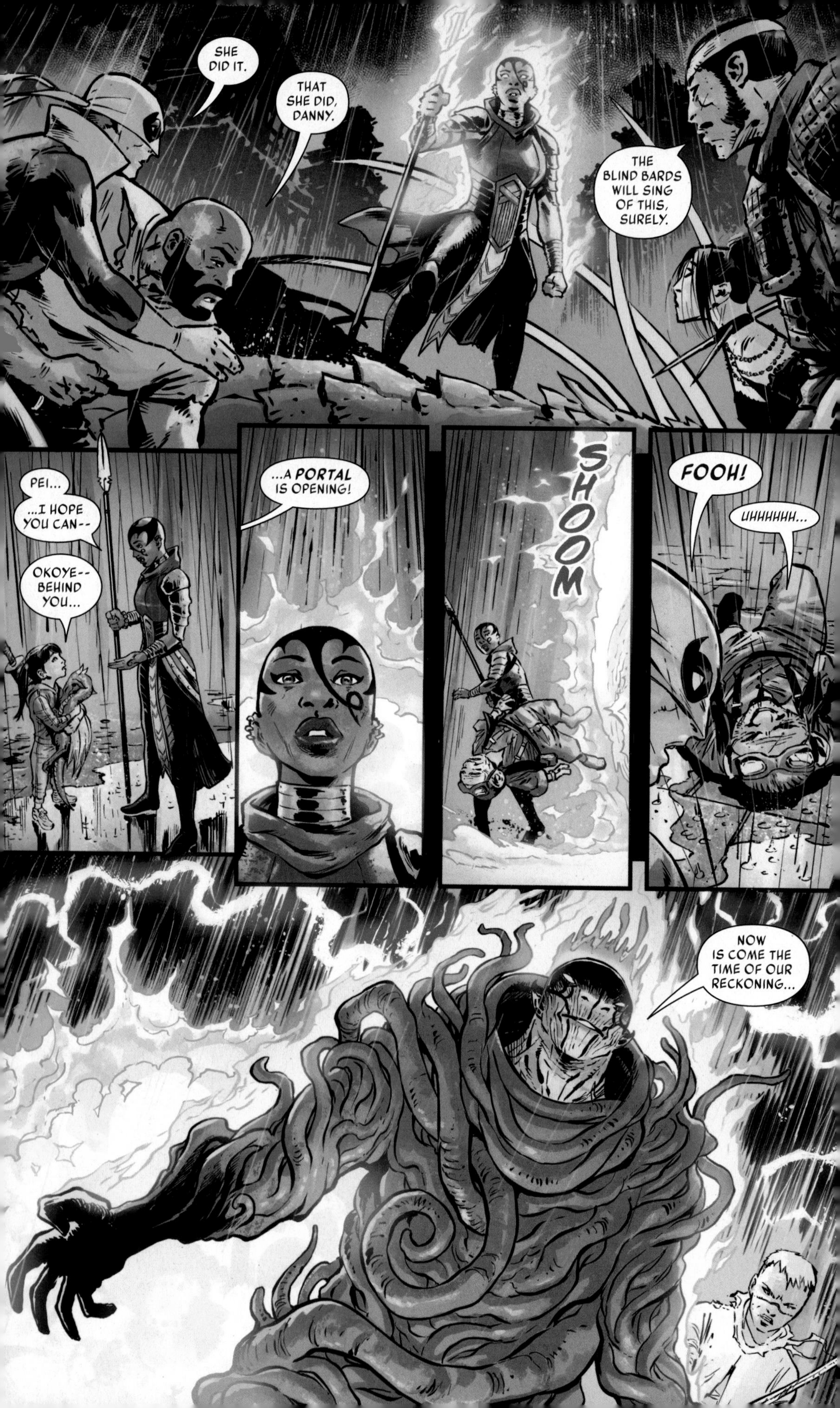

SHE DID IT.
THAT SHE DID, DANNY.
THE BLIND BARDS WILL SING OF THIS, SURELY.
PEI...
...I HOPE YOU CAN--
OKOYE--BEHIND YOU...
...A PORTAL IS OPENING!
SHOOM
FOOH!
UHHHHHH...
NOW IS COME THE TIME OF OUR RECKONING...

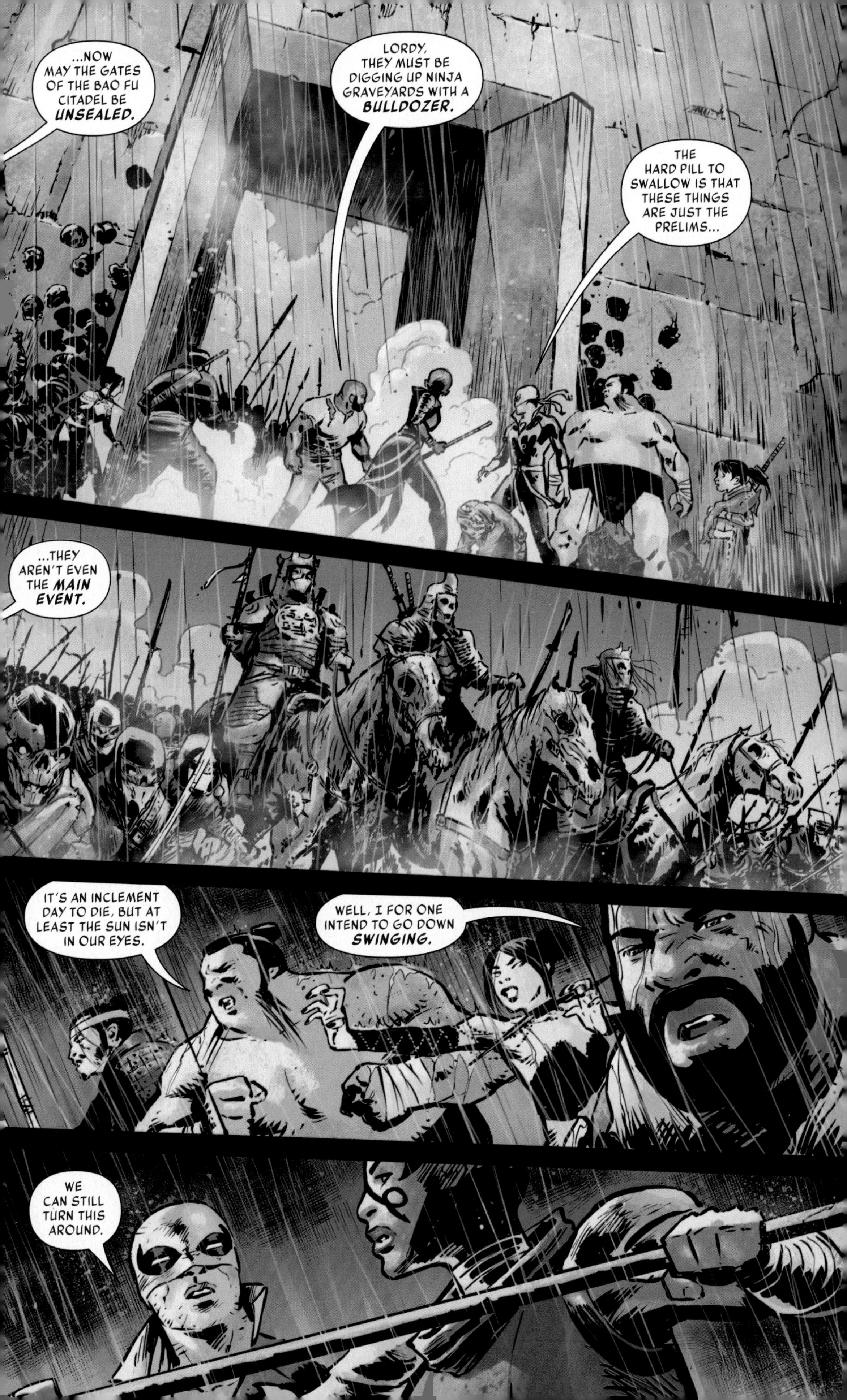
...NOW MAY THE GATES OF THE BAO FU CITADEL BE UNSEALED.
LORDY, THEY MUST BE DIGGING UP NINJA GRAVEYARDS WITH A BULLDOZER.
THE HARD PILL TO SWALLOW IS THAT THESE THINGS ARE JUST THE PRELIMS...
...THEY AREN'T EVEN THE MAIN EVENT.
IT'S AN INCLEMENT DAY TO DIE, BUT AT LEAST THE SUN ISN'T IN OUR EYES.
WELL, I FOR ONE INTEND TO GO DOWN SWINGING.
WE CAN STILL TURN THIS AROUND.

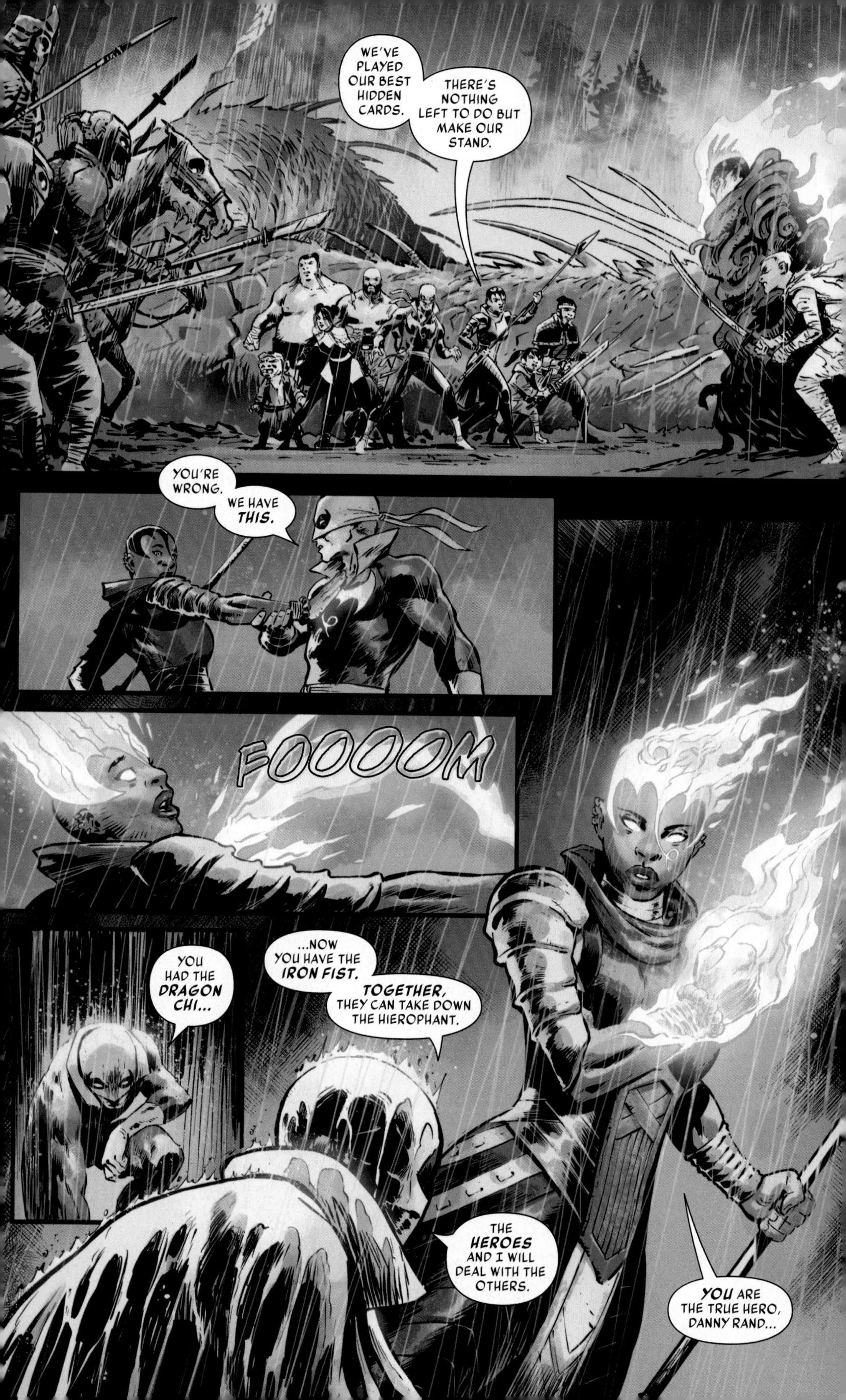
WE'VE PLAYED OUR BEST HIDDEN CARDS.
THERE'S NOTHING LEFT TO DO BUT MAKE OUR STAND.
YOU'RE WRONG.
WE HAVE THIS.
FOOOOM
YOU HAD THE DRAGON CHI...
...NOW YOU HAVE THE IRON FIST.
TOGETHER, THEY CAN TAKE DOWN THE HIEROPHANT.
THE HEROES AND I WILL DEAL WITH THE OTHERS.
YOU ARE THE TRUE HERO, DANNY RAND...

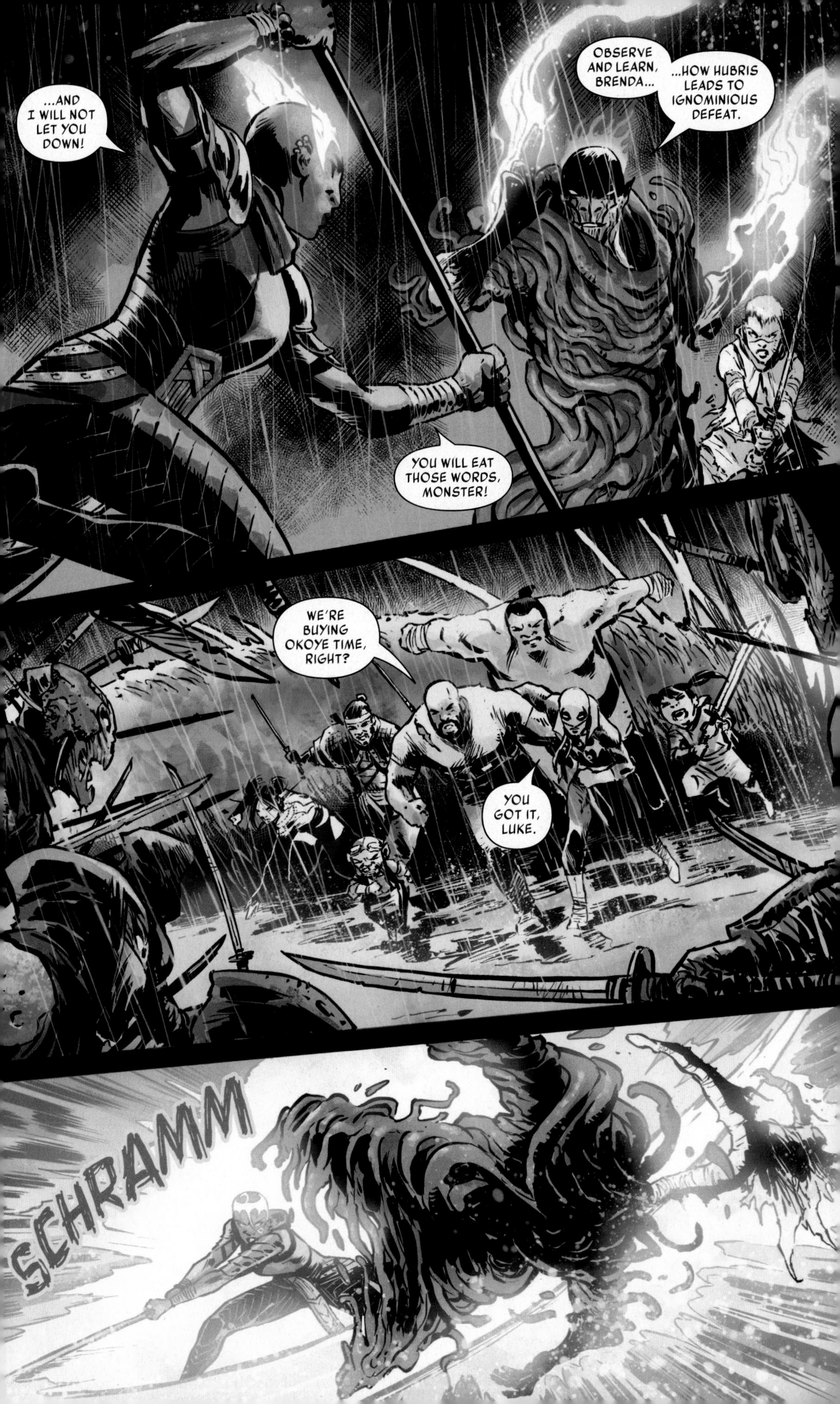
...AND I WILL NOT LET YOU DOWN!
OBSERVE AND LEARN, BRENDA...
...HOW HUBRIS LEADS TO IGNOMINIOUS DEFEAT.
YOU WILL EAT THOSE WORDS, MONSTER!
WE'RE BUYING OKOYE TIME, RIGHT?
YOU GOT IT, LUKE.
SCHRAMM

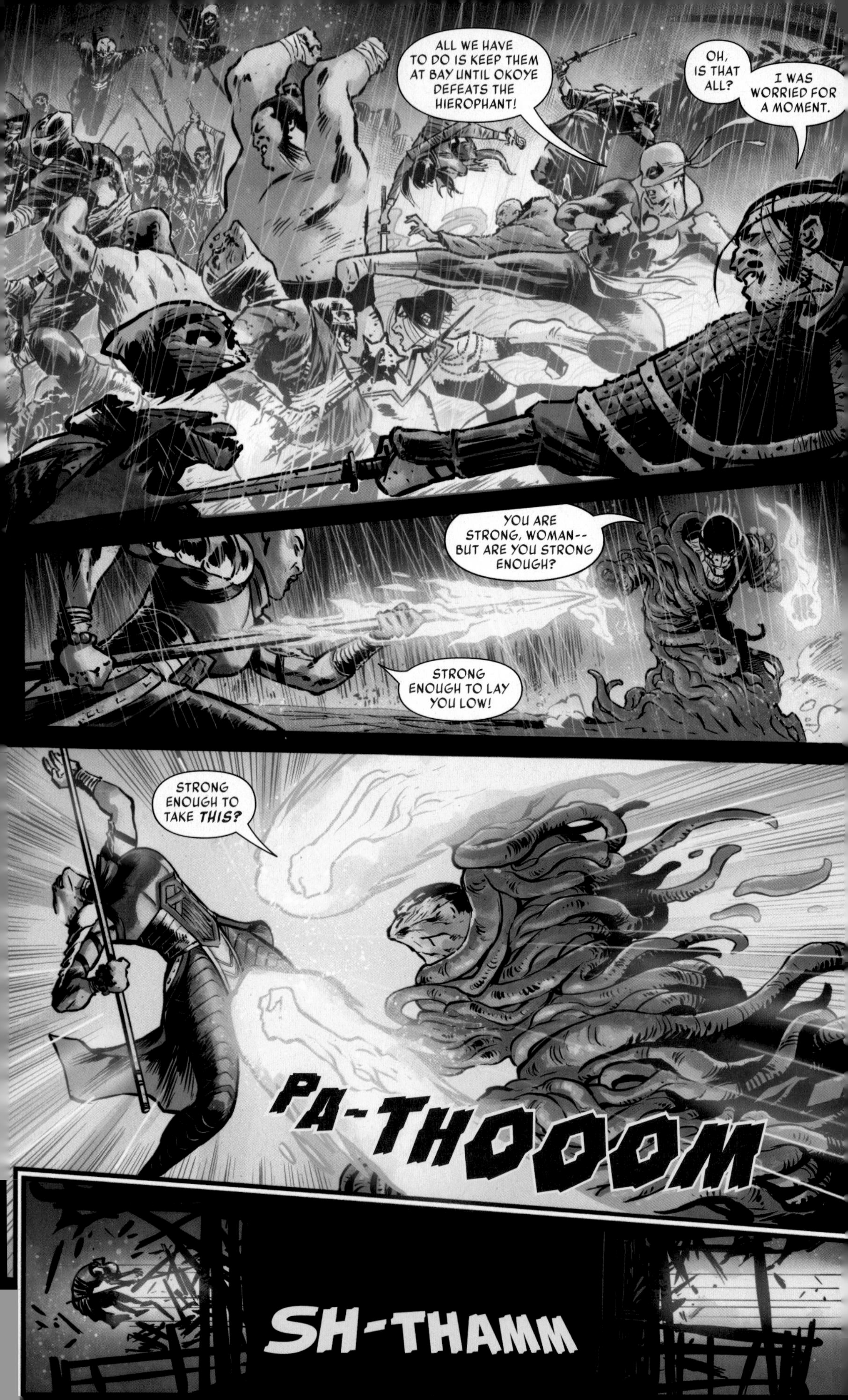
ALL WE HAVE TO DO IS KEEP THEM AT BAY UNTIL OKOYE DEFEATS THE HIEROPHANT!
OH, IS THAT ALL?
I WAS WORRIED FOR A MOMENT.
YOU ARE STRONG, WOMAN-- BUT ARE YOU STRONG ENOUGH?
STRONG ENOUGH TO LAY YOU LOW!
STRONG ENOUGH TO TAKE THIS?
PA-THOOOM
SH-THAMM

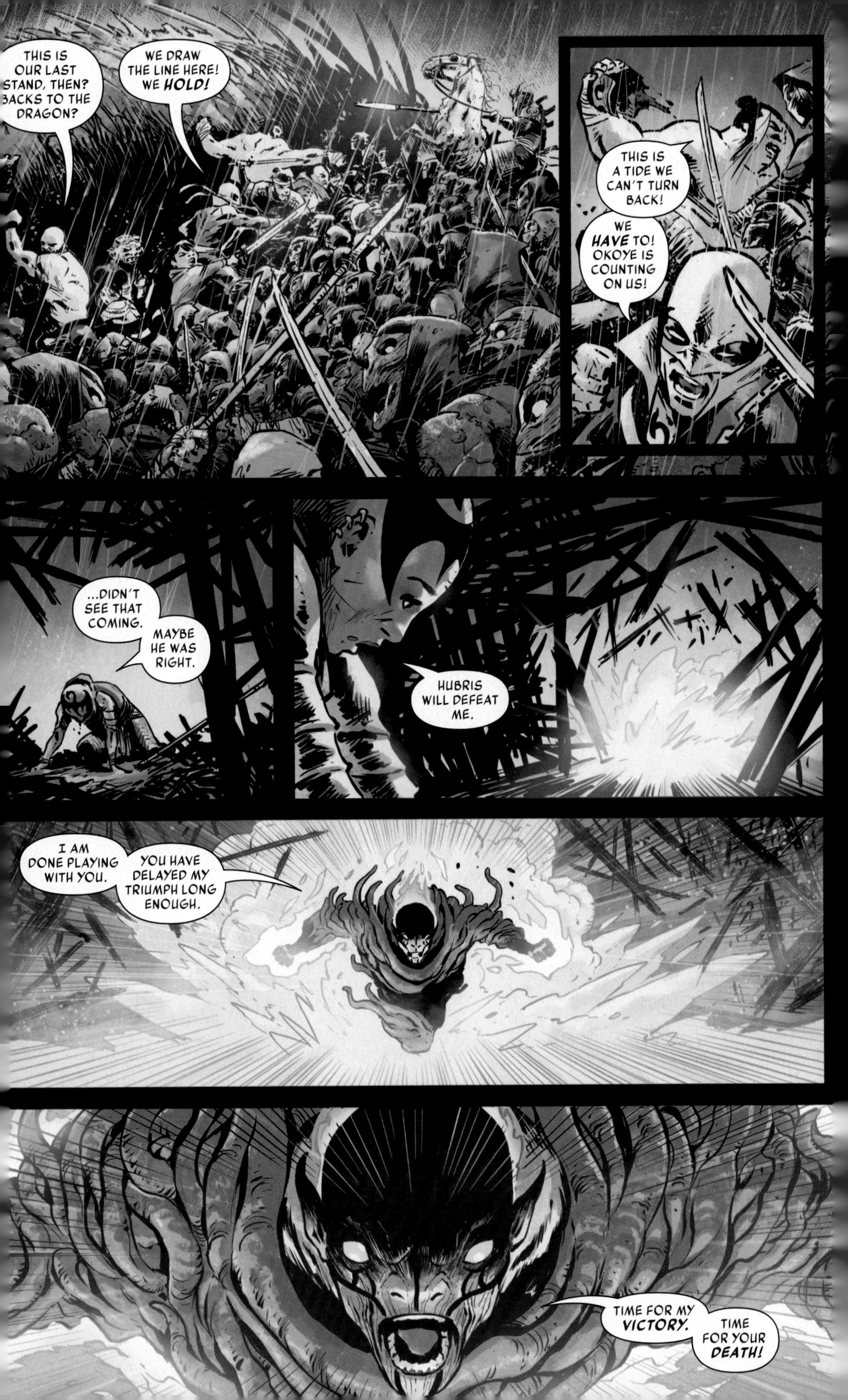
THIS IS OUR LAST STAND, THEN? BACKS TO THE DRAGON?
WE DRAW THE LINE HERE! WE HOLD!
THIS IS A TIDE WE CAN'T TURN BACK!
WE HAVE TO! OKOYE IS COUNTING ON US!
...DIDN'T SEE THAT COMING.
MAYBE HE WAS RIGHT.
HUBRIS WILL DEFEAT ME.
I AM DONE PLAYING WITH YOU.
YOU HAVE DELAYED MY TRIUMPH LONG ENOUGH.
TIME FOR MY VICTORY.
TIME FOR YOUR DEATH!

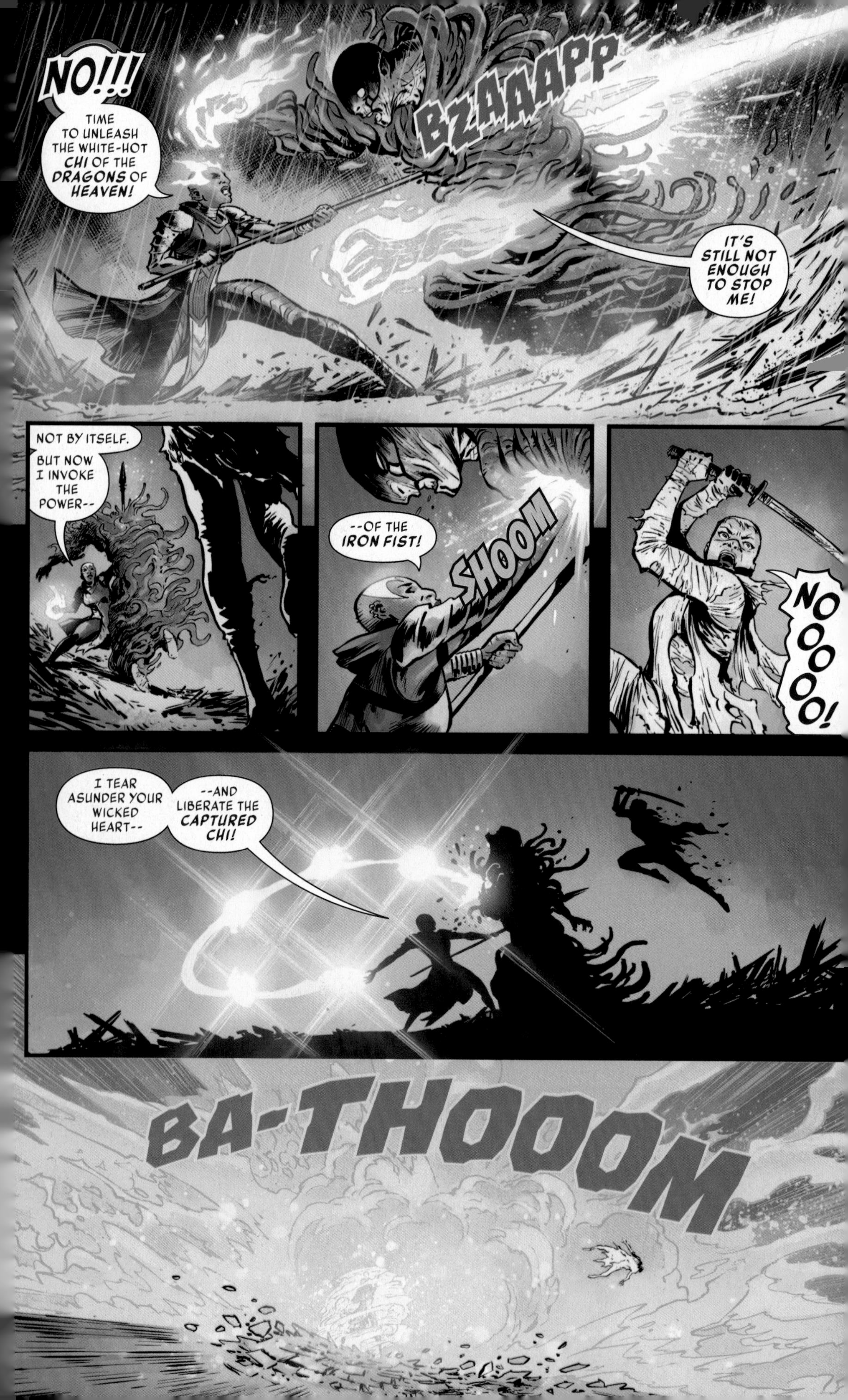
NO!!!
TIME TO UNLEASH THE WHITE-HOT CHI OF THE DRAGONS OF HEAVEN!
BZAAAAPP
IT'S STILL NOT ENOUGH TO STOP ME!
NOT BY ITSELF.
BUT NOW I INVOKE THE POWER--
--OF THE IRON FIST!
SHOOM
NOOOOO!
I TEAR ASUNDER YOUR WICKED HEART--
--AND LIBERATE THE CAPTURED CHI!
BA-THOOOM

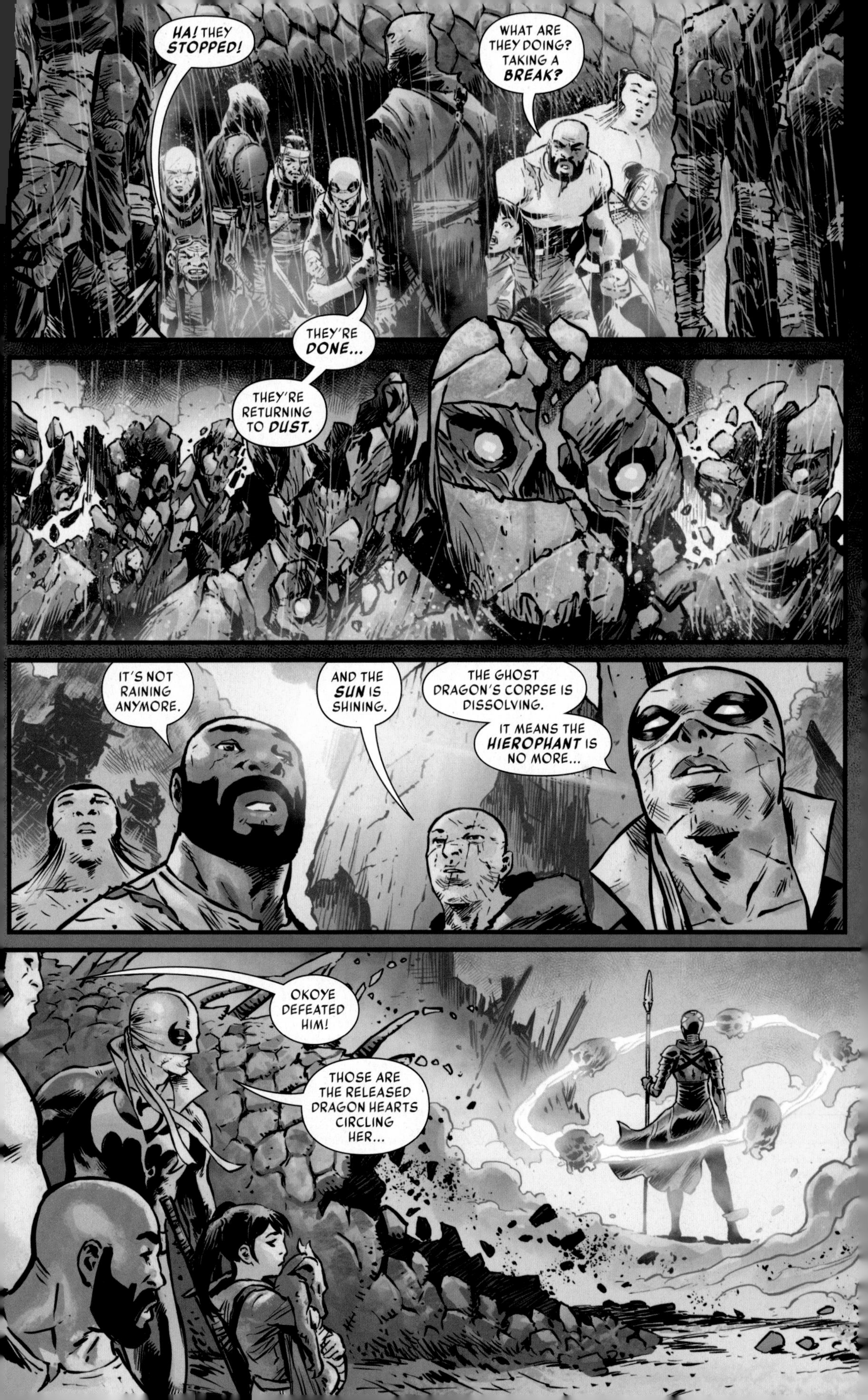
HA! THEY STOPPED!
WHAT ARE THEY DOING? TAKING A BREAK?
THEY'RE DONE...
THEY'RE RETURNING TO DUST.
IT'S NOT RAINING ANYMORE.
AND THE SUN IS SHINING.
THE GHOST DRAGON'S CORPSE IS DISSOLVING.
IT MEANS THE HIEROPHANT IS NO MORE...
OKOYE DEFEATED HIM!
THOSE ARE THE RELEASED DRAGON HEARTS CIRCLING HER...

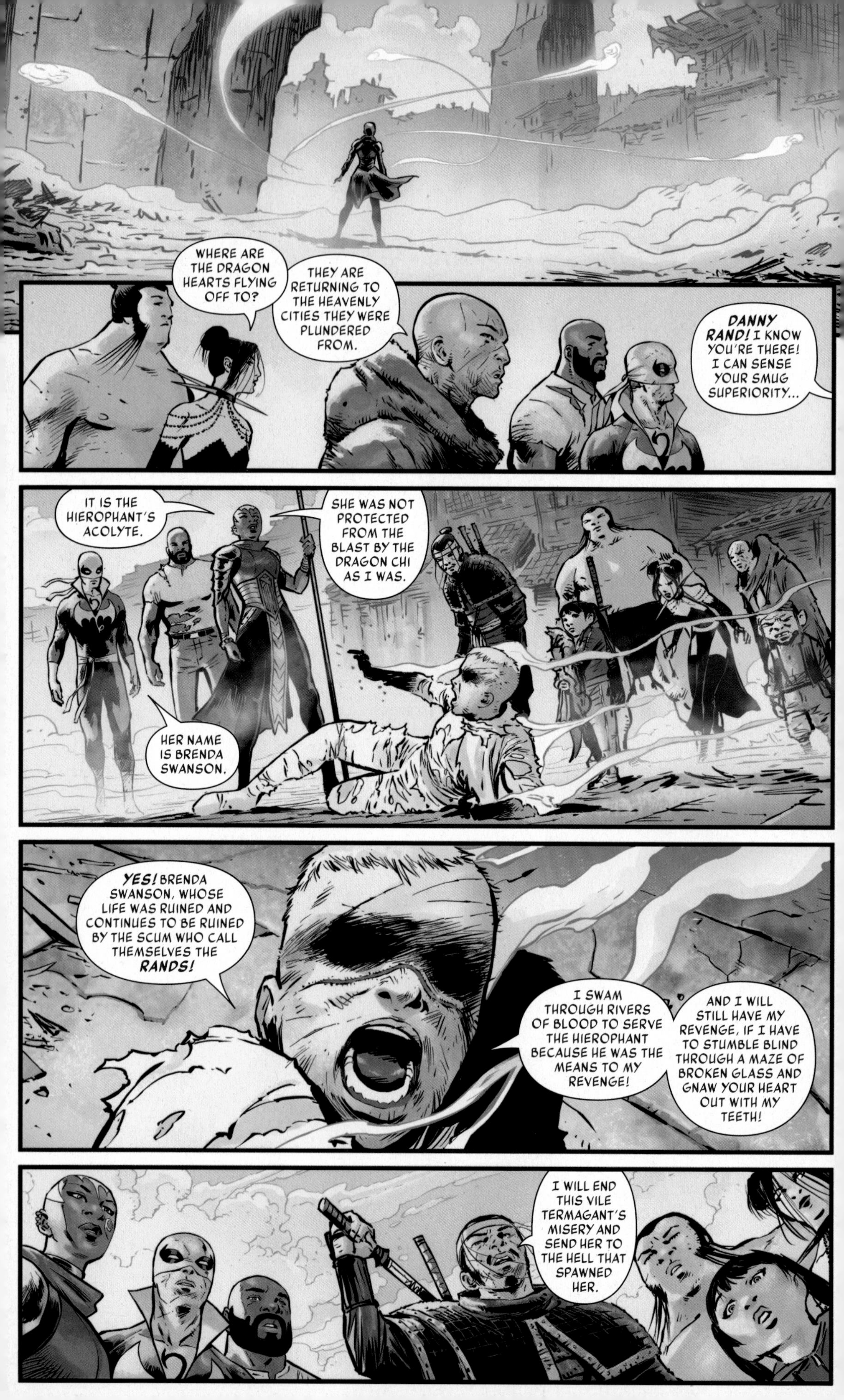
WHERE ARE THE DRAGON HEARTS FLYING OFF TO?
THEY ARE RETURNING TO THE HEAVENLY CITIES THEY WERE PLUNDERED FROM.
DANNY RAND! I KNOW YOU'RE THERE! I CAN SENSE YOUR SMUG SUPERIORITY...
IT IS THE HIEROPHANT'S ACOLYTE.
SHE WAS NOT PROTECTED FROM THE BLAST BY THE DRAGON CHI AS I WAS.
HER NAME IS BRENDA SWANSON.
YES! BRENDA SWANSON, WHOSE LIFE WAS RUINED AND CONTINUES TO BE RUINED BY THE SCUM WHO CALL THEMSELVES THE RANDS!
I SWAM THROUGH RIVERS OF BLOOD TO SERVE THE HIEROPHANT BECAUSE HE WAS THE MEANS TO MY REVENGE!
AND I WILL STILL HAVE MY REVENGE, IF I HAVE TO STUMBLE BLIND THROUGH A MAZE OF BROKEN GLASS AND GNAW YOUR HEART OUT WITH MY TEETH!
I WILL END THIS VILE TERMAGANT'S MISERY AND SEND HER TO THE HELL THAT SPAWNED HER.

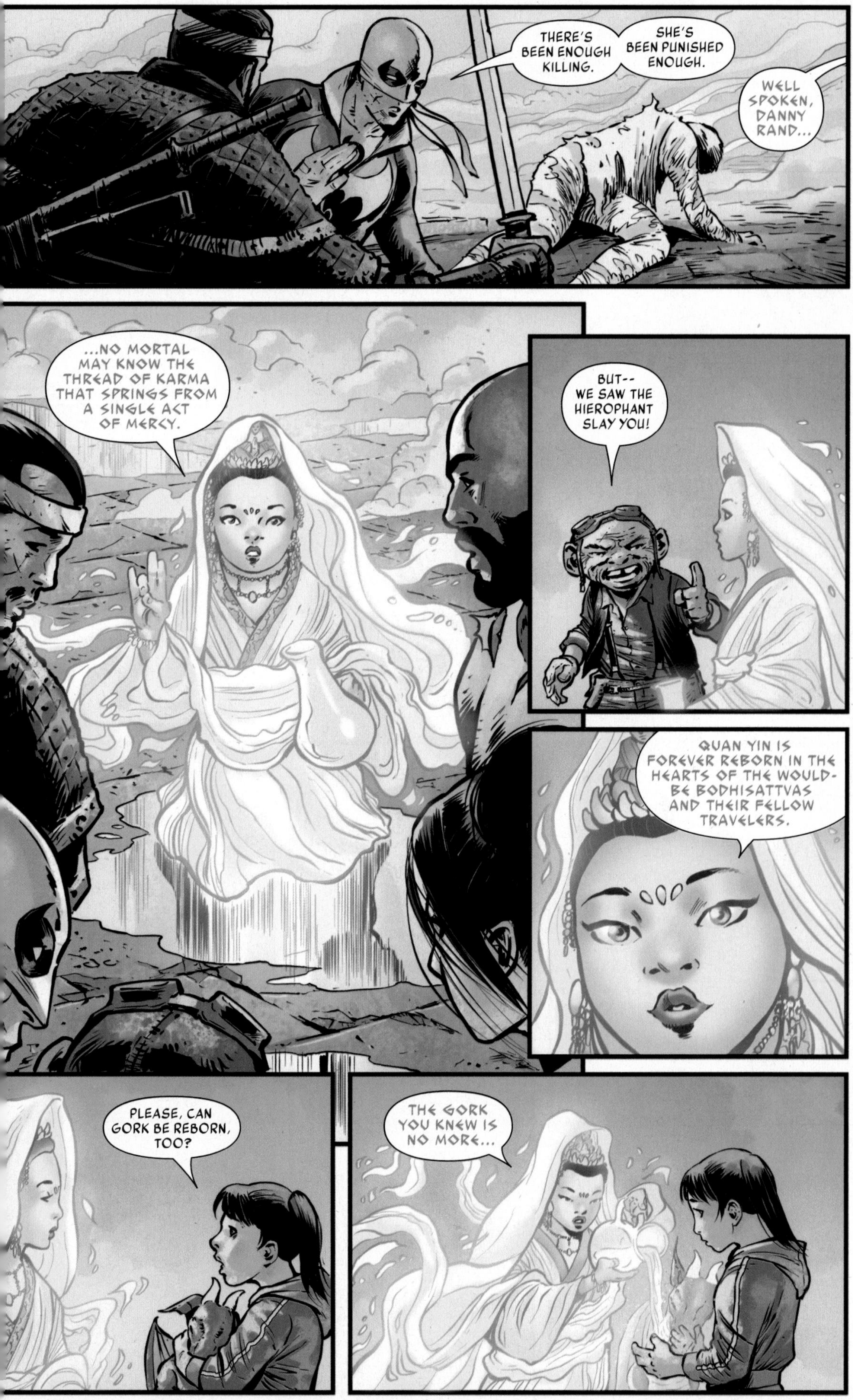
THERE'S BEEN ENOUGH KILLING.
SHE'S BEEN PUNISHED ENOUGH.
WELL SPOKEN, DANNY RAND...
...NO MORTAL MAY KNOW THE THREAD OF KARMA THAT SPRINGS FROM A SINGLE ACT OF MERCY.
BUT-- WE SAW THE HIEROPHANT SLAY YOU!
QUAN YIN IS FOREVER REBORN IN THE HEARTS OF THE WOULD-BE BODHISATTVAS AND THEIR FELLOW TRAVELERS.
PLEASE, CAN GORK BE REBORN, TOO?
THE GORK YOU KNEW IS NO MORE...

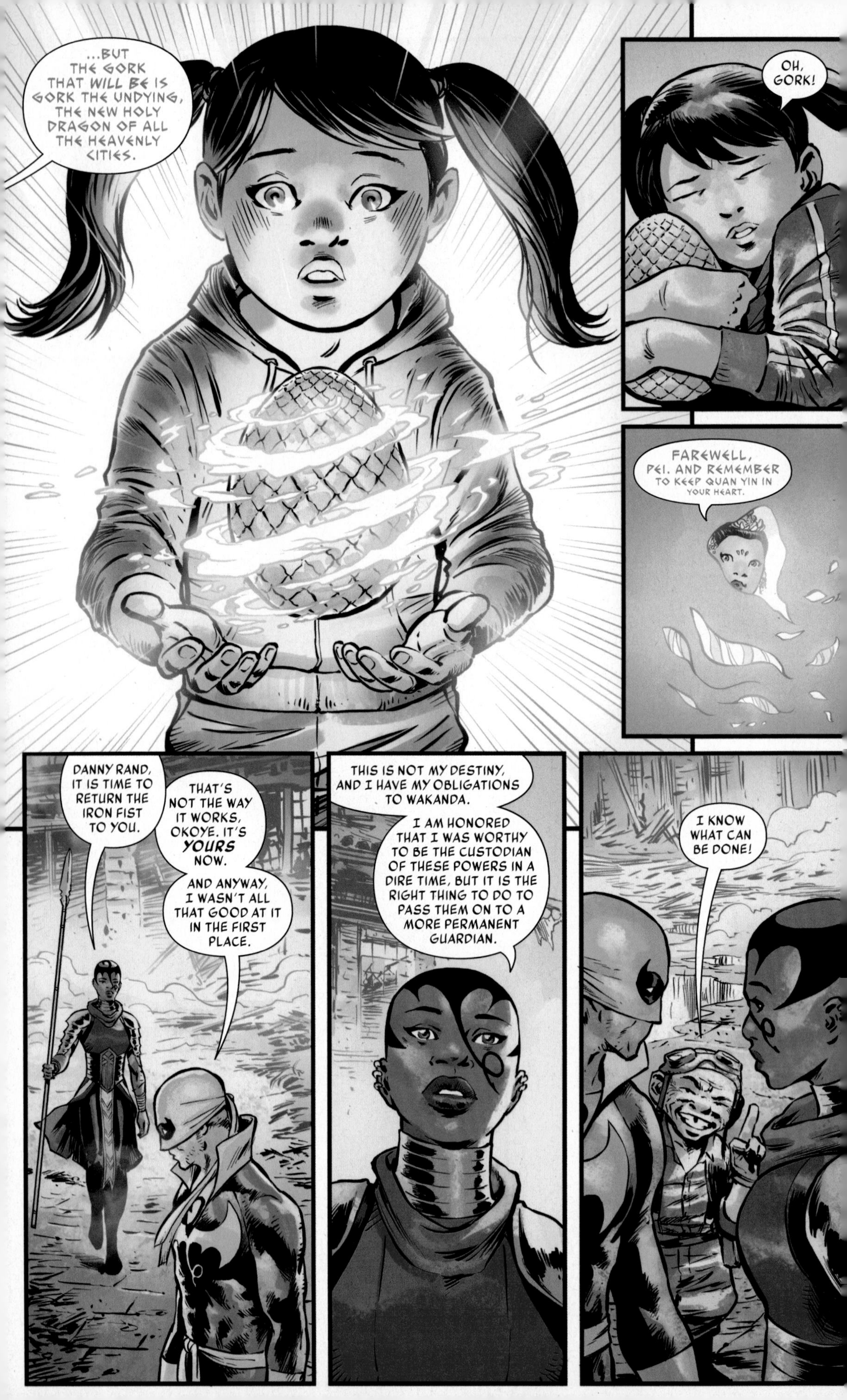
...BUT THE GORK THAT *WILL BE* IS GORK THE UNDYING, THE NEW HOLY DRAGON OF ALL THE HEAVENLY CITIES.
OH, GORK!
FAREWELL, PEI. AND REMEMBER TO KEEP QUAN YIN IN YOUR HEART.
DANNY RAND, IT IS TIME TO RETURN THE IRON FIST TO YOU.
THAT'S NOT THE WAY IT WORKS, OKOYE. IT'S *YOURS* NOW.
AND ANYWAY, I WASN'T ALL THAT GOOD AT IT IN THE FIRST PLACE.
THIS IS NOT MY DESTINY, AND I HAVE MY OBLIGATIONS TO WAKANDA.
I AM HONORED THAT I WAS WORTHY TO BE THE CUSTODIAN OF THESE POWERS IN A DIRE TIME, BUT IT IS THE RIGHT THING TO DO TO PASS THEM ON TO A MORE PERMANENT GUARDIAN.
I KNOW WHAT CAN BE DONE!

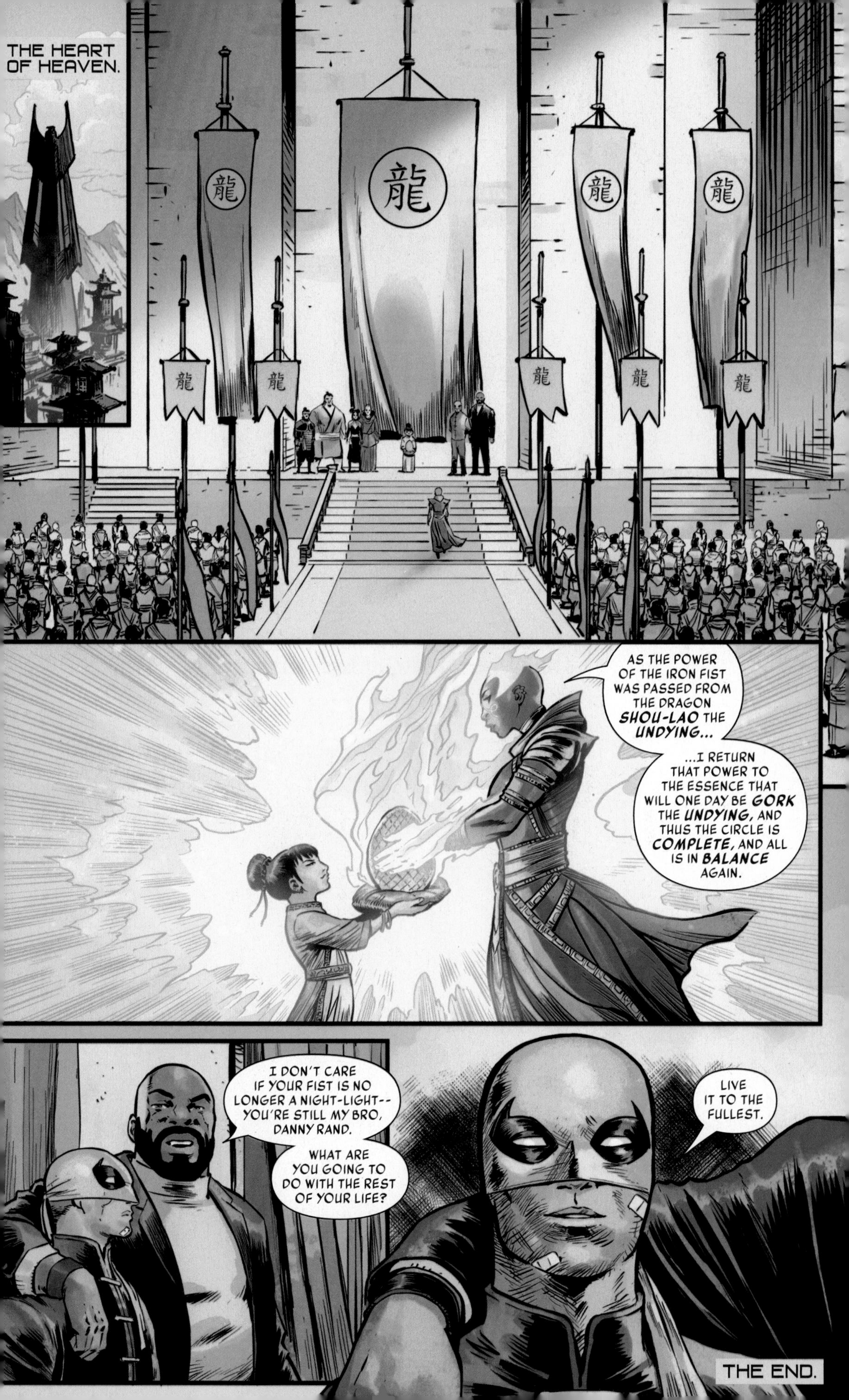
THE HEART OF HEAVEN.
龍
龍
龍
龍
龍
龍
龍
龍
龍
AS THE POWER OF THE IRON FIST WAS PASSED FROM THE DRAGON SHOU-LAO THE UNDYING...
...I RETURN THAT POWER TO THE ESSENCE THAT WILL ONE DAY BE GORK THE UNDYING, AND THUS THE CIRCLE IS COMPLETE, AND ALL IS IN BALANCE AGAIN.
I DON'T CARE IF YOUR FIST IS NO LONGER A NIGHT-LIGHT-- YOU'RE STILL MY BRO, DANNY RAND.
WHAT ARE YOU GOING TO DO WITH THE REST OF YOUR LIFE?
LIVE IT TO THE FULLEST.
THE END.

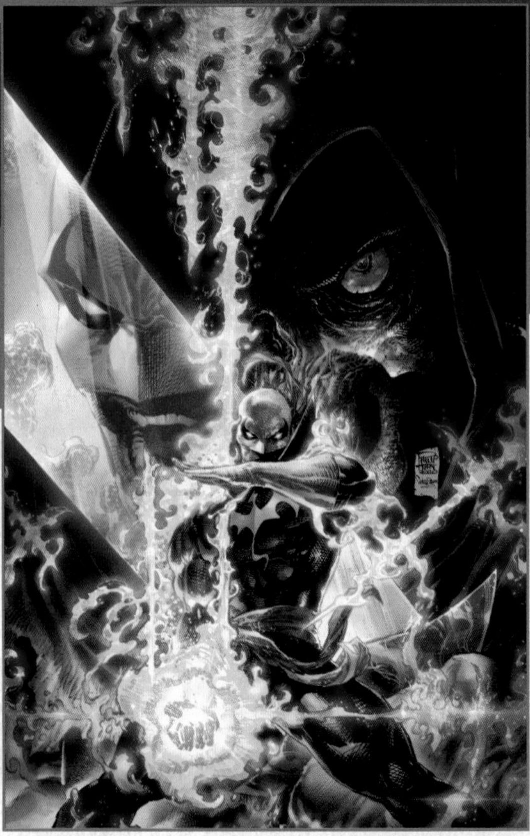

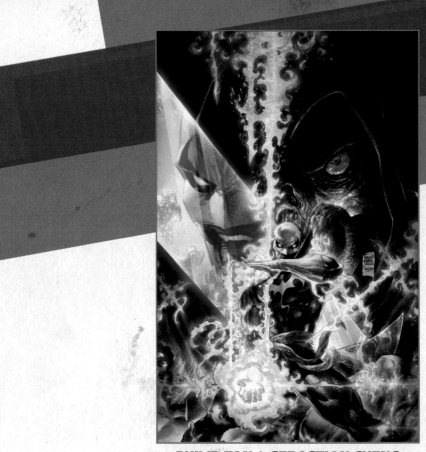

**PHILIP TAN** & **SEBASTIAN CHENG**
*#1 Variant*

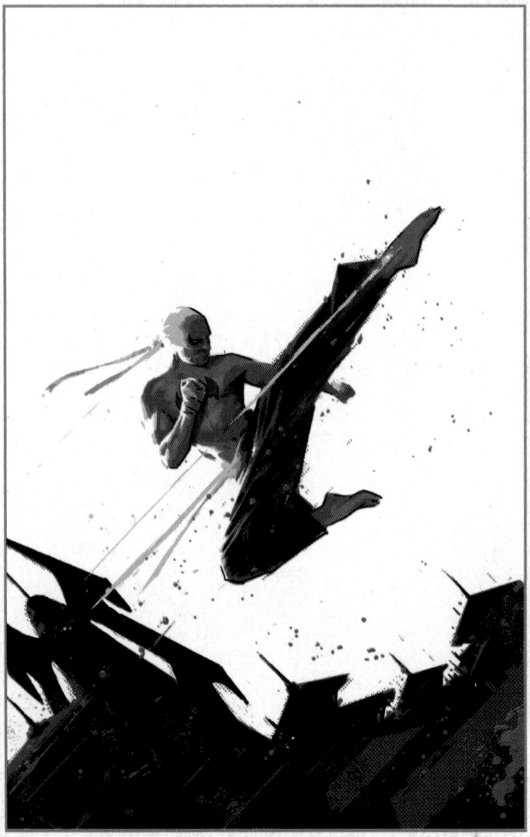

**DAVID AJA**
*#1 Variant*

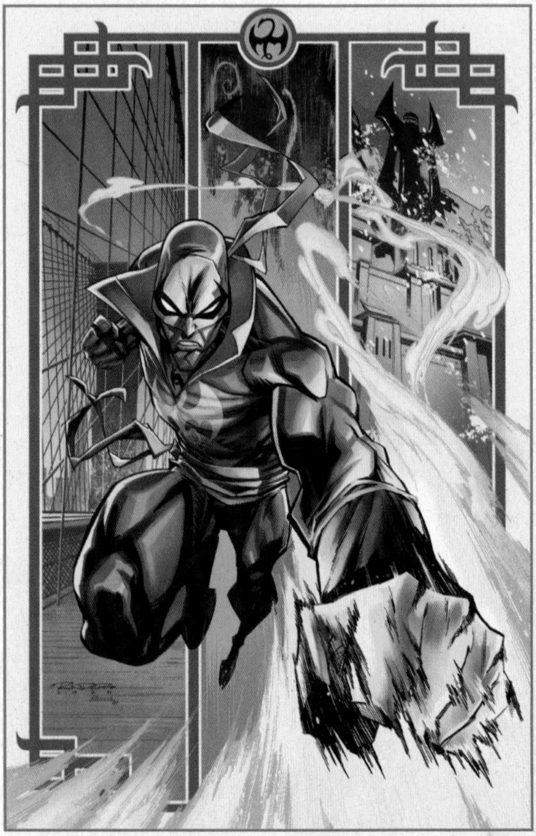

**KHARY RANDOLPH** & **EMILIO LOPEZ**
*#1 Variant*

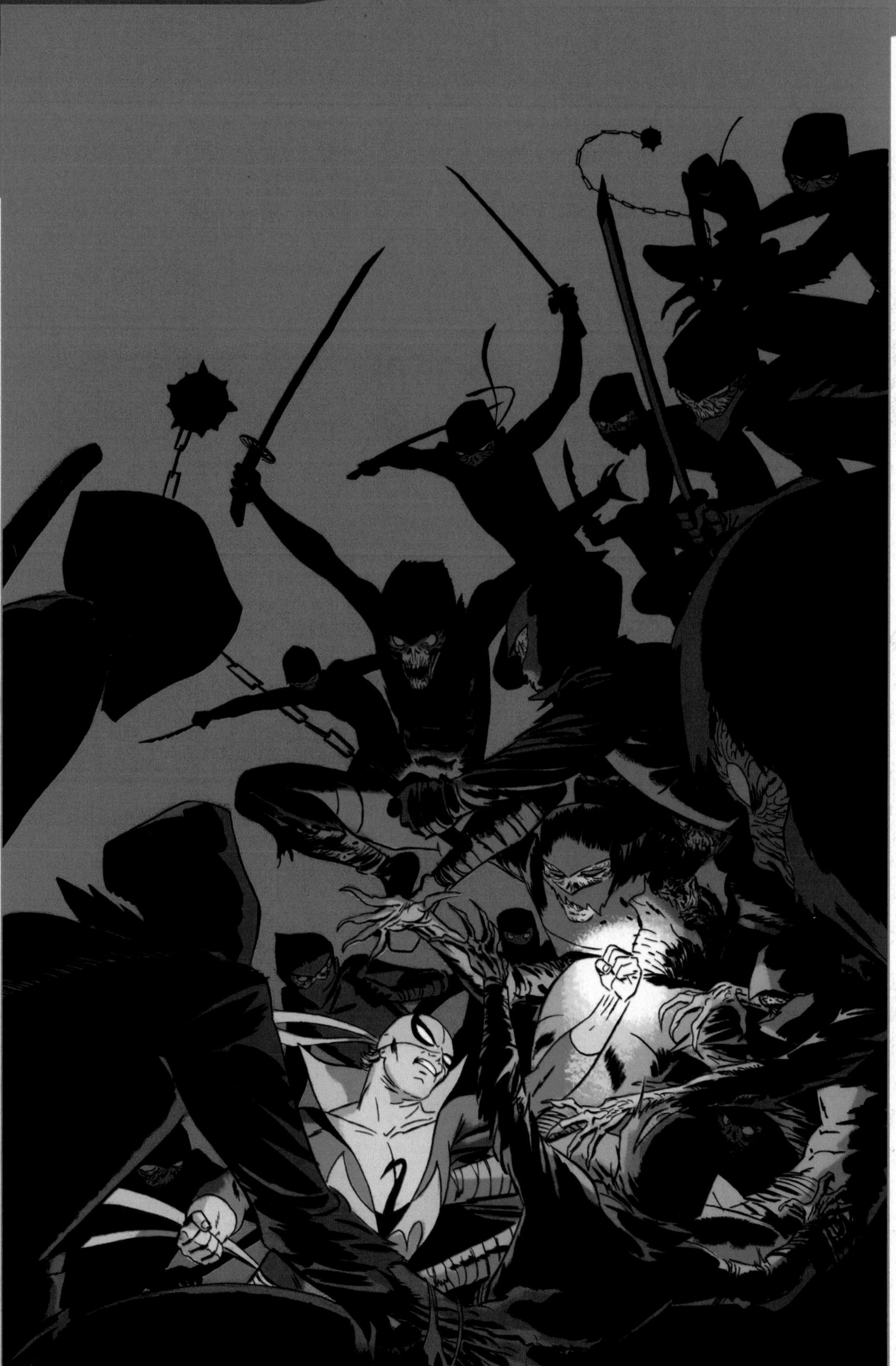

**MARCOS MARTIN**
*#2 Variant*

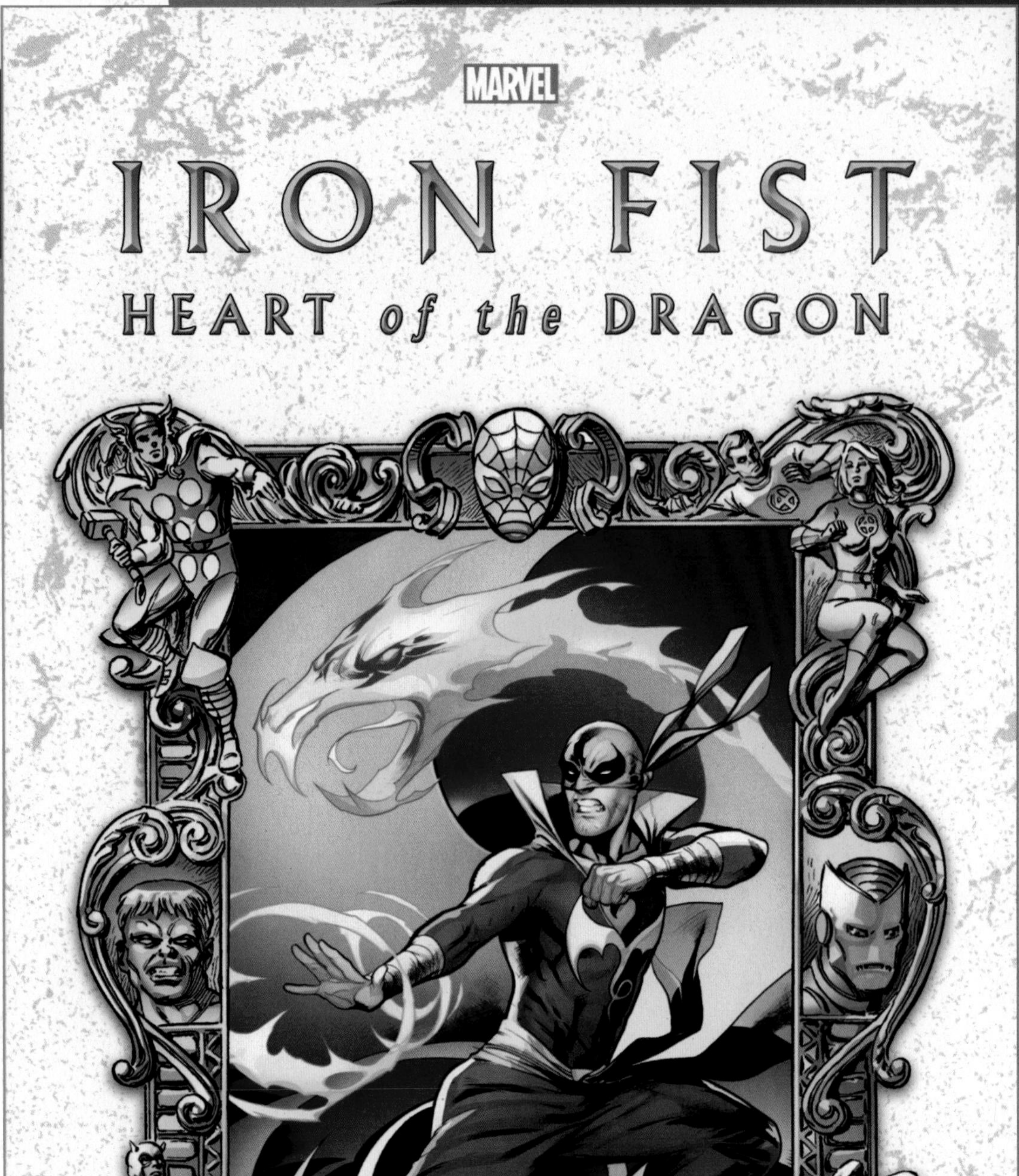
MARVEL
IRON FIST
HEART of the DRAGON

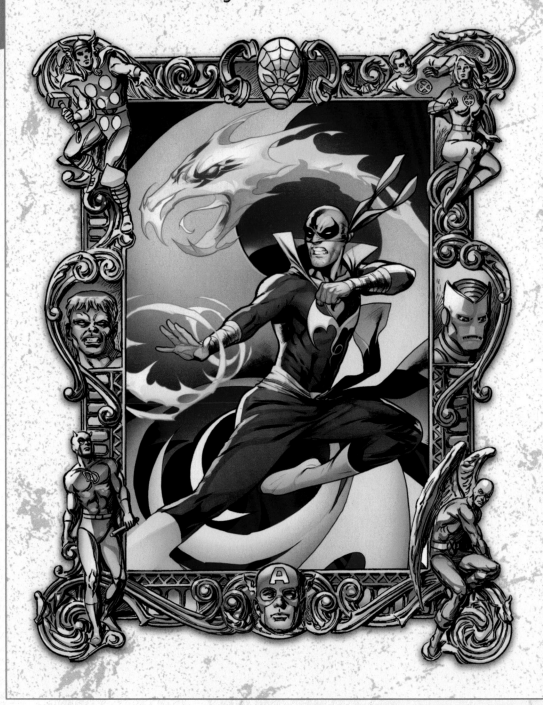

**EMA LUPACCHINO & DAVID CURIEL**
*#2 Marvel Masterworks 300th Anniversary Variant*

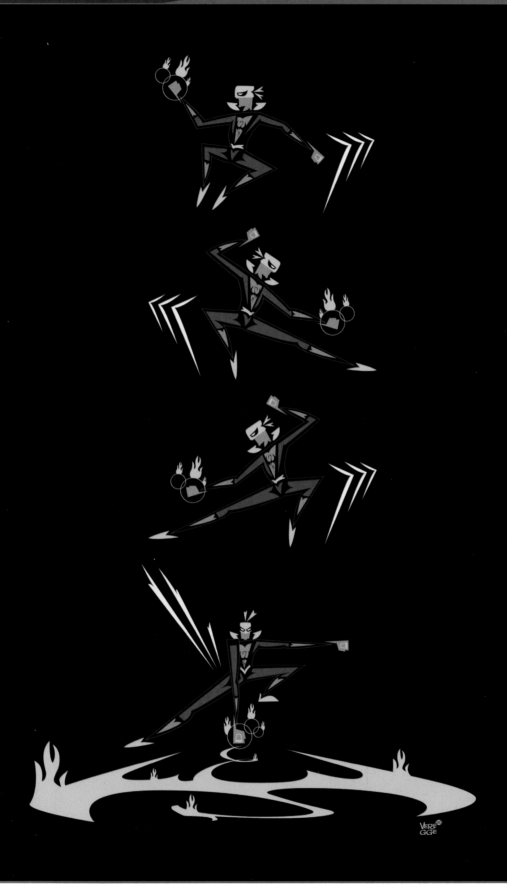

**JEFFREY VEREGGE**
*#3 Variant*

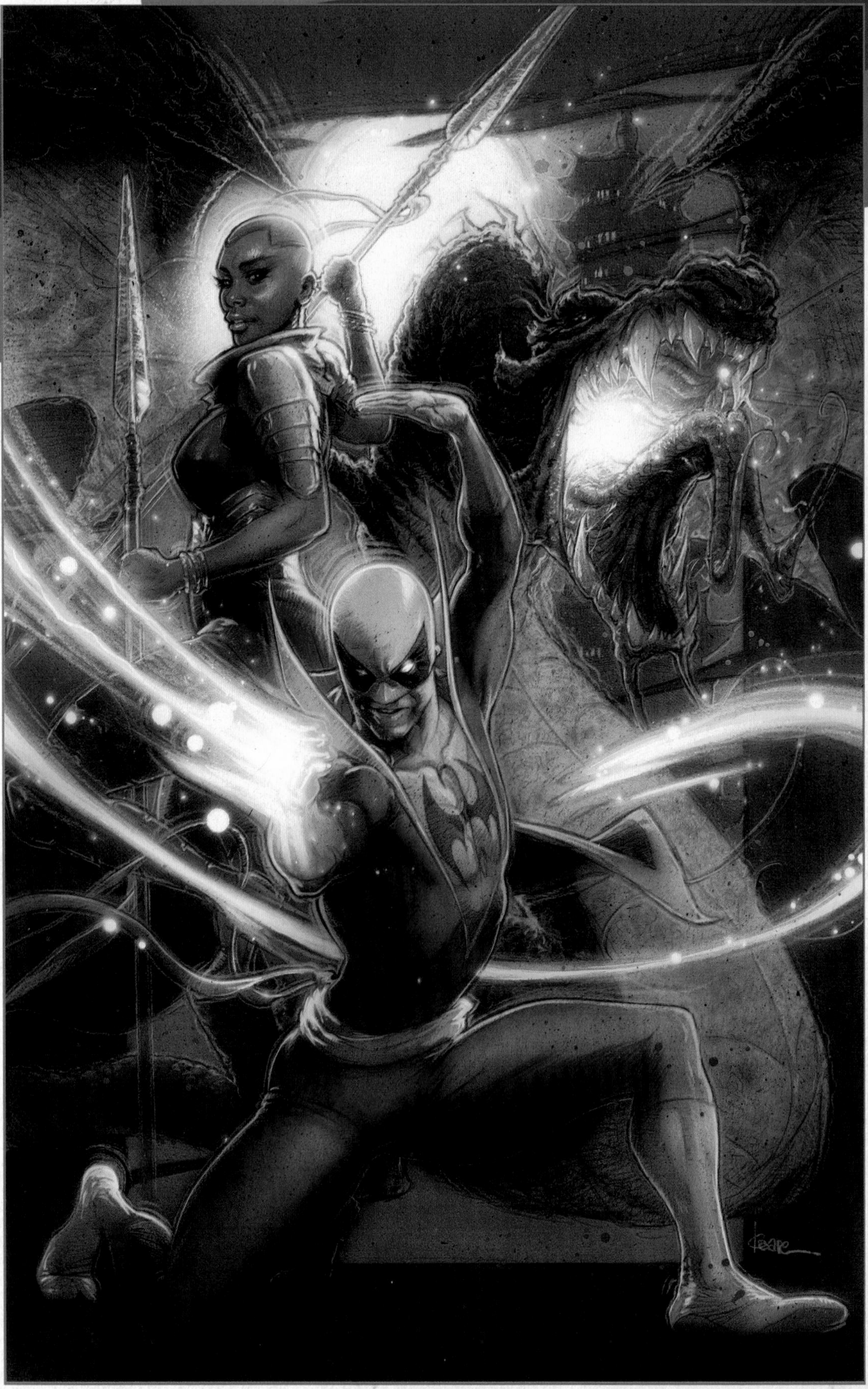

**KAARE ANDREWS**
*#4 Variant*

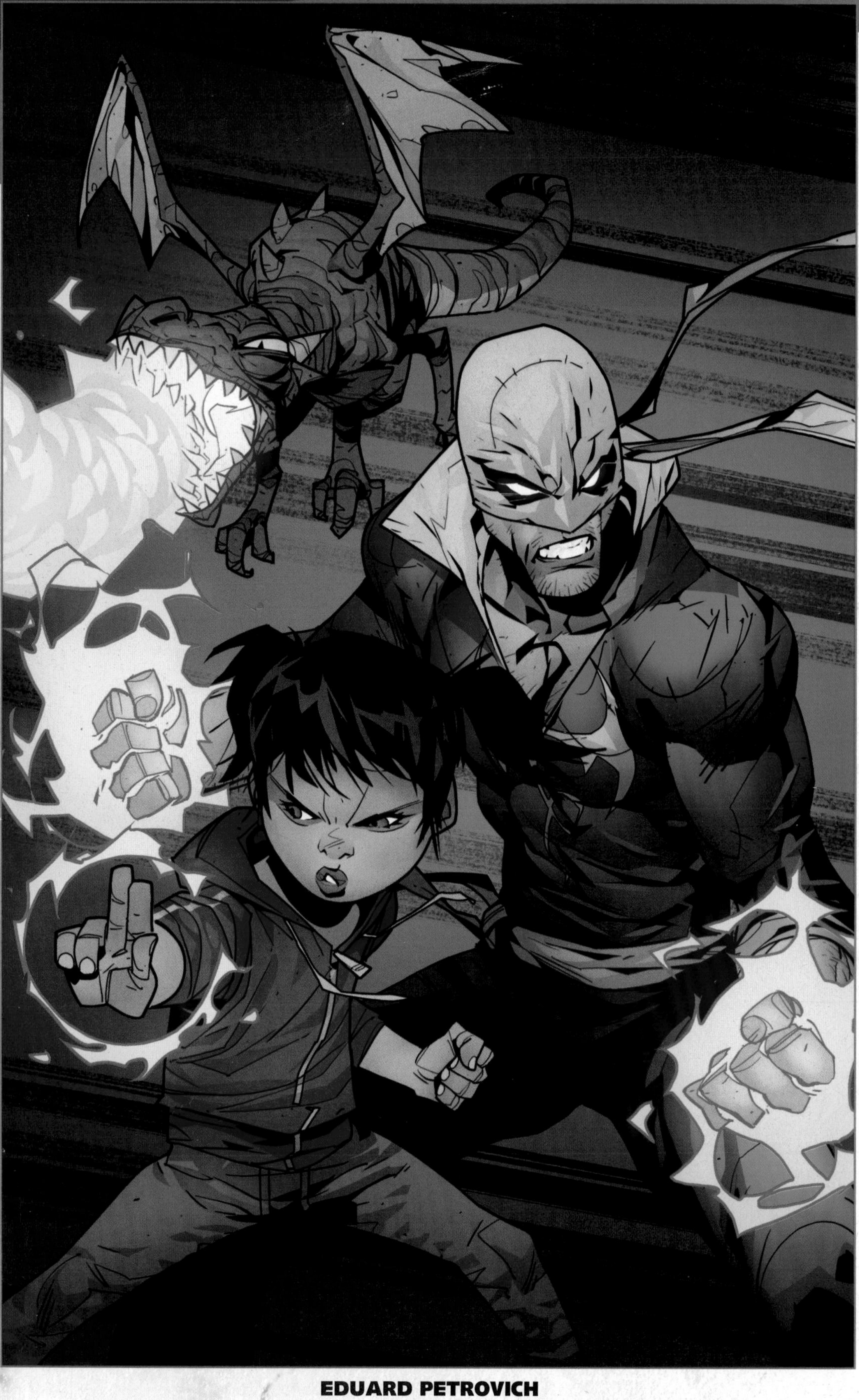

**EDUARD PETROVICH**
*#5 Variant*

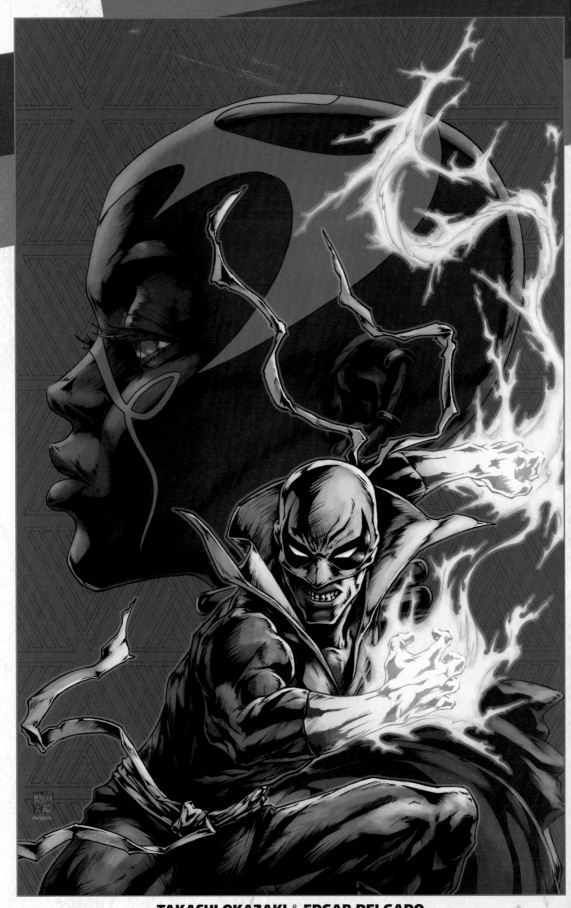

**TAKASHI OKAZAKI** & **EDGAR DELGADO**
*#6 Variant*